SOCIAL FOUNDATIONS
OF POSTINDUSTRIAL ECONOMIES

Social Foundations of Postindustrial Economies

GØSTA ESPING-ANDERSEN

OXFORD

UNIVERSITY PRESS

OXFORD

UNIVERSITY PRESS

Great Clarendon Street, Oxford OX2 6DP

Oxford University Press is a department of the University of Oxford.
It furthers the University's objective of excellence in research, scholarship,
and education by publishing worldwide in

Oxford New York

Auckland Cape Town Dar es Salaam Hong Kong Karachi
Kuala Lumpur Madrid Melbourne Mexico City Nairobi
New Delhi Taipei Toronto Shanghai

With offices in

Argentina Austria Brazil Chile Czech Republic France Greece
Guatemala Hungary Italy Japan South Korea Poland Portugal
Singapore Switzerland Thailand Turkey Ukraine Vietnam

Published in the United States
by Oxford University Press Inc., New York

British Library Cataloguing in Publication Data

Data available

Library of Congress Cataloging in Publication Data

Esping-Andersen, Gøsta 1947– .
Social foundations of postindustrial economies / Gøsta Esping-Andersen.
Includes bibliographical references and index.
1. Welfare economics. 2. Capitalism. I. Title. II. Title.
Social foundations of post-industrial economies.
HB846.E778 1999 330.12—dc21 98–43147

ISBN 0–19–874200–2

9 10 8

Printed in Great Britain
on acid-free paper by
Biddles Ltd., King's Lynn, Norfolk

ACKNOWLEDGEMENTS

The material in this book has been repeatedly tested on a non-random cross-section of student populations: at the European University Institute, the University of Trento, the Juan March Foundation in Madrid, New York University, the University of Wisconsin-Madison, the Faculty of International Economics at Maastricht, and at the University of Pompeu Fabra. Chris de Neubourg, Wolf Heydebrand, and Vicente Navarro deserve thanks because their invitations to lecture on the welfare state at Maastricht, the New York University, and Pompeu Fabra respectively, helped me test the coherence of the argumentation that follows.

Students are excellent cannon-fodder on the global academic battle-field. I do have some sympathy with my students at Trento when they lament that my lectures are incomprehensible. They are, of course, the front-line recipients of any new idea that comes to mind. To my students, therefore, a genuine, if collective, appreciation.

Many of the papers and talks that eventually coagulated into this monograph were written in response to criticism of my earlier work, a heavy dose of which came from the feminists. What I caught from their attacks was not so much the overarching salience of gender as the analytical power that a re-examination of the family can yield. A thank you, therefore, to one more collectivity: the feminist critics.

You often need a nudge from someone to bring that endless mass of papers you have been writing into a coherent book. For this I must thank Colin Crouch, who generously proposed that I put together an updated, re-thought, and revised study on comparative welfare states and publish it in his series at Oxford University Press. I must also apologize for the fact that what you see here is a far cry from what we initially agreed upon.

I did indeed have an endless mass of papers to go on, but I soon discovered that they did not add up to much. No wonder, many of them were the kind of stuff that airport-academics concoct between check-in and arrival on the nth seminar journey: the same argument or the same data recycled over and over again. Those that have found their way into this book in one shape or another were the ones that took real effort. Two such were my study for the United Nations (UNRISD) 1995 Social Summit in Copenhagen, and the study for the OECD Conference on *Towards 2000* in Paris, 1996. Here is my chance to acknowledge my debt to Dahram Gai, Cynthia Hewitt (both at UNRISD), and Peter Sherer (at the OECD) for the opportunity to make myself clear also to a non-academic audience.

I cannot honestly claim that everything that the reader will find in this book are the fruits of my own hard labour. There are two groups whose generosity has been decisive. One helped me with data and statistical analysis. Ivano Bison at Trento, Koen Vleminckx at LIS, and Axel West Pedersen at FAFO in Oslo have been outstandingly generous. The second group helped me think more clearly on various questions. Jens Bonke and Anne-Mette Sorensen helped me think about the household economy; Gotz Rohwer, Hans Peter Blossfeld, and Karl Ulrich Mayer helped me think about the life course. Carles Boix, Colin Crouch, Ian Gough, Axel Leijonhuvud, Frances Piven, Adam Przeworski, Jill Quadragno, and Vicente Navarro all helped me with thoughtful suggestions across the entire spectrum. John Myles, as always, helped me think about what, in the first place, I was doing, and why.

But there is only one person in the world to whom I really wish to dedicate this book, namely Paula Adam.

Gøsta Esping-Andersen

Barcelona
June 1998

CONTENTS

LIST OF TABLES

1

Introduction

We social scientists have some difficulty keeping pace with history. Most of us were bred on the notion that this has been the century of victorious pluralism, social citizenship, and welfare capitalism. Yet, we now look back with heavy nostalgia on the decades of Golden Age Capitalism when all seemed to work better. Today it seems that one after another of those constituent elements that once assured harmony and happiness are sliding into irreversible crisis and decay. Europe will herald in the new century with 15-odd million unemployed; North America, with about the same number of low-wage workers. The welfare state, arguably one of modern history's most spectacular reformist achievements, may no longer be sustainable in the kind of economic order that is unfolding.

The problems that beset the welfare state are intimately connected with the malfunctioning of labour markets and families. Both function badly because they are in the throes of revolutionary change. The former is seemingly incapable of furnishing full employment and equality at the same time; the latter, once the nucleus of social integration, is now unstable and, in many countries, seemingly on a fertility strike. We are, in brief, entering a new political economy wracked with dilemmas and trade-offs. Postindustrial society may hold the promise of many wonders, but equality is probably not among them. Hence our growing nostalgia for the Golden Age.

Still, how golden was it really? True, we can probably not expect the dizzying growth rates of the past to resurface, but we are none the less much richer today. Since the first OPEC oil crisis, the OECD countries have, on average, added 50 per cent to real per capita GDP; since 1960, a full 84 per cent. True, most advanced nations suffer from chronic mass unemployment, yet we should not forget that this occurs on the backdrop of much higher participation rates than in the past. Unlike before, we must now include women in a nation's full employment promise. And if we date the Golden Age to the 1950s and 1960s, that was surely not an epoch of mature welfare states and generous social rights. Most nations had yet to achieve anything close to universal coverage, benefit adequacy, or the levels of employment protection that today are taken for granted.

More than anything else it is the crisis of the welfare state which symbolizes the contemporary malaise. But, as Hugh Heclo (1981) once remarked, it would appear that the welfare state was destined to be in crisis from day one. Table 1.1 illustrates the long sequence of welfare state crises.

TABLE 1.1. *Major symptoms in the perennial welfare state crisis*

1950s	1960s	1970s–80s	1990s
Creates inflation Harms growth	Fails to produce equality Too bureaucratic	Stagflation Unemployment Post-materialism Government overload	Globalization Unemployment Rigidities Inequalities, social exclusion Family instability

Source: Esping-Andersen (1997*b*).

Table 1.1 may be overly schematic, but it suffices to impart a few basic lessons. Firstly, even if the welfare state is doomed to a life of endless crises, at least the maladies always change. In the 1950s, the attack came from the right and from economists worried that rapid public sector growth would stifle the market. A decade later, the pendulum shifted to the left which saw lingering inequalities everywhere notwithstanding that, by the 1960s, the welfare state edifice was declared completed. By the late 1970s and early 1980s we arrive at the third crisis, this time meriting an international high-level conference (OECD, 1981), from which I have synthesized the principal symptoms. Unemployment emerges for the first time as a major welfare state failure, there was widespread fear that governments were being overloaded with demands and responsibilities, that society had become ungovernable. The new social movements, preoccupied with cultural value changes, saw the welfare state as fossilized, incapable of adapting itself to true needs. The present crisis stands out for being rather less partisan, but also more comprehensive and, once again, it merited an international conference (OECD, 1997*a*).

The second lesson is that all earlier crises dissipated with time. The promised collapse of growth in the 1950s turned into a spectacular economic boom—all the while that public spending grew. From the 1960s to the 1970s, welfare states everywhere undertook major steps to assure benefit adequacy and reduce inequalities. Indeed, and this is a vital point to stress, this—and not the 1950s—was the true period of welfare state consolidation. This was the era of affirmative action, of anti-poverty programmes, of across-the-board benefit upgrading, and, generally, of cementing the rights of social citizenship. The response to the egalitarian assault was truly massive.

In fact, it was precisely this which triggered the third crisis. From 1960 to the mid-1970s, total public expenditure (as a percentage of GDP) jumped on average 30 per cent, almost exclusively due to social spending growth.[1] True, 'government overload' (as well as unemployment) may not have disappeared since the early 1980s, but its meaning and implications have changed. For one, social expenditures have almost everywhere been stagnant since the 1980s. This contradicts the then popular thesis that citizens' appetite for benefits, and politician's craving for office, are insatiable and that government growth is accordingly unstoppable. Moreover, the main issue that worries today's critics is less 'overload' and more 'rigidities'.

The third lesson is that the contemporary crisis differs notably from its forebears. Until now, the crisis was invariably *endogenous* to the welfare state—it was doing things badly or bringing about unwelcome consequences. The present crisis is, in contrast, essentially a manifestation of *exogenous* shocks that put into question the longer-term viability of the welfare state. The new global economy, it is said, undercuts polities' discretionary use of fiscal and monetary policy, necessitates greater employment and wage flexibility, and especially the less skilled will be condemned to unemployment unless wages and social benefits are reduced. The ageing of populations means that our commitments to social security must be rethought. Family instability implies, on the one hand, that households' traditional caring capacities are eroding and, on the other hand, that poverty risks are mounting—all the while that families are asked to absorb the new risks that come from labour markets. Above all, such exogenous shocks combine to create painful policy dilemmas: if, as in most of Europe, welfare states are committed to uphold existing standards of equality and social justice, the price is mass unemployment; to reduce unemployment, Europe appears compelled to embrace American-style deregulation. This will inevitably bring about more poverty and more inequality.

In the contemporary diagnosis, rigidities appear as a sole, but none the less severe, 'endogenous' symptom of crisis. Basically, the welfare state produces too much protection where flexibility is needed, too much equality where differentiation is the order of the day.

The various symptoms in the novel welfare state crisis may, or may not, be grounded in solid empirical fact. In any case, they are often poorly specified. Demographic ageing is primarily an issue of low fertility, and it is therefore this that we must analyse. The growing risks of poverty and

---

[1] Here, and above, the growth rates are calculated from OECD, *Historical Statistics*, various issues.

social exclusion are not necessarily inherent and inevitable features of our society. They spring from two 'malfunctioning' institutions: the labour market and the family.

AIMS OF THIS BOOK

This book is an attempt to come to grips with the 'new political economy' that is emerging. For lack of a better term, I refer to it as the postindustrial economy. One premiss of my analyses is that 'postindustrial' transformation is institutionally path-dependent. This means that existing institutional arrangements heavily determine, maybe even over-determine, national trajectories. More concretely, the divergent kinds of welfare regimes that nations built over the post-war decades, have a lasting and overpowering effect on which kind of adaptation strategies can and will be pursued. Hence, we see various kinds of postindustrial society unfolding before our eyes. Welfare states responded quite energetically, although far from uniformly, to past crises. This is certainly also happening today.

There is a crucial addendum to make to this general proposition: the decisive period in which the basic components of post-war welfare regimes were put in place, when welfare capitalism was institutionalized so to speak, was not the post-war decades but during the 1960s and 1970s. This was when strong worker protection and labour market regulation emerged, when social citizenship was fully affirmed. And this was when the core features of welfare states crystallized. The essential differences between the Nordic, social democratic, the Continental European, and the Anglo-Saxon liberal welfare states were affirmed in these years.

This said, we hardly need historians to remind us that the timing was auspicious: the consolidation and maturation of post-war welfare capitalism coincided with the onset of the new, post-OPEC economic realities of slow growth and rising structural unemployment. It also coincided with accelerating economic globalization and family instability. No wonder that many interpret this historical coincidence as a one-way causality: exaggerated welfare statism is what catapults Eurosclerosis, poor economic performance, mass unemployment, and, indeed, rising poverty (Giersch, 1985; Lindbeck, 1992; Murray, 1984).

The book pursues a set of interlinked arguments. The first addresses the so-called welfare state crisis. Contemporary debate has been far too focused on the *state*. The real crisis, if there is any, lies in the *interaction* between the composite parts that, in unison, form contemporary welfare 'regimes': labour markets, the family, and, as a third partner, the welfare *state*. We should not forget that the sum-total of societal welfare derives from how inputs from these three institutions are combined. Some regimes, in particular the liberal, Anglo-Saxon, are market-biased; others, especially the Southern European or the Japanese, are powerfully familialistic. And still others put the accent on state delivery of welfare. This way of defining the problem implies that what most commentators see as a welfare *state* crisis, may in reality be a crisis of the broader institutional framework that has come to regulate our political economies.

The second line of argument is that the 'real' crisis of contemporary welfare regimes lies in the disjuncture between the existing institutional construction and exogenous change. Contemporary welfare states and labour market regulations have their origins in, and mirror, a society that no longer obtains: an economy dominated by industrial production with strong demand for low-skilled workers; a relatively homogenous and undifferentiated, predominantly male, labour force (the standard production worker); stable families with high fertility; and a female population primarily devoted to housewifery. Welfare regimes are built around a set of egalitarian ideals and risk profiles that predominated when our parents and grandparents were young. If we wish to understand the travails of welfare regimes today, we must begin with the recognition that the risk structure is changing dramatically.

The third line of argument is a follow-up on the second: the emerging risks of postindustrial society come primarily from the revolution that is unfolding in both labour markets and households. We sorely need a better conception of what, today, drives family behaviour and service employment. According to most analyses, the driving force is of the macroscopic, global kind. This is certainly one part of the story, but there is also a potent microscopic force at play, namely families' and, in particular, women's economic decisions.

I agree that the new political economy presents trade-offs that make it exceedingly difficult to harmonize *some* egalitarian goals with a return to full employment. Existing welfare regimes tend to be captive in their own institutional logic and, hence, the ways in which they respond to and manage emerging dilemmas will yield different outcomes and produce varying 'postindustrial' scenarios. Our common tendency to regard postindustrial society as a largely convergent global process impairs our analytical faculties tremendously. Besides the well-known juxtaposition of nations which create jobs through deregulation, and those which create mass unemployment through strong social protection, emerges adjunct dilemmas. One such is a potential 'low-fertility equilibrium' trap that springs from the incapability of women to harmonize careers and family obligations. Low fertility is, of course, a major reason for why welfare states may not be sustainable. Another is the 'low-wage, low-skill equilibrium' that easily accompanies deregulation.

Behind these lines of analysis lurks my key hypothesis, namely that the household economy is *alpha and omega* to any resolution of the main postindustrial dilemmas, perhaps the single most important 'social foundation' of postindustrial economies.

To proceed, we need to tackle a number of problems. We have to re-examine social risks and the welfare state; the family as welfare consumer and producer; the functioning of labour markets and what drives service employment. We are operating on slippery territory because we are examining the passage from one well-known social order—let us call it welfare capitalism—to another—let us call it postindustrial society—the contours of which are still unfolding. One method of dealing with this problem is to hold the parameters of change up against well-known historical constants. The book therefore begins with 'the past', a re-examination of welfare capitalism; the era of what Lipset (1960) called the democratic class struggle.

There are four phenomena which, together, form the unifying theme of this book: equality, risks, jobs, and the 'new political economy'. 'Risks' and 'jobs' will be dealt with in separate chapters. Here I shall limit myself to some brief remarks on 'equality' and the 'new political economy'.

THE PROBLEM OF EQUALITY

The concepts of equality and welfare state have become almost synonymous, and both have become shorthand for post-war welfare capitalism. If postindustrial society is driven by a trade-off between equality and other goals, it would seem necessary to understand better just exactly which kind of equality is involved. If we must sacrifice equality, what kind?

There exist few concepts with such variegated meanings as equality. It can denote fairness and justice (that is, issues of equity), the distribution of opportunities, resources, and capabilities (which address equality of life chances), the allocation of rewards and the differentiation of living conditions (a more static, 'here and now' equality), or permanent social cleavages (a question of class formation). Equality is also invoked when, for example, social reformers or trade union organizers call for universalism and solidarity—issues of equality or rights and duties.[2]

In the broadest meaning possible, equality is the major 'leitmotif' of social science. In economics, the stress is on the distribution (and utilization) of scarce resources; in political science more on power; and in soci-

---

[2] Equity and equality are often used indiscriminately. Given their more individualistic view of the economic world, it is hardly surprising that economists tend to imply equity when they use the word equality. For a recent example by a sophisticated thinker on this subject, see Le Grand (1991). For an overview of the meanings and implications of egalitarian concepts (and an appeal to study equality in terms of capabilities), see especially Sen (1992).

ology on social stratification. Issues of equality are contentious and for this reason Gunnar Myrdal's (1954) old warning about the value premisses of social scientists cannot be easily ignored. Social science parallels politics with its perennial battle between anti- and pro-egalitarians. Yet, such labels are not especially informative when we consider the multifaceted character of the concept. Certainly, the pros or the cons rarely agree on what kind of equality should be optimized or done away with.

The substantive meaning of equality or inequality is powerfully bound by nation and epoch. Not only are some societies or cultures more intolerant of inequities or social differentiation, but what is implied by equality or fairness may differ qualitatively. In a recent study, Svallfors (1998) shows that popular assessment of what is a just income ratio between top and bottom hovers around 4-to-1 in Scandinavia compared to 12-to-1 in the United States. Korpi (1980*a*) once showed how differently Americans and Scandinavians view poverty: Americans will see the poor in categorical terms, as a distinct substratum ('the losers'); to a Scandinavian, poverty is a question of how unequally resources are distributed. And ever since Marx and Sombart it has been repeatedly observed that Americans see equality in terms of individual meritocracy (or in terms of levelling living standards) while Europeans are more likely to think in class terms (Lipset, 1991).

The meaning of equality changes across historical epochs. In the first part of the twentieth century, the problem of equality was, consciously or unconsciously, explicitly or implicitly, an echo of the Marxist question of class. The governing strata were preoccupied with the 'Arbeiterfrage" or the 'Soziale Frage' (in Germany), 'la question sociale' (in France), and, in Britain, Disraeli spoke of the 'Two Nations'. The socialists, in turn, used the language of class struggle and, when less Marxist, spoke of social emmiseration. The post-war embrace of Keynesianism and the welfare state appeared to have resolved the 'social question' once and for all and, hence, equality became more individualized, a matter of mobility chances.

Welfare capitalism became the reigning political economy in the advanced economies over the past half century. It would probably be futile to search for a precise definition of this concept considering that it basically serves to capture the *Zeitgeist* of an era.[3] Regardless, it signals the arrival of four constituent institutional innovations in the history of capitalism. The first and foremost was the welfare state with its promise of universal social citizenship, of a new social solidarity. The notion of a welfare state points immediately to the second, namely full democracy. In its

---

[3] The notion of 'welfare capitalism' actually dates back to the 1920s when the American Right sought to deflect the demand for European-style social insurance by encouraging voluntary, company-based welfare plans.

English usage, the welfare state was coined by the Archbishop of York during World War Two as a programmatic antidote to the Nazi warfare state (Briggs, 1961). Nowhere did the democratic content of welfare states find stronger expression than in T. H. Marshall's (1950) assertion that civil and political rights are only democratically meaningful if complemented with social rights. In other words, democracy and the welfare state are sewn from the same fabric.

The full recognition and consolidation of trade unionism and what we today call modern industrial relations systems was the third pillar of welfare capitalism, not only because this regularized labour market conflict, introduced an element of employment rights and job protection, or nurtured a more consensual approach to bargaining, but also because it introduced a modicum of democracy 'behind the factory gates', as Swedish socialists used to say. Finally, welfare capitalism would have been incomplete were it not for the fourth pillar, the rights to education and the expansion of modern mass education systems.

Thus was born a new egalitarian agenda. By the 1950s, the 'social question' had vanished from the political vocabulary, and the working class question no longer impassioned politics. American society had become 'middle class', and Europe discovered the 'affluent worker' (Zweig, 1971). The issue of equality was reformulated because, it seemed, class differences had ceased to be of importance. It was this which Lipset (1960) sought to describe with his notion of the 'democratic class struggle'. The four pillars of welfare capitalism appeared to guarantee that achievement and merit would reign supreme.

The recast egalitarian agenda presents a wholly new mix of collectivism and individualism. On one side, social citizenship prevails over old class solidarities. On the other side, the raw *laissez-faire* call for individual self-reliance was pushed aside and liberals linked arms with social democrats in a battle for equal opportunity. In effect, welfare capitalism was often a synthesis of liberal and social democratic egalitarianism.

This synthesis took variegated forms, not only because the liberal ethos was stronger in some nations (especially in the Anglo-Saxon world), and the social democratic stronger in others (Scandinavia especially). But also because in many countries, like Japan and much of Continental Europe, both liberalism and socialism were decidedly peripheral compared to their conservative competitors, whether they were etatiste, corporativist, or guided by Confucian or social Catholic teachings. Whereas the new politics of equality assumed a strong individualistic form in Scandinavia and in the Anglo-Saxon nations, this was not so in East Asia or much of Continental Europe where the unit of social protection, of social rights, and of redistributive attention, was more likely an economic status group ('corporation') or the family (via the male bread-winner).

At century's end, the epoch of welfare capitalism as we know it is in decline. Its constituent elements seem all in crisis, unable to adequately address emerging needs and problems. We find that longstanding norms and practices are losing their carrying power, that conventional formulae seem not to work. If the literature has diagnosed the situation correctly, we appear to face concomitant welfare state, labour market, training, and family 'failure'.[4]

Post-war social science built a powerful conceptual and theoretical apparatus to help us understand the workings of welfare capitalism. It is, however, ill-equipped to deal with the kind of world that is now unfolding. Take unemployment, which used to be a fairly straightforward concept. To most it meant that a person (usually a male) was temporarily out of a job because of frictional or cyclical adjustments. What does it mean today? Is housewifery, early retirement, or, for that matter, prolonged education unemployment in disguise? And Richard Freeman (1996) is not joking when he claims that incarcerated American males are the functional equivalent of the long-term unemployed in Europe. Or take productivity. Fred Block (1990) suggests that we may be caught in a kind of neo-physiocratism: we have no difficulty recognizing the productive contribution of metal workers, but what about caring for someone else's children? The value-added of public employment is routinely measured as equal to the cost of the input. Many feminists insist that unpaid domestic labour is a productive contribution to aggregate welfare. Some argue that working mothers' true productivity is negative when we count in the costs of leave schemes and daycare (Rosen, 1996).

The concept of equality finds itself in a similar conundrum. In the first post-war decades, education was widely considered the *panacea* of equality of opportunity. The egalitarian critique of welfare states in the 1960s was in large measure based on the realization that social equality requires more than the expansion of mass education. Hence, both scholarly and political debate began to re-theorize equality, now stressing the importance of cultural and social capital, and the unequal distribution of resources. More importantly, the politics of egalitarianism changed: some welfare states began to promote a more aggressive assault on income and resource differences (equality here-and-now) and/or on life chance equalization (affirmative action, sponsored mobility, or quotas). The upshot, as we see today, is that welfare states find themselves barraged from two sides at once. One side protests that redistributive, here-and-now equality has progressed too little, that some groups have been left behind; another side sees that exaggerated commitments to equalize everything has produced nothing but inequity and inefficiency. Most

---

[4] For an overview, see Esping-Andersen (1997*b*).

writers on the welfare state underestimate the inherent tension between equity and equality.

Welfare states today face multiple egalitarian tensions. On one side, there is the problem of how to balance equality and equity; on the other side, how to combine egalitarianism with full employment. In both cases, one of the two may have to give. Yet, we have no yardstick, no oracle, that could help us decide how much, or what kind of, equality must be sacrificed—if any. And we lack any coherent formula for how to manage the consequences of whatever decision we make. We all know that globalization, the new service economy, or the new demography threaten received notions of equality, but do we have any formula for rewriting the egalitarian agenda? Can we conceive of a new social contract that would befit a 'postindustrial' society?

Some of the losers in contemporary society are easily discernible. The less skilled, youth, and single-parent families are becoming high-risk groups almost everywhere. But one thing is momentary under-privilege, another life-long entrapment. There are signs that some losers are forming into long-term socially excluded strata. Europe is ripe with popularly coined new social classes: the 'A-team' and 'B-team' in Denmark, the 'two-thirds society' in Germany, the 'two-speed society' in France, the new 'underclass' in Britain and the United States. What most members of the various B-teams have in common is that they had much less to fear a few decades ago.

The design of contemporary welfare states reflects a risk structure that is closer to that of our fathers and grandfathers than of young families today. In this nexus, the welfare state is embattled from three sides at once. There are those who oppose any change whatsoever, citing the inviolability of achieved rights. There are those who wish to rescue the welfare state by altering it so that it may, once again, address real needs and risks and perhaps even give a new push to economic efficiency. And, as a powerful third force, there are those who insist that the only way to guarantee a future 'good society' is to dismantle the welfare state.

POLITICAL ECONOMIES

Robert Merton once observed that contemporary social scientists may see more clearly because they stand on the shoulders of giants. My favoured giants tend to be political economists. Yet, how far I shall be able to see, what I shall see, and how I eventually interpret that which I manage to see, all depends on my choice of giant. Political economy has very different meanings.

By political economy, some mean public, or rational choice, theory. This is truthfully more a (often powerful) methodological than theoretical approach. Indeed, public choice is an analytical preference that ranges from quite conservative scholars such as Tullock and Buchanan, to writers with a Marxist intellectual inspiration such as Adam Przeworski.

Political economy can also be shorthand for what is being studied—the interplay of public and private, state and market. The mix of politics and economy often generates disciplinary colonization. To economists, political economy often means the application of economic theory to political phenomena; to political scientists, vice versa.

It can, however, also imply a particular theoretical framework for analysing society. The starting point here is to offer an alternative to the supposedly disembodied treatment of economic life typical of mainstream economics. The market, to a political economist, is neither sovereign nor natural, but a construction suspended between collective force and social institutions.

As theoretical approach, political economy is a medley of traditions. One derives from Marxism and sees politics and power in class terms, the economy as a fount of contradictions, exploitation and, hence, of collective conflict. In this tradition the welfare state takes on two forms: to some it is a (problematic) instrument of social legitimation, as in O'Connor (1973) and Offe (1972); to others it is a (possibly contradictory) democratic implant in a capitalist body, as in Gough (1979) and in the writings of many radical economists.

A second follows the lead of European institutional thought. The echoes of Joseph Schumpeter, Max Weber, and Karl Polanyi are particularly strong. It often shares with Marxism a keen eye for issues such as power, inequalities, and conflict but does not automatically assume that 'class struggle' is the motor of change or that capitalist institutions, per definition, are repressive. Indeed, its great analytical asset lies in its sensitivity to historical transformation and cross-national variation. With one huge reservation, this is the guiding perspective of the present book.

My reservation has to do with the blindness of virtually all comparative political economy to the world of families. It is, and always has been, inordinately macro-oriented. It occupies itself with macroscopic constructions, such as welfare states, world trade, international finance, or trade unions, and with similarly huge outcomes, such as inflation, employment, inequality, or growth. A major belief that underpins this book is that a sound understanding of postindustrial society must be anchored in the household economy.

THE THREE WORLDS OF
WELFARE CAPITALISM REVISITED

Most social scientists, like the societies they study, are hard put escaping from their own path dependencies. I am certainly no exception. It is therefore inevitable that this work flows from earlier. Indeed, the present project began as an attempt to revisit *The Three Worlds of Welfare Capitalism* (Esping-Andersen, 1990) in light of numerous criticisms. Also that book was an exercise in political economy, defining welfare regimes in terms of the mix of public and market provision and, subsequently, explaining international variations in terms of state traditions and dominant patterns of power mobilization. Labelling the three principal welfare regimes as 'social democratic' (basically the Nordic countries), 'conservative' (Continental Europe), and 'liberal' (the Anglo-Saxon nations) served to identify their roots as well as their character.

Two among many criticisms stand out because, if unresolved, further analytical progress will be hampered. The first is principally a classificatory critique (are there more than, simply, three models?). I shall address this issue, but not exhaustively. The second has to do with my failure to recognize gender differences and, more generally, with my severely underdeveloped analysis of the family. This critique shall receive considerable more attention, first of all because it is a sorely needed reminder that the household is a core component of any welfare regime. It is evident that the Mediterranean (and Japanese) welfare model is powerfully *familialistic*, a feature which, as we shall see, has immense consequences for both welfare and employment.

For decades, the family—both as social institution and as decision-maker—was largely assumed away. As the notion of a 'second demographic revolution' indicates, and as all statistics demonstrate, the changing role of women and evolving new household forms are an intrinsic—possibly leading—part of the socio-economic transformation around us. Our grandfathers were male bread-winners; our grandmothers most likely housewives. Very few children today grow up in this kind of family. Household forms are being revolutionized even if some welfare states do not seem fully aware of it.

PART I

VARIETIES OF
WELFARE CAPITALISM

Why do we now think of post-war welfare capitalism as such a successful social order? Basically because it succeeded in unifying social citizenship, full employment, mass education, and well-functioning industrial relations systems. This institutional configuration proved itself capable of absorbing huge masses of de-ruralized workers while, simultaneously, raising real earnings and living conditions for the vast majority of people. The same cannot be said for today as de-industrialization and the service economy seem to generate mass unemployment and stagnant earnings. What has happened? How can we account for this historical turnabout?

All epochs have their catchwords, their peculiar leitmotif, that help us grasp the essence of the world around us. Post-war welfare capitalism was the era of 'pluralism', of the 'end-of-ideology' (Bell, 1960), of the 'waning of oppositions' (Kirscheimer, 1957), and of the 'affluent worker' (Zweig, 1971). Lipset's (1960) notion of the 'democratic class struggle' managed perhaps better than any other to invoke the spirit of the times. That spirit was a hopeful one, primarily because it juxtaposed a problematic past. The pathologies of totalitarianism and extremism had been cured, class differences had faded. Welfare capitalism had put an end to the old 'Arbeiterfrage'.

Pluralist theory is now less persuasive. Instead of a middle-mass of affluent workers, new extremisms raise their heads and we seem to be reverting back to the kind of social polarization that we so successfully escaped. Few continue to believe in a harmony of egalitarianism, growth, and full employment; a social-democratic 'third way' appears no longer possible. Instead, we seem to be entering a world where one goal must be sacrificed for another: if we desire full employment, we must scale back social citizenship and job rights. If we wish to restore full employment, we may have to accept levels of inequality that neither pluralist theory nor welfare state ideology would have found acceptable.

The contemporary pessimists, like the post-war optimists, often see the world governed by overpowering universal forces. To the pluralists, modernization, 'the logic of industrialism', the nuclear family, and a triumphant middle-class society were inescapable universals. Their modern-day equivalents are unstoppable globalization and the great 'equality-or-jobs' trade-off.

Universalizing theory is powerful when it captures the empirical essence of an epoch. Pluralism was powerful because there was an undeniable decline of ideological and social polarity in post-war welfare capitalism— certainly when compared to the pre-war era. The contemporary 'great trade-off' appears equally compelling because inequality, marginaliza- tion, and mass unemployment have become defining characteristics of our present epoch. Yet, universals often appear less valid when put to the test of comparative empirical analysis.

In the subsequent two chapters, I revisit the political economy within which post-war welfare regimes emerged, matured and, now, appear crisis- ridden. The 'Golden Age' could certainly not have come about had it not been for the rise of welfare states. What has been less recognized in the literature is that the *modus operandi* of labour markets and the structure of families were equally detrimental forces.

2

The Democratic Class Struggle Revisited

Lipset's (1960) 'democratic class struggle' depicts a society where consensual bargaining has replaced naked class war, where meritocracy and equal life chances prevail over inherited privilege and ascription. This was a credible imagery because inequalities did in fact decline and material betterment was in fact quite universal. Mass consumption, growth, and modest unemployment brought middle-class living standards to workers and, to their offspring, a sense of upward mobility into white-collar jobs.

We habitually believe that it was Keynesianism and the welfare state that rendered the 'democratic class struggle' possible. However, with the aid of hindsight we can see that this was only one side of the coin. The other side was that families were stable and the economy dynamic. Even low-skilled workers could count on well-paid and secure jobs and real wages grew year after year. The new society appeared middle class because the kind of income security that was once a privilege of the few was now enjoyed by most; the average working-class family could now aspire to home ownership, household goods, and full-time housewifery—all symbols of the comfortable middle-class life. Full employment growth nurtured strong trade unions and, in their wake, worker protection and diminished pay inequalities.

The importance of the welfare state during the immediate post-war decades lay not so much in its effects on employment and redistribution as in its capacity to lessen economic insecurity during peoples' inactive years. Until the 1970s most social security systems were, in reality, still quite rudimentary in terms of the range of social risks covered, the population included, or the level of income replacement. Even in the vanguard Nordic welfare states, the principle of guaranteed full income replacement emerged only in the mid-1960s. Similarly, the attainment of full employment was not necessarily the result of Keynesianism. Full employment arrived in avowedly Keynesian regimes, like Sweden, but also in staunchly 'monetarist', anti-Keynesian polities, like Germany. And in some nations, like Italy and the United States, *de facto* full employment never really arrived. Besides, the massive employment-generating effect of welfare state expansion in education, health, and social services occurred—once again—from the mid-1960s onward.

In any case, more equality and jobs did not abolish social class once and for all. Factory workers were still factory workers, regardless of pension rights and homeownership. What had happened, according to Lipset, was that the conflict-producing *correlates* of class had disappeared. With lifetime job security, high pay, and welfare guarantees, Seebohm Rowntree's notion of a distinct 'working-class life cycle of poverty' seemed now a relic of the distant past. Class differences appeared to narrow also because each new generation received more education, attained middle-class jobs, and earned more than did its parents (Levy, 1988). Europe's 'affluent worker' and America's 'middle class' were the same phenomenon (Myles and Turegun, 1994). The 1950s and 1960s were the years of the 'great compression', as Goldin and Margo (1991) call it. For the average manufacturing worker in general, and for the unskilled worker in particular, the world was undoubtedly a much better place to live. Still, the 'class-correlates' did not erode similarly across all advanced nations, and this is where differences in welfare state and industrial relations construction matter.

VARIETIES OF THE DEMOCRATIC CLASS STRUGGLE

In an important reappraisal of Lipset's thesis, Korpi (1983) argues that distributional outcomes depend on wage-earner unity and power mobilization. His balance-of-class power argument does in fact help explain broad variations in post-war labour market performance. Where trade unionism was less centralized and coverage limited, as in the United States, the result was more segmentation, dualism and, hence, inequality. When also the welfare state is residual and social protection highly privatized—again as in the United States—market inequalities are unlikely to be affected much by social redistribution.

In contrast, market distribution is likely to be more egalitarian where trade unionism is centralized and coverage comprehensive as in much of Europe, but especially in Scandinavia. This is particularly the case in centralized, economy-wide, and co-ordinated bargaining systems which, as a vast literature has shown, constitute the best possible institutional infrastructure for harmonizing wage-equalization, full employment, and growth.[1] Clearly, where also the welfare state is strongly universalistic, the distribution of resources and life chances should be additionally egalitar-

---

[1] Highly co-ordinated bargaining means that unions must represent the universal, rather than narrower group interests. Potentially inflationary rent-seeking bargaining is thus kept to a minimum, unions are better capable of guaranteeing wage discipline, and the result should be fewer externalities. The evidence in favour of the beneficial effects of encompassing interest organizations and highly co-ordinated industrial relations is massive (Garret and Lange, 1986; Calmfors and Driffill, 1988; Hicks, 1988; Soskice, 1990; 1994). For an overview, see Esping-Andersen (1994).

ian, creating homogeneity not only within the working class, but also between the social classes.[2] Hence, the new 'affluent worker' probably became a more universal phenomenon in Europe.

For these very same reasons, post-war European politics remained more solidly anchored in class organizations than pluralist theory allowed for. Where social democracy and trade unionism was especially powerful there emerged encompassing systems of 'social partnership', of class and interest representation within a framework of tripartite consultation and interest inter-mediation.[3] Hence, the 'great' social classes, rather than disappearing, became institutionalized agents of collective action.

Many nations, of course, developed neither nationally co-ordinated and centralized, nor decentralized, collective bargaining. Yet, they were hardly pluralist in the American sense. Instead, they were *dirigiste*, as in France, pillared polities, as in the Netherlands, clientelist, as in Italy, or corporatistic dictatorships, as in pre-1975 Portugal and Spain. The real world of pluralism was in fact rather small.

The welfare state combines with industrial relations to form the principal institutional infrastructure for labour market behaviour. Indeed, there exists a very close connection between systems of interest representation and welfare state construction. Comprehensive, universalistic welfare states almost invariably go hand-in-hand with centralized, nation-wide and co-ordinated bargaining (Denmark, Norway, Finland, and Sweden); residual welfare states, with decentralized and weak unionism (the United States, Canada, and now also the UK). Welfare state construction has profound, mainly indirect, effects on labour market outcomes.

The liberal, Anglo-Saxon welfare state emphasis on targeted means-testing for the poor and private occupational plans for core workers will reinforce rather than mute market-based stratification. Core, unionized workers typically combine modest-level public entitlements with a fairly extensive package of private benefits and rights. The relative size of the 'core' is obviously of great importance in terms of the net stratificational outcome. This is precisely Castles' point when he insists on a sharp distinction between American welfare state residualism and the implicit universalism within the Australian 'wage-earners' welfare state (Castles, 1996; Castles and Mitchell, 1993). In the United States, employee coverage under company welfare programmes was about 50 per cent for pensions and 70 per cent for health care at the height of occupational benefit

---

[2] This has been widely documented in stratification, poverty, and income distribution research (Erikson and Aberg, 1985; Palmer, 1988; Mitchell, 1991; Smeeding *et al.*, 1990). Comparative data also point to a considerably greater degree of inter-class equality in Scandinavia compared to the rest of Europe, mainly due to Scandinavia's much more universalistic and egalitarian welfare states (Mitchell, op.cit).

[3] For an overview, see Goldthorpe (1984), Streeck (1992), and Regini (1992).

expansion in the 1970s (Bureau of Labor Statistics, 1987). At the other extreme, the most vulnerable will find themselves locked into a combination of low public benefits and few, if any, private entitlements. In contrast, Canadian workers came to enjoy universal health care, and Australians a *de facto* universal system of occupational welfare (Castles, 1996).

Continental Europe's status divided social insurance systems influence labour market stratification very differently. The narrower communities of social citizenship create more pronounced differentials according to occupational status. Also, the strong link between benefits and employment record creates a stronger gender-segmentation with profound secondary effects. Since entitlements assume stable, uninterrupted careers, the labour market becomes constructed around the male bread-winner, while wives and family members will depend on derived rather than personal social rights. Family welfare, in other words, depends on the bread-winner. This kind of system is bound to produce generous rights, heavy labour costs, and pervasive job protection for the core worker. The second-order consequence is heavy hiring and firing costs and, hence, barriers to entry. Hence, familialistic, social insurance-based social policy regimes are likely to produce a divide between labour market insiders and outsiders.

Yet another configuration emerges in the comprehensive Scandinavian welfare states. The accent on universal benefits and services creates a more homogenous population in terms of the distribution of social resources. Its stress on individual rights and, even more importantly, on promoting women's employment (since the 1960s) has *de facto* replaced the conventional male bread-winner model with the double-earner, dual-career family. And the massive apparatus of collective social services has created an essentially female, occupational hierarchy in the welfare state. Hence, probably nowhere else are women and the welfare state so dominant in the evolution of the postindustrial economy—with the unintended side-effect of unusually strong job sex-segregation.

The consolidation of these divergent welfare capitalisms occurred at the very same moment when the political economy changed, when full employment industrialism was replaced by the twin process of de-industrialization and tertiarization. Industrial workforce redundancies, women's employment growth, and service sector development do not merely follow universal laws of motion. Rather, postindustrial society is being created by an antecedent institutional infrastructure. In this chapter, I shall focus on the labour market components of this infrastructure: the nature and strength of trade unionism, and variations in labour market regulation.

Models of Industrial Relations

Table 2.1 summarizes the main cross-national differences in industrial relations structure in terms of the scope of bargaining coverage, centralization, and degree of co-ordination.[4] Coverage rates are usually a function of degree of co-ordination and centralization in collective bargaining. The greater the coverage, co-ordination, and centralization level, the more likely is it also that bargaining will produce more homogeneous, across-the-board egalitarianism in terms of wages and conditions. Vice versa, very decentralized structures with only marginal levels of coverage—as in North America and the United Kingdom—are apt to result in greater differentials and segmentation. We can note a certain degree of decentralization in the past decades, most clearly in Denmark, Sweden, and the UK.

We know from collective action theory (Olson, 1982) that the degree of co-ordination affects outcomes. Little or no co-ordination means that individual unions are more likely to pursue egoistic, rent-seeking, 'insider' wage bargaining while highly co-ordinated bargaining is more likely to harmonize general wage developments with economy-wide constraints (Alvarez, Garret, and Lange, 1991; Bruno and Sachs, 1985; Crouch, 1985; Calmfors and Driffill, 1988; Soskice, 1990).

The relationship between collective bargaining and labour market performance is often depicted as a 'hump-shaped' curve. In this view, desirable collective goals, such as price stability and low unemployment are more likely to result if unionism is either very weak (hence market forces will predominate) or very strong (consensual solidarity will predominate). The worst-case scenario occurs where unions have muscle but no capacity for co-ordination (Calmfors and Driffill, 1988; Soskice, 1990; OECD, 1997b). The gains from co-ordination should also extend to economies' capacity to minimize equality–jobs trade-offs. Thus centralization and co-ordination seem better able to sustain wage equality or strong worker rights without adverse employment or inflationary effects, primarily because of unions' capacity for across-the-board wage restraint (OECD, 1997b, Tables 3.5 and 3.6).[5]

Contrary to what is often believed, there is no uniform trend towards trade union decline. Our data do not permit long-term comparisons but, according to Visser (1996, Table 2), coverage rates have remained fairly stable in all countries except the United States and Britain. There is,

---

[4] We should focus on union coverage rather than actual membership since it is the former that really matters from the point of view of bargaining results. Union density figures may seriously misrepresent a nation's collective bargaining practice, as is most dramatically evident in France where union membership is insignificant (10 per cent of the labour force) while coverage under collective contracts is over 80 per cent (OECD, 1994a, ii, 10).

[5] These issues will be examined more closely in Part II of this book.

TABLE 2.1. *A comparison of labour market institutions*

	Union coverage	Centralization		Co-ordination
	1990s	1970	1990s	1980s
Australia	80	Medium	High	High
Canada	35	Low	Low	Nil
UK	47	Medium	Low	Nil
USA	15	Low	Low	Nil
Denmark	80+	High	Medium	Some
Finland	95	High	High	Some
Norway	75	High	High	High
Sweden	83	High	Medium	Some
Austria	98	High	Medium	High
Belgium	90	Medium	High	Some
France	82	Medium	Medium	Some
Germany	90	Medium	Medium	High
Italy	70	Medium	Medium	Some
Netherlands	81	Medium	Medium	Some
Portugal	79	Medium	Medium	Some
Spain	70+	Medium	Medium	Some

Notes: Coverage is the percentage wage-earners *de facto* covered under collective agreements; centralization reflects dominant locus of bargaining: company, sector, or economy-wide level; co-ordination implies synchronization of bargaining across individual unions.

Sources: Visser, 1996, Table 2; and OECD, 1994*a*, Part II, Tables 5.9 and 5.14. Data on Italy based on personal communication with M. Regini.

however, a notable fall in centralization and co-ordination within those nations that once were considered the epitome of neo-corporatism: Austria and Scandinavia.

The coherence of employer organizations may also be detrimental to collective bargaining. Swenson (1989) argues that trade union attributes are basically a derivative of employer organization. In fact, the cross-national rank-order of employer organizational density or cohesion is almost identical to that of trade union density and centralization: very low in Britain on both counts; high or medium-high in both the Nordic and Continental European countries. There are, however, two exceptions— Italy and Portugal—where fairly high levels of union cohesion coincide with weak employer organization (Visser, 1996).

In any case, there is some evidence that types of welfare states and industrial relations systems go hand-in-hand. The simple correlation between levels of co-ordination and a dummy variable for the social democratic, liberal, and conservative welfare state model is, respectively: +.45, −.25, and −.13. And for union centralization, the respective correlation is: +.41, −.52, and +.15. These are weak correlations, but they do indicate that social democratic welfare regimes stand out for their greater degree of co-ordinated and centralized bargaining systems; the liberal for the opposite. There is clearly no prevailing pattern among the conservative welfare states.[6]

Employment Regulation and Worker Rights

At the core of the contemporary 'Eurosclerosis' debate and, more generally, of the attack on the welfare state, lies the problem of labour market regulation. There is the widespread view that excessive rigidities contribute to, and probably cause, persistent mass unemployment, long-term unemployment, and sluggish job growth across Europe (Giersch, 1985; Siebert, 1997; OECD, 1994a; Scarpetta, 1996).[7]

The regulatory framework of labour markets consists of three main types of 'rights', each in principle conducive to the promotion of rigidities.[8] There are, firstly, social benefits. These may have a double effect. On the supply side, a high reservation wage (and tax-wedge) may entrap people in unemployment or assistance dependency; on the demand side, an expensive welfare state imposes high fixed labour costs on employers. The second has to do with wage structure and, in particular, with the minimum wage. If wages are too undifferentiated and/or the minimum is too high, the less productive workers will find themselves priced out of the market, and employers are more likely to opt for labour substitution investments. This will most likely affect weaker groups such as youth, women, and increasingly, the less skilled.[9] And the third has to do with job rights and, in particular, with the cost of worker dismissals. In this case, the link to employment outcomes is more indirect since rigidities of this kind will primarily affect turnover across business cycles.[10]

[6] The data refer to 1980, that is before the contemporary era of widespread deregulation and occasional trade union decay. In OLS regressions, the coefficients are significant for the social democratic welfare state and for the liberal welfare states *only* as regards the co-ordination variable.

[7] The empirical validity of these claims will be examined in Part II of this book. For an overview of the debate and evidence, see Alogoskoufis *et al.* (1995), Nickell (1997), and Esping-Andersen (1998).

[8] Rigidities is a rather unfortunate concept with pejorative overtones. Most economists seem to use it to describe practices and regulations that inhibit automatic market clearing. I use it here and elsewhere mainly as shorthand for measures which inhibit employer prerogatives. It is evident that it has affinities to concepts like de-commodification.

[9] A recent and balanced overview can be found in Dolado *et al.* (1996) and in Card and Krueger (1995).

[10] For a discussion, see Buechtemann (1993), OECD (1994a), Blank (1994), and Bentolila and Bertola (1990).

Varieties of Welfare Capitalism

As Buechtemann (1993) and many others have noted, this complex of regulations and 'rights', whether legislated or bargained, is of very recent vintage. Most countries' regulatory framework dates back to the late 1960s and early 1970s, when trade union bargaining power was at its strongest and worker militancy at a peak. It coincides, in other words, with welfare state maturation *and* with the end of the post-war growth-boom.

On all three measures, there is no doubt that Europe as a whole exhibits pervasive regulation in comparison to the Anglo-Saxon countries in general, and the United States in particular. The reservation wage is typically more generous, the minimum wage relatively higher, and dismissal protection much stronger. For an overview, see Table 2.2.

TABLE 2.2. *Labour market regulations and worker job rights*

	Unemployment benefit as a percentage of APW[a]	Minimum wage as a percentage of average[b]	Synthetic rigidity ranking[c]
Australia	32	—	4
Canada	32	35	3
New Zealand	31	45	2
UK	23	40	7
USA	14	39	1
Denmark	60	54	5
Finland	45	52	10
Norway	40	64	11
Sweden	30	52	13
Austria	43	62	16
Belgium	57	60	17
France	48	50	14
Germany	43	55	15
Italy	5	71	21
Netherlands	58	55	9
Portugal	42	45	19
Spain	41	32	20
Japan	10	—	8

[a] APW = average production worker. Unemployment benefits are net, after tax as a percentage of average production worker earnings, for single person for 1991. *Source*: OECD, 1994*a*, Part II, Table 8.B.1.

[b] The data refer to 1993, except Canada and New Zealand (1991). *Source*: Dolado *et al.*, 1996, Table 1; and OECD, 1994*a*, Part II; Chart 5.14.

[c] This is an average index based on four different rankings of employment protection, and refers to the situation in the late 1980s–early 1990s. *Source*: OECD, 1994*b*, Part II, Table 6.7.

As Table 2.2 shows, Europe's social minima are in general appreciably higher than in the liberal, Anglo-Saxon world. Vice versa, European countries score much higher in terms of 'rigidities'.[11] There are, however, several important qualifiers. The first is methodological. These are all 'stylized' measures. Unemployment benefit rates refer only to single persons; the minimum wage estimates do not include special low-pay provisions, for example for apprentices. And the measure of job protection (rigidity) is a composite of dismissal and hiring rules (cost of dismissal, periods of notification, and so on). These indicies are also static which is problematic since most European countries have undergone waves of labour market deregulation over the past ten years.

The second qualifier is substantive. Not only do nations differ as to whether employment regulations are negotiated, legislated, or simply customary, but it is realistic to assume that official rigidities coincide with, and are offset by, informal flexibilities (and vice versa). Powerfully regulated labour markets, such as the Italian, introduce flexibility through the back door, be it in the form of black economy activity, under-declaration of wages, franchise work, or self-employment on contract. Unregulated labour markets, like the American, may officially permit hiring-and-firing at will, but in reality at least the primary, core workforce enjoys benefits and rights that are not that different from common European experience.

The third qualifier is comparative. As shown, the Continental European countries are invariably rather 'rigid'; the Nordic, rather less so. Indeed, Denmark would appear quite deregulated in any comparison. Superficially this seems to contradict a standard 'working-class mobilization' hypothesis. Why have the Scandinavian labour movements not translated their (erstwhile) immense bargaining power into worker protection? How is it that comparatively weak labour movements, such as the French or Spanish, have seemingly been victorious? The answer is that 'power' can translate into diverse protection strategies. The modest levels of 'rigidity' in the Nordic group reflect a strategy of harmonizing flexible employment adaptation with individual security through full-employment promotion, active labour market policy, and welfare state guarantees. In contrast, the unusually high levels of worker security that characterize especially Southern Europe reflect an implicit familialism in labour market management, namely the urgency of safeguarding the earnings and career stability of the male bread-winner.[12]

---

[11] Italy's very low unemployment benefits reflect its dual approach to unemployment protection. Most experienced workers will receive Cassa Integrazione at roughly 80 per cent of normal wages. Inexperienced workers have no real claims on benefits.

[12] Hence in Italy and Spain, married males with children are given privileged treatment in virtually all industrial relations matters, especially in hiring-and-firing decisions.

FROM DE-RURALIZATION TO
POSTINDUSTRIALIZATION

Post-war welfare capitalism presided over the era of high industrialism. While mass production was booming, agricultural decline produced a massive outflow of rural populations. We are, today, in a parallel situation. The tertiary economy evolves on the backdrop of 'de-industrialization' which, once again, casts off masses of relatively low-skilled workers. In fact, present-day job destruction hardly appears dramatic when confronted with its predecessor. As we shall see, our ability to offset industrial job decline with tertiary jobs today is not inferior to past experience—on the contrary. De-ruralization failed to produce a social trauma because labour markets were bouyant, cohorts were small, and because women remained at home.

What has changed can be summarized in three factors: one, less skilled and inexperienced workers are increasingly difficult to absorb in the new employment structure; two, women's altered roles imply that the clientele for a full employment commitment has been vastly augmented; and, three, the presence of welfare states and strong unions means that the management of employment dislocation is radically different.

In most advanced economies de-ruralization coincided with the end of World War Two. Hence, labour markets had to simultaneously absorb a vast agrarian surplus and millions of demobilized soldiers. Yet, a relapse into pre-war, depression-level unemployment failed to materialize because factory and construction employment boomed. Bolstered by liberalized trade (and, in Europe, the Marshall Plan) and insatiable consumer demand, masses of low-qualified workers were thus absorbed in well-paid, secure jobs—which, in turn additionally fuelled demand and employment. But also embryonic welfare state expansion helped. The growth of mass education helped absorb labour surpluses, and in the United States the importance of the G.I. bill cannot be overestimated.

There are several reasons why a similarly favourable dialectic does not operate in our epoch of de-industrialization and tertiarization. Foremost among these is altered demographics. The cohorts that entered in the 1950s were lean due to low fertility in the 1930s; the 1980s had to absorb the bloated baby-boom generations. Altered female behaviour is equally crucial. The rise in female employment began in earnest during the 1960s and exploded during the subsequent two decades, exactly at the moment when male factory jobs were disappearing. The tertiary sector may be capable of creating huge numbers of new jobs. But, since service productivity grows slower than in industry, strong wage growth becomes more difficult to sustain. And the service sector is less likely to provide well-paid first-entry employment to youth and low-skilled workers. Hence the widespread belief that full employment will necessitate unequal wages, slower real-wage growth, and less worker security.

The exodus from agriculture in the post-war decades was, in most countries, easily managed through job growth in industry and distribution. Neither demographic pressures nor rising female activity rates exceeded nations' net capacity for job expansion. As can be seen in Table 2.3, this was less the case in France, and even less so in Spain and Italy, two nations with retarded de-ruralization. The timing of de-ruralization in Spain has been especially unfortunate since it coincides almost perfectly with de-industrialization and demographic pressures—hence Spain's presently record-high unemployment levels and unusually low activity rates (Jimeno and Toharia, 1994; Toharia, 1997).

While industrial job decline over the past two decades is on a scale that is reminiscent of de-ruralization a generation ago, service growth is even brisker than was once industrial job growth. Why, then, do we now seem to have an especially acute employment problem? The reason does not lie in service growth *per se*, but in a combination of possible circumstances. The most cited reason has to do with labour market regulation and rigidities ('Eurosclerosis'). The case in favour of Eurosclerosis is rather weak, but there are two additional explanations.[13] One refers to the nature of services and service employment; the other to the growth and composition of labour supply.

Table 2.3 presents data for the two decades in which a given country experienced its sharpest decline in rural employment and, in a parallel manner, for the past two decades of de-industrialization. The third column for each epoch presents the net surplus or deficit of industrial (service) job growth versus agrarian (industrial) job loss as a percentage of the labour force in the last year. The fourth column gives the difference between change in labour supply and employment growth as a percentage of the labour force, again as measured in the last year.

Most advanced economies reached the pinnacle of industrialism and the culmination of de-ruralization in the 1960s. Literally millions of agricultural jobs were lost in the brief span of two decades. If we adopt a longer-range view, their share of total employment declined from 32 to 9 per cent in Germany, and from 25 to 8 per cent in the United States from the 1930s to 1960. France started with 30 per cent in 1949, but it took until the 1980s to arrive below 10 per cent (Marchand and Thelot, 1997: 219). In Italy, the really massive rural out-migration lagged by ten years; in Spain, by twenty. Italian agricultural employment dropped from 32 per cent of total in 1959 to 21 per cent in 1968, and 7 per cent in 1993 (Paci,

[13] The issue of labour market rigidities and contemporary unemployment will be examined in Chapter 6.

TABLE 2.3. *The waves of (a) de-ruralization, and (b) de-industrialization*

(a) De-ruralization

	Rural decline (000s)	Industry growth (000s)	2–1 (% labour force)	Employment minus labour force growth (% labour force)
	(1)	(2)	(3)	(4)
Germany (1947–67)	–3,200	+4,360	+4.3	+1.6
France (1946–68)	–4,340	+1,920	–11.6	–0.4
Sweden (1945–65)	–344	+300	–1.3	+0.6
United States (1946–67)	–4,280	+7,950	+4.4	–1.3
Italy (1955–76)	–4,240	+1,500	–13.6	+7.6
Spain (1960–82)	–2,700	+785	–13.1	–18.2

(b) De-industrialization

	Industrial decline (000s)	Service growth (000s)	2–1 (% labour force)	Employment minus labour force growth (% labour force)
	(1)	(2)	(3)	(4)
Germany (1973–90)	–1,010	+3,960	+9.3	–10.8
France (1973–93)	–1,740	+4,370	+10.7	–9.4
Sweden (1973–93)	–415	+980	+13.1	–5.9
United States (1973–93)	–1,495	+32,015	+25.0	–3.4
Italy (1973–93)	–770	+4,110	+14.8	–5.1
Spain (1973–93)	–1,320	+1,965	+4.2	–20.4

Source: ILO, *Yearbook of Labour Statistics*, current vols. Geneva: ILO.

1973; Censis, 1995); and Spanish from 42 per cent in 1960 to 25 per cent in 1970 and 10 per cent today (Espina *et al.*, 1985: 153).[14]

Had these masses of largely unskilled workers not been so painlessly absorbed, the likely result would have been more social polarization and a downward pressure on wages. Such a scenario would hardly have brought us strong unions, a 'democratic class struggle' and declining class-correlates. In Germany, Sweden, and the United States, manufacturing or total employment expansion more than compensated for de-ruralization *plus* labour force growth. But where there was a notable manufacturing job deficit, as in France and subsequently in Italy, there was also less of a democratic class struggle in Lipset's terms. Indeed, these were the very same polities that social scientists diagnosed as 'exceptional', stubbornly 'ideological', 'oppositional', and polarized (Dahl, 1966; Blackmer and Tarrow, 1975; Crouch and Pizzorno, 1978; Lange, Ross, and Vanicelli, 1982). While economists such as Bentolila and Dolado (1994) point to inflexible labour markets and a strong insider–outsider divide as the chief reason for Spain's persistently high unemployment levels, the real culprit may simply be the rotten timing of structural change (Marimon and Zilibotti, 1996).

In any case, 'high industrialism' produced an occupational structure that mirrored the national mix of manufacturing, construction, and distribution. Where, as in the United States, mass consumption was more developed and manufacturing productivity levels higher, the bias in favour of clerical and sales jobs became stronger. In contrast, Europe became considerably more 'industrial'. Peaking in the 1960s, the German, British, and Scandinavian manual working class accounted for roughly 40–42 per cent of the labour force, compared to only 34 per cent in the United States.[15]

Family Behaviour and Full Employment

It is equally unlikely that full employment would have been achieved had it not been for housewifery. Had de-ruralized women—like men—sought employment, it is possible that post-war Sweden, Britain, or America would have looked more like Spain today. Fortunately for the full-employment commitment, there was very little growth in labour supply; in part because of sheer demographics (small birth cohorts); in part because of family behaviour: the post-war urban working class embraced the male bread-winner, female housewife model.

[14] Britain, of course, was an exception given that agricultural decline occurred much earlier.
[15] Delayed de-ruralization in Italy meant also that the industrial working class proper remained smaller. At the height of Italian industrialism, say 1971, industrial workers accounted for only 34 per cent (Paci, 1973: 310).

The economic status of women in these decades was, in reality, less straightforward. Participation rates of *un*married women were hardly affected at all whereas a dramatic, albeit dualistic, change occurred among married mothers. On one side, masses of previously active 'rural' or working-class women now chose to remain at home, a choice made possible by their husbands' ability to earn a steady family wage. We thus register a sharp reduction in female activity rates in countries as different as France, Italy, and Sweden. On the other side, this was also the epoch that catalysed married women's integration in the economy. First in America and later in Europe, booming mass consumption created a ready-made female labour market of sales and clerical jobs. As married women's presence in the labour market grew, eventually also so did demand for personal and social services.

Still, on balance the low birth rates of the 1930s and 1940s, combined with little growth in women's labour supply, were key factors in the post-war full employment performance. High fertility in the 1950s and 1960s, combined with the ensuing explosion of female employment, are probably more important than labour market rigidities in accounting for today's employment deficit. A comparison of columns 3 and 4 in the upper and lower half of Table 2.3 summarizes the epochal shift: in the post-war decades, the industrial boom absorbed the effects of de-ruralization, and full employment was achieved because of feeble labour supply growth. Today, service growth more than compensates for de-industrialization but there is mass unemployment because of an explosion in supply. Viewed historically, then, the contemporary postindustrial job disease is not necessarily the result of rigidities, equality, or 'Eurosclerosis'. The real problem is simply that Europe is comparatively less capable of managing the postindustrial family in general, and women's desire to work in particular. It is this which demands explanation.

The apparently contradictory behaviour of married women in the post-war years is best explained by class differences. It is not surprising that de-ruralization causes a decline in female employment. In agriculture women typically work, so if the wives of millions of urbanized males choose housewifery, the result is that the male bread-winner family becomes a mass phenomenon. There is some evidence that households' post-war employment choices were class-distinct: that the full-time housewife option was prevalent in the working class, while the career option was at first the preference of better-educated middle-class women. Basically, working-class families emulated the middle-class norm of housewifery at the very moment that middle-class women began to distance themselves from it. The 'Ozzie and Harriet' model seemed to depict the standard American middle-class family; in reality, it was more of a working-class phenomenon.[16]

[16] For a treatment of married women's employment behaviour in the 1950s and 1960s, see Goldin (1990) for the United States, and Tilly and Scott (1987) for Britain and France. In

The post-war political economy, then, was built around a set of family prototypes that are now becoming marginal if not outright extinct. The post-war woman was assumed to be a housewife, and the male a 'standard production worker', meaning a semi-skilled, manufacturing worker who is sole provider of family income and social entitlements. It was further built on a life course prototype: women would cease to work with marriage and childbirth, and thus be available to care for, first, children and, later, aged parents. This assured that families were largely self-sufficient in the production of personal and social service needs. And men would follow a rigid sequence of schooling until age 16, uninterupted employment until age 65, followed by some years in retirement.[17] Of course, prototypes are meaningful only if they adequately represent a critical population mass; only if living conditions and life chances are sufficiently homogenous.

The Declining Correlates of Class

Welfare capitalism undoubtedly did homogenize the distribution of welfare everywhere. But here we must consider two factors. One, the prototypical division of family labour began to unravel with accelerated pace from the 1960s onward. Two, there never was a universal 'standard production worker' that fitted all countries precisely because, as previously argued, institutional differences matter. This can be seen in prevailing pay inequalities. As the full-employment, industrial era reached its climax, say around 1970, European workers in the lowest quintile earned roughly 65–70 per cent of the median, compared to only 41 per cent in the United States.

The concommitant upgrading of social security systems in the 1960s and 1970s produced a similar kind of national bifurcation. As the European welfare states moved towards universalism and from minimum to full income maintenance, they created also a fundamental homogenization of life chances and welfare. A similar leap did not occur in the liberal, Anglo-Saxon welfare states (Skocpol, 1995). To a degree, private and especially company benefit plans compensated for stagnant public commitments. But strong dualisms emerge if, as in the United States, occupational benefits remain limited to the more privileged primary

Sweden, arguably one of the least 'familialistic' of societies, women's employment rate declined from 43 per cent in 1930 to 35 per cent in 1950 (OECD, 1994c: 130). Hard data do not exist, but working-class women's declining activity rates are connected to de-ruralization and possibly also to the early waves of 'de-industrialization' which, incidentally, hit female industries like textiles and leather. The class specificity of women's post-war employment behaviour is also argued by Lipset and Bendix (1959) and Fuchs (1983).

[17] The 'standard production worker' concept has been applied by organizations such as the OECD for the purpose of assembling internationally comparative statistics, and of estimating the economic position of a typical household.

economy workers. As we have seen, by the 1970s only half of the American workforce was entitled to occupational pensions; about two-thirds to a health-care plan.[18]

But to some extent the impact of nationally specific inequalities was muted by sustained, across-the-board real earnings growth. From 1949 to 1969, the average American factory worker saw his real annual earnings increase by 65 per cent (Levy, 1988, Table 7.2). In Europe, the rise in prosperity began a little later but was even more phenomenal; from 1960 to 1973, average real manufacturing wages in Europe rose by 76 per cent (calculated from OECD, *Historical Statistics, 1960–1990* (1995)).

If not identically, the correlates of class did decline and this, in turn, gave credibility to the pluralist ideal of a middle-class society. This ideal was in reality a composite of truths and assumptions. Among the former was a decisive democratization of lifestyles: the vast majority could now enjoy a consumption standard that once had been the prerogative of the upper strata (such as homeownership, washing machines, and automobiles). To this we should add the elimination of traditional working-class risks of poverty, insecurity, and want. The main assumption, of course, was that upward class mobility was possible for all with talent, drive, and acumen, regardless of social origin.

The promise of upward class mobility remained more of a nirvana. Indeed, Lipset and Bendix's (1959: 165) data from the 1950s show that 80 per cent of American workers spent their entire working life in manual occupations. There was certainly social mobility, but it was mainly confined to moves between different manual jobs, or to the attainment of a white-collar job by working-class children. The lion's share of intergenerational upward mobility has been due to changes in occupational structure (more white-collar jobs) rather than greater openness (Erikson and Goldthorpe, 1992). A similar picture emerges with regard to educational achievement. The great push towards educational expansion in the postwar era was meant as a policy of equal opportunity. Certainly, a massive across-the-board upgrading in educational levels has occurred everywhere. The proportion of a cohort which has attained at least upper secondary schooling has, in many countries, doubled since the 1950s. Yet, raising the stakes seems not to have affected class differentials. All evidence suggests that patterns of class recruitment have changed very little (Shavit and Blossfeld, 1993).

---

[18] The wage data discussed in the text derive from OECD (1993, Table 5.2) and refer to male wage-earners only. The uniformity of European wage profiles is brought out by the rather narrow variance between countries. The most egalitarian was the Netherlands (with 78 per cent of median pay), and the most inegalitarian France (with 61 per cent). Virtually all other nations hover around 70 per cent.

7 CONCLUSION

Before we turn to the welfare state it is important, once again, to underline that the post-war achievement of less inequality with, typically, full employment and rising prosperity was probably more due to well-functioning labour markets and fortunate demographics than to the coming of the welfare state itself. As far as the first two post-war decades are concerned, the chief impact of welfare states on equality and employment was limited mainly to the consolidation of social citizenship rights. Where welfare states made a huge difference was their ability to guarantee against social risks.

3

Social Risks and Welfare States

INTRODUCTION

National welfare states espouse radically different notions of equality, but variant conceptions of equality coexist also within individual welfare states. Some welfare states (or programmes) put the stress on individual equity. This is evident in traditional, contribution-defined social insurance: you receive in proportion to what you paid in. Status-segmented social insurance, which is the norm across Continental Europe, follows a corporatist logic. Means-tested benefits will easily provoke stigma and dualisms, while universal programmes deliberately aim to eliminate any kind of status distinction. Some welfare states, the Nordic in particular, vocally battle gender inequality with the aid of social services and paid-leave schemes; others pursue a similar objective through quotas or affirmative action. The 'egalitarian' result is unlikely to be similar.

What is to be equalized differs also. The Scandinavian social democrats have now for decades defined their target as the equalization of social resources, a multidimensional across-the-board programmatic effort to level social capital; in contrast, the liberal Anglo-Saxon approach is selective, singling out disadvantaged groups for 'sponsored mobility'.

There is an argument to be made that egalitarianism is a derivative consequence of what is and always was the foremost objective behind social policy, namely insuring the population against social risks. How, to what degree, and which kinds of risks are pooled collectively will certainly have immediate—but none the less derivative—consequences for poverty, income distribution, economic opportunities and, more generally, for social solidarities and stratification outcomes. It is accordingly useful to begin with social risks. Indeed, the controversial issue of welfare state de-commodification, and the debate on models of solidarity are, in the last instance, intrinsically bound up with the management of social risks.

The distribution of social risks varies by social class, sex, and age, just to mention a few. It also changes across history. The post-war welfare state has been noticeably successful in minimizing many of the risks that plagued our parents' generation, particularly those related to old age. As we shall see, postindustrial society is altering the risk structure in dramatic ways; in part because new inequalities are emerging; in part because of labour market and demographic transformation. To address these issues, let us begin with a retrospective.

The welfare state is one among three sources of managing social risks, the other two being family and market. How risks are pooled defines, in effect, a welfare regime: the state's role can be defined as residual and minimalist or, alternatively, as comprehensive and institutional as regards the range of risks that is to be considered 'social', or the collectivity of people that is to be considered eligible for protection. Until the twentieth century, most risks were not considered social, that is, a matter of state. For one, nineteenth-century society was still predominantly rural. Additionally, the infrastructure of public administration, statistical bookkeeping, and taxation remained inadequate to the task of collectivizing social risks on a mass scale (Wilensky, 1975).

What we call the welfare state may have its roots in, but certainly does not begin with, late nineteenth-century social reformism. The welfare state is a peculiar historical construction that began to unfold between the 1930s and 1960s. Its promise was not merely social policy to alleviate social ills and redistribute basic risks, but an effort to rewrite the social contract between government and the citizenry. When, therefore, we today debate the pros and cons of the welfare state it is absolutely necessary that we keep in mind that it was built to cater to an historically specific population distribution with its historically specific risk structure.

The post-war welfare state was premissed upon assumptions about family structure and labour market behaviour that, today, are largely invalid. Risks that in the 1950s or 1960s were assumed away are now becoming dominant. Vice versa, the post-war welfare state being the child of the 1930s Depression and the 'workers question', was moulded on a society in which the prototypical client was a male production worker. This client is now rather hard to find. A first step towards an understanding of the contemporary welfare state crisis must begin with: (a) a diagnosis of the changing distribution and intensity of social risks, and (b) a comprehensive examination of how risks are pooled and distributed between state, market, and family.

THE STATE IN THE WELFARE NEXUS

Welfare state research is often guilty of conceptual confusion. Some speak of welfare states, some of welfare regimes, some simply of social policy as if the meaning were the same. It is not. Social policy can exist without welfare states, but not the other way around. Social policy has existed as long as there has been some kind of collective political action in address to a social risk. It was social policy, not a welfare state, when the Romans meted out food to the poor; when the church, guilds, or nobility distributed charity and alms; or when nascent nation states and absolutist monarchs legislated poor relief (and welfare plans for public employees).

We usually date modern social policy (and often also the welfare state) to Bismarck's social insurance laws in the late nineteenth century. But does the existence of a pension scheme, even if complemented with sickness and unemployment insurance, imply the birth of a welfare state? Bismarck, *in persona*, would probably have answered in the negative because his stated ideal was a monarchy of subservient subjects, not of citizens endowed with democratic rights.

The welfare state is something other than whatever menu of social benefits a state happens to offer. Many would date the arrival of welfare states to the moment when a basic repertoire of social policies was in place. In this case, Britain was a welfare state in 1920, as was Nazi Germany, and Franco's Spain in the 1960s. But if it is to have any meaning at all, the welfare state is more than social policy; it is a unique historical construction, an explicit redefinition of what the state is all about.

Without usually giving it much thought we tend to equate the welfare state with post-war capitalism: since the war, we live in a 'welfare state'. The term ushered in a new political commitment, a rewritten social contract between the state and the people. As T. H. Marshall (1950) put it, this implied a recognition of citizens' social rights and a promise to bridge the divisions of class. We cannot separate the welfare state ideal from its historical context.

Roosevelt's New Deal and Swedish social democracy's 'Peoples' Home' were parallel efforts to rewrite the relationship between citizen and state, an affirmation that welfare and capitalism need not be incompatible. Western nations became self-proclaimed welfare states in the post-war decades, perhaps to underline their social reformist enthusiasm, but certainly also because the Cold War rivalries necessitated a visible attention to equality, full employment, and social welfare.

Studying just the welfare *state* leaves a huge 'welfare residual' unaccounted for. During the 1980s, there emerged a large comparative literature which sought to remedy this by examining the interplay of public and private provision.[1] By so doing, the term 'welfare state' became misleading since what was being studied was the broader package of welfare production and distribution. Hence emerged the practice of using terms like 'welfare regimes'. A welfare regime can be defined as the combined, inter-

---

[1] Representatives of this, so-called 'second-generation' welfare state research include Stephens (1979), Korpi (1980b, 1983), Myles (1984), Castles (1986, 1993), Palme (1990), and Kangas (1991). Explicit and systematic efforts to identify the public–private mix include Rein and Rainwater (1986), Esping-Andersen (1990), West Pedersen (1994) and, most recently, Shalev (1996).

dependent way in which welfare is produced and allocated between state, market, and family.[2] The family, however, tends to disappear within the perspective of comparative political economy. Political economy needs to become more sociological.

The Misunderstood Family

Take any sociology textbook, and the family is defined as a core societal institution, the micro-foundation of society. The same textbook will, most likely, inform us that once the principal locus of production, consumption, and reproduction, the family's productive role was eclipsed with industrialism. Its most important remaining function is to provide emotional integration: it has become a 'haven in a heartless world', to quote Lash (1977). If this were an adequate depiction of reality, the standard political economy approach would remain valid. However, the single most compelling critique that comes from feminist scholars is that everywhere women's unpaid domestic work remains a major—and in some countries, dominant—source of welfare; that the family never ceased being a producer. In fact, the post-war welfare state's male- and income-transfer bias could be upheld because of households' own social servicing.[3]

The Welfare Triad

The family, then, cannot be dismissed as a haven of intimacy and consumption. It is an all-important actor whose decisions and behaviour directly influence, and are influenced by, the welfare state and the labour market. Welfare regimes must be identified much more systematically in terms of the inter-causal triad of state, market, and family.

It is vital to recognize that these represent three radically different principles of risk management. Within the family, the dominant method of allocation is, presumably, one of reciprocity. To be sure, this does not necessarily imply full 'equality' in the intra-household allocation of

---

[2] To this triad we should rightfully add the 'third sector' of voluntary, or non-profit, welfare delivery. In some countries, the voluntary sector (often run by the Church) does play a meaningful, even significant, role in the administration and delivery of services. Thus, in Germany and Austria a large part of health care is, like the American Blue Cross-Blue Shield plan, non-profit. Cross-national comparisons are rare indeed, and this obviously hampers any attempt at systematic examination. Salamon and Anheier (1996) suggest its role is largest in the USA, the UK, and Germany, and very small in Italy; that typically more than half its workforce are paid employees, and that the lion's share of revenue comes from fees and from public subsidies. However, social services generally account for only a small proportion of its total activities (on average 40 per cent).

[3] By 'third generation' I here mean the literature that blossomed in the 1990s, to an extent dominated by feminist critiques of what they call the preceding 'mainstream', male view. This literature will be discussed in more detail below. For an overview, see O'Connor (1996).

resources.[4] Markets, in contrast, are governed by distribution via the cash nexus, and the dominant principle of allocation in the state takes the form of authoritative redistribution—which, again, does not imply egalitarianism.[5]

It would be easy to assume that the three welfare pillars are functional equivalents and, therefore, mutually substitutable: markets will pick up where the state and family leave off, and vice-versa. This is a hazardous assumption. Markets can and do fail; only the most naïve romantic can believe that the family's historical monopoly of care and self-help can be resurrected; and not even Stalin assumed that the state could do everything. The basic reason has to do with the variable capacity of the three institutions to manage and pool social risks.

At the macro-level, the welfare production of either of the three components is obviously related to what happens in the other two. And at the micro-level, individuals' welfare depends on how they manage to 'package' inputs from the three. To exemplify, a traditional male bread-winner family will have less demand for private or public social services than a two-career household. But, when families service themselves, the market is directly affected because there will be less labour supply and fewer service outlets. In turn, if the state provides cheap daycare, both families and the market will change: there will be fewer housewives, more labour force participation, and a new demand multiplier caused by double-earner households' greater propensity to purchase services.

The household is the ultimate destination of welfare consumption and allocation. It is the unit 'at risk'. How social risks are managed and distributed between state, market, and families themselves makes a huge difference.

THE FOUNDATIONS OF WELFARE REGIMES: RISK MANAGEMENT

Social policy means public management of social risks. Some risks are perennial, some come and go with the flow of history. People have, throughout modern civilization, faced poverty, homelessness, handicaps, violence, and sudden death, but not always unemployment or nuclear radiation. Some risks, such as old age infirmity, are 'democratic' because

---

[4] Nor does reciprocity imply that exchange is a matter of unselfish giving. It is altogether possible that reciprocity means unavoidable obligations, an act of investment with a view to future returns, or a perceived compulsion to pay back 'debts'.

[5] Some insist that the triad should rightfully be presented as a diamond, with a fourth leg reserved for the 'third sector' such as charity, co-operatives, and voluntary associations. In principle, I would have no objections. In practice, it may make little empirical difference. As we shall see below, where its role is more than peripheral it is because it is subsidized by the state—i.e. a semi-public delivery agency.

they will afflict us all; others, such as unemployment and poverty, are socially stratified. Still other risks are life-course specific, income loss in old age for example.

One does not have to be a functionalist to recognize why the management of risks has become increasingly collective. An individual risk becomes 'social' for three reasons. Firstly, this happens when the fate of an individual (better, many individuals) has collective consequences; when the welfare of society is at stake. Herein lies, in fact, the most compelling reason why social protection is a precondition for economic efficiency. If, for example, people without social security risk unemployment they are more likely to resist any kind of technological change that would augment that risk.

Secondly, risks become social simply because society recognizes them as warranting public consideration. And thirdly, the growing complexity of society itself means that an ever larger share of risks originates from sources beyond the control of any individual. This is a compelling explanation for why mobilized political power has, over the past century, struggled to de-individualize and also de-familialize the burdens of risks.

Dependency on market income is a primary catalyst of generalized risks because survival itself is at the mercy of conditions over which individuals have little say; markets cannot guarantee an income, nor a job. Because market economies are dynamic, workers may find themselves technologically redundant; because they are competitive, the less endowed may find themselves marginalized. Mass unemployment is a phenomenon unique to wage-earner societies.

Family and Market 'Failures'

The more that risks are generalized, the more it is likely that family *and* market will 'fail'; rendered incapable of adequately absorbing risks. The pre-industrial family internalized most social risks by pooling resources across generations. The starting point of functionalist welfare state historiography is that industrialism renders this model unworkable. This is then what brought about the welfare state.

There is one problem in this causal reasoning, namely that it seems to assume that the market was never an effective alternative to family. But why not? If capitalism implies the triumph of all kinds of markets, then why not also for social risks? Of course, no one would deny that markets always have played a role in social protection. There exist however a number of well-known theoretical reasons why markets are problematic and ultimately insufficient.[6]

---

[6] The following discussion is indebted to the work of Barr (1993).

Firstly, as Polanyi (1944) so forcefully argued, an unfettered labour market may jeopardize societal survival. The pure market is unlikely to 'clear' unless all participants are effectively commodified, meaning that they adjust perfectly to demand and supply. Distortions will emerge if people command alternative sources of welfare, such as a guaranteed income. The *contradiction* is that if individuals do not have access to non-market guarantees, their capacity to be free, unconstrained, market agents is reduced, even nullified. A first principle in free exchange is that the actor has the possibility of withholding the product until the 'price is right'. However, this is not possible if basic existence is at stake. The labour market can therefore only be a real market when, paradoxically, it has been distorted, reduced, and tamed; when participants have access to sources of welfare other than earnings.

Trade unionism and collective bargaining have historically been the major instrument of taming the market and freeing the worker; but not of securing a guarantee of welfare independent from the market.[7] Collective bargaining is only powerful if the individual members can permit themselves the luxury of being solidaristic, and this means that the opportunity cost cannot be too high. There exist, in fact, three fundamental theoretical reasons why markets are insufficient: imperfect competition, market failure, and information failure.

Imperfect competition, due generally to monopolistic or collusive practices, will distort prices. Customers of welfare services, medicine, or private pension plans may, for example, be forced to be price (or quality) takers if supply is controlled or prices fixed. Similarly, monopolistic trade union bargaining on behalf of the insiders may exclude the outsiders; employer blacklisting of, say, trade unionists or other undesirables is a similar case. Imperfect competition makes a case for public regulation of price setting, but not for a welfare state.

The case for a welfare state is substantially stronger when we consider market failure. A commonly cited example are externalities which occur when someone (say a polluter) imposes costs (such as cancer) on innocent others. A more serious source of market failure stems from the unequal distribution of risks. Some risks are 'good'; some are *de facto* uninsurable. Private insurance companies are usually happy to insure a young, educated, and healthy citizen against almost anything at an affordable rate. Older, disabled, and unskilled workers will, however, find it difficult to

---

[7] Until the 1930s, trade unions (and socialist movements more generally) saw themselves as direct providers of social protection and in many countries (including the United States) their role was quite substantial. However, the economic depression of the 1930s testified to their fragility. Inherently, workers' friendly societies can only function well when members' risks are few. Mass unemployment easily causes bankruptcy. For a discussion, see Esping-Andersen (1990).

purchase an insurance that they can pay. Or, think of private risk pooling along occupational lines: voluntary private unemployment insurance for software programmers would most likely cost and spend little; a similar one for miners would, today, charge exorbitant rates and still face bankruptcy. The problem is that 'bad' risks are often the ones that are most desperately in need.

Orthodox liberals, and the Malthusians in particular, advocate 'self-help'; 'bad risks' should fend for themselves. This is not necessarily evidence of human cruelty, only of strict adherence to a theory that believes that public aid to the indigent yields nothing but more indigence. Whether social aid creates poverty traps and negative work incentives is one matter. It is another matter if it also leads to society-wide dis-utility. In essence this is what the 'reformed liberals', like John Stuart Mill, came to realize. A telling example was the dismal performance of the British during the Boer war, the principal reason being the downtrodden quality of working-class recruits.

Hence, even leaving ideology aside there exist purely rational reasons in favour of a welfare state solution. But what kind? Barr (1993) argues that if market failure is confined to select bad risks, a sufficient solution would simply be a residual welfare state on behalf of those who are barred from, or discriminated by, the market. There is no a priori reason why social policy should cater to the good risks. Such is in practice the philosophy that underpins liberal, Anglo-Saxon welfare regimes, and especially the American.

The problem of information failure, if taken seriously, can however only be resolved with a comprehensive and universal welfare state. Why? Economic theory of markets assumes perfect knowledge, yet the real world of risks precludes this almost by definition. Few individuals have the means to forecast the business cycle, predict a calamity, or to shop around for the best offer in liver transplants. We must seek the advice of experts. The experts, like doctors or insurance brokers, are often the very same that wish to sell us their welfare product. How can we have faith in their advice unless we, too, are experts?

But, expert or not, the error margin in the calculus of social life is huge. Even if it is common knowledge that divorce is on the rise, young newlyweds cannot be blamed if they believe in everlasting marital bliss. Few teenagers can envisage themselves with Alzheimer's disease later in life. No freshly trained typesetter in 1960 could have imagined that computers would eliminate, a few years later, his entire profession. If it is difficult for one-fifth of adult Americans to understand the instructions on an aspirin bottle, as OECD (1996a) shows, information failure is not just an individual but a national problem.

If, as social policy-makers, we assume that most citizens lack (and cannot obtain), the kind of information needed for private welfare markets to work fairly and efficiently, we would be compelled towards a welfare state design that is universalistic and comprehensive.

THE DISTRIBUTION OF RISKS
AND MODELS OF SOLIDARITY

Social risks are the building blocks of welfare regimes. Some risks are purely random, but most occur with sociological regularity. These can be classified along three distinct axes; 'class risks', 'life-course risks', and 'intergenerational risks'. They can all be internalized in the family, allocated to the market, or absorbed by the welfare state, but it can easily be demonstrated that class and intergenerational risks require a welfare state solution. Where the state absorbs risks, the satisfaction of need is both 'de-familialized' (taken out of the family) and 'de-commodified' (taken out of the market).

Class Risks

The notion of 'risk classes', to follow Baldwin (1990), implies that the likelihood of a social risk is unevenly distributed across social strata. Miners are more prone to occupational injury than are college professors; the unskilled are particularly vulnerable to low earnings and unemployment; lone mothers run a high risk of poverty. High-risk strata will, almost by definition, find it difficult to obtain affordable insurance in the market and the family is unlikely to be an effective alternative considering that the risk profile of household members is apt to be similar. The way that welfare states manage risk inequalities is therefore also a politics of solidarity, of social stratification.

We can here distinguish three distinct models of welfare state solidarity. These reflect historically dominant constellations of collective political mobilization (Baldwin, 1990; Esping-Andersen, 1990). One is a residual approach which limits its aid to targeted ('bad') risk strata—say, lone mothers, the disabled, or the demonstrably poor. A residual approach to risk pooling divides society into them and us: on one side, a self-reliant majority of citizens which can obtain adequate insurance through private means; on the other side, a minoritarian and dependent welfare state clientele. Residual programmes are typically needs-tested and generally destined to be ungenerous since the median voter is unlikely to extend much support to benefits of scarce personal relevance.

The second, corporativist approach pools risks by status membership. Occupational differentiation is, for two reasons, the most typical expression of corporativism. Firstly because professional status usually captures similar risk profiles; secondly because occupations are a primary source of social closure and collective mobilization. To assure closure and maximize corporativist solidarities, such programmes are usually premissed on compulsory membership. Their concrete articulation depends very much on the history of collective mobilization—on the degree of segmentation. The manual, non-manual divide has been the chief axis in German social policy; France and Italy exhibit a tradition of much narrower occupational closure as witnessed by the one hundred-plus occupationally separate pension plans.

The third, universalistic approach is premissed on the idea of pooling all individual risks, bad or good, under one umbrella. It implies a solidarity of the 'people'. In some cases, such as with national health-care systems, this is because the risk *is* universal. In other cases, such as the Nordic 'peoples' pensions' or universal family allowances, the idea is more that the risk *should* be shared universally. Universalism has its historical roots in two seemingly contradictory political legacies. Reformist liberals (such as Beveridge) often advocated universalism on the grounds that it minimizes bureaucracy and competitive distortions; socialists and trade unionists, because it helps overcome invidious divisions and strengthens broad solidarities.

Life-Course Risks

Social risks are also distributed unequally across the life course. This was the fundamental insight behind Rowntree's (1901) notion of the 'working-class life cycle of poverty'; the observation that poverty is especially concentrated in childhood (particularly in large families) and in old age (because earnings decline). The life cycle of poverty is closely associated with the lack of correspondence between age-specific needs and earnings: young families have costly needs and low incomes, earnings rise later on (when children have left), and then they decline sharply in old age.

The family has, traditionally, been the main locus of pooling life-course risks. The classical intergenerational contract implied that the young would care for the aged in exchange for the transfer of wealth. Also markets manage life-course risks, as in the case of life insurance and private pension savings. Because high incomes in 'prime age' working life permit most individuals to save, old age security is possible to buy in the market. But the same does not obtain for young child families whose savings capacity is severely reduced.

It is not surprising that traditional welfare state coverage of life-course risks has concentrated on the two 'passive' tail ends of life: on children (via family allowances) and old age (pensions). To a liberal, these reflect 'deserved' needs. More generally, since the post-war welfare state assumed stable male bread-winner families, its social protection efforts were directed to their job security. Women's 'risk' of motherhood was not a pressing social policy concern because women were presumably house-wives; hence few maternity or parental leave provisions.

The emerging outlines of postindustrial society, with heightened family instability, widespread unemployment, and more insecure careers, suggest that life-course risks are now bundling in youth and prime age, adult life. Concepts such as the 'two-thirds society' and the new underclass suggest also that entrapment in inferior life chances is a rising possibility. There is therefore easily a gap between conventional welfare state design and emerging needs that is not easy to fill with either familial or marketized welfare.

Intergenerational Risks

Textbook sociology often sees modernization as the passage from ascription to meritocracy. Of course, race and ethnic discrimination testify to lingering ascriptive practices. The life chances of some groups are system-atically inferior. Such inequalities appear normally as 'class risks', but if they are also inherited, the problem is one of intergenerational risk trans-mission. Inheritance and markets are usually mutually reinforcing. We know that occupational and educational attainment remains powerfully over-determined by social origin (Erikson and Goldthorpe, 1992; Shavit and Blossfeld, 1993). Also poverty is easily inherited. In a re-study of Rowntree's families in York in the 1970s, Atkinson (1983) found that the children from poor families were 2.6 times more likely than others of also becoming poor. Likewise, children of American welfare mothers face dis-proportionate risks of dropping out of school, of unemployment, and of becoming second-generation welfare dependants (Mclanahan and Sandefur, 1994).

Inherited disadvantage becomes inequalities of 'social capital'. Since such inequalities are produced in the family and are then compounded in the market, intergenerational risks are unlikely to diminish unless the wel-fare state actively redistributes life chances. 'Class' and 'life-course' risks are primarily a question of social protection and income security, and the principal kind of equality that is involved is one of universalizing rights. Intergenerational risks, however, demand a very different and more explicit commitment to egalitarianism, primarily in the form of equal-opportunity policies.

There is substantial variation in how welfare states have interpreted equal opportunity. To simplify, we can distinguish a minimalist and max-imalist interpretation. The former, which has been the conventional basis of policy everywhere, lies close to the notion of 'equity', or fairness. It is based on the admission that society systematically discriminates against certain groups, and thus denies them an equal, fair chance. This was the classical thinking behind the expansion of universal, compulsory education: assuring equal access to human capital would annul inherited inequalities. The premiss here was, of course, that human capital is the decisive factor of life chances.

The growing realization that educational attainment remains unequal and that a narrow human-capital policy is inadequate produced, in the 1960s, a watershed in the history of welfare state egalitarianism.[8] As a consequence, many welfare states enlarged and redefined their commitment to equal opportunity. Some, mainly the liberal Anglo-Saxon, retained what we could call the 'minimal' definition, but with the introduction of new 'residual' affirmative action programmes targeted to socially disadvantaged groups (such as 'Head Start' in the United States). Other welfare states, especially the Nordic, adopted a more aggressive, broader, and more comprehensive approach to equal opportunity. Here the underlying principle was that disadvantage can stem from multiple sources and that, in principle, all groups face risks. Inherited disadvantage, then, goes far beyond mere human capital and comes to embrace any resource which can be considered vital for life chances. According to this formula, the problem to be solved is not merely lingering, isolated inequities but the systematic reproduction of inequalities. The attack, therefore, came to involve human capacities in general, peoples' command of the entire complex of social resources necessary to function optimally. Indeed, the Scandinavian push to provide public social services since the 1960s must be seen in this light.[9]

De-commodification Reconsidered

The concept of de-commodification has been much debated in recent welfare state research. Originally derived from Polanyi (1944), and later developed by Offe (1972, 1984), it is meant to capture the degree to which welfare states weaken the cash nexus by granting entitlements independent of market participation. It is one way of specifying T. H. Marshall's notion of social citizenship rights (Esping-Andersen, 1990, ch. 2).

[8] Here the Coleman report (Coleman *et al.* 1966) and the work of Jencks *et al.* (1982) stand out.
[9] Indeed, the famous Scandinavian 'level of living' studies were initiated (in the late 1960s) explicitly for the purpose of monitoring trends in social-resource distribution across the population (for a presentation, see Erikson *et al.*, 1991). With hindsight, it is clear that equality in Scandinavia has been inordinately directed towards women, but there is some evidence that—at least in Sweden—the effect of class inheritance has been weakened. Sweden is a unique case where educational attainment has become somewhat decoupled from class origin (Shavit and Blossfeld, 1993). The same holds for social mobility (Erikson and Goldthorpe, 1992).

Inherently, the concept presupposes that individuals—or their welfare acquisitions—are already commodified. It is precisely this presupposition which has guided much subsequent criticism (see especially Orloff, 1993). It may adequately describe the relationship between welfare states and the standard, full-career male worker, but it is not easily applicable to women considering that their economic role is often non-commodified or at least only partially commodified. The issue to many feminists is that most welfare states, at worst, reproduce women's imprisonment in their pre-commodified status or, at best, do too little to alleviate the dual burden of employment and family responsibilities. The concept of de-commodification is inoperable for women unless welfare states, to begin with, help them become commodified.

The conservative tradition that permeated Continental European social-policy evolution highlights, like none other, the conceptual problem. As emerged in my earlier comparisons, most Continental European welfare states score quite high on indicies of de-commodification (Esping-Andersen, 1990) and, yet, they are also very familialistic. Historically speaking, conservative reformers feared raw market capitalism because it creates atomistic individualism or its dialectical opposite, socialism. To conservatives of the absolutist, Hegelian mould, it was mainly hierarchy and state authority that was under siege. In the Catholic (or East Asian Confucian) tradition, however, communitarian-familial solidarities were at stake. A conservative 'politics against the market' is a struggle to reproduce pre-capitalist institutions in a commodified world; to harmonize wage work with traditional ideals of social integration and mutualism; to combat the penetration of the cash nexus into the realm of human need and family. Hence, to a Confucian or Catholic social reformer de-commodification is desirable if it bolsters familial piety and interdependency. But it is suspect, indeed ruinous, if it encourages individualism and independence. The Catholic principle of subsidiarity in its present-day form means strong welfare guarantees to the male bread-winner so as to cement familialism.

This duality of de-commodification is crucial. Social democrats and conservatives differ not only in terms of who should be made independent of market compulsion but also in terms of how. In principle—but not necessarily in practice—socialist reformers always emphasized universal individual efficacy, autonomy, and economic independence. Since Friedrich Engels and, later, the Myrdals, equality between the sexes has been a *sine qua non* in socialist thought.

Principle and reality are, of course, not always bedfellows and this is evident in the evolution of social democratic policy. Until the 1960s, the universality of the male bread-winner family was everywhere assumed. The Beveridge report which guided post-war British Labour policy held that

'. . . the great majority of married women must be regarded as occupied with work which is vital though unpaid, without which their husbands could not do their paid work, and without which the nation could not continue' (Beveridge, 1942: 49). The first to abandon this view were the Nordic countries, but not until the late 1960s. And the policy shift came not so much from the commanding heights of the labour movement as from a massive popular campaign led by women's organizations.

In any case, the concept of de-commodification has relevance only for individuals already fully and irreversibly inserted in the wage relationship. In practice, this means that it increasingly does speak to women, too. Yet, it remains a fact that a large proportion of women (and some men) are institutionally 'pre-commodified'; their welfare derives from being in a family. The functional equivalent of market dependency for many women is family dependency. In other words, female independence necessitates 'de-familializing' welfare obligations.

Familialism and De-familialization

Words like these will easily promote confusion. To an American, 'profamily' politics imply a Christian conservative effort to restore traditional family values (whatever that means). But to a Scandinavian, the term implies what Hernes (1987) calls a women-friendly welfare state: an active policy committed to lessening the caring burdens of the family.

In this book 'familialism' is used to denote the former. A familialistic welfare regime is therefore one that assigns a maximum of welfare obligations to the household. And I shall use 'de-familialization', yet another admittedly awkward word, to capture policies that lessen individuals' reliance on the family; that maximize individuals' command of economic resources independently of familial or conjugal reciprocities. It is, like the concept of de-commodification, empirically more a matter of degree than of an 'either–or'. Given that women's (or at least mothers') family responsibilities easily restrict their ability to gain full economic independence solely via work, their de-familialization, as many studies have shown, depends uniquely on the welfare state.

In Chapter 4 I shall demonstrate that welfare state variations in terms of 'de-familialization' are as great as for de-commodification. The Nordic welfare states remain the only ones where social policy is explicitly designed to maximize women's economic independence. This distinguishes them sharply from the liberal regimes in that they offer a supplementary or alternative income guarantee to that of the market. The contrast with the conservative approach is even sharper since it actively encourages women's full-time, life-long participation in the labour market by lessening the familial burden. Conservative-Catholic (and Confucian) policy is not averse to 'de-commodifying' the male bread-winner via income guarantees (the 'just wage') because this is a way to strengthen, or at least reproduce, patriarchy and traditional family dependencies: women's economic dependence on the male; and males' social reproduction dependency on the female (Saraceno, 1996; Bettio and Villa, 1995).

Minimizing family dependencies implies a radically recast welfare state. Basically, via the de-familialization of welfare responsibilities, the social democratic welfare state helps commodify women (and so lessens the dependence on males) so that it can then de-commodify them.

We have now come full circle: a better specification of what the politics of de-commodification imply in different regimes converges with the critique of gender-blindness in much comparative welfare state research. As in my *Three Worlds*, welfare state regimes were generally too narrowly specified through income maintenance programmes, the duality of state and market, and through the lens of the standard male production worker. Still, as we shall see in the next two chapters, an empirically based re-examination along these lines confirms more than it disconfirms the validity of a simple conservative, liberal, and social democratic regime trichotomy.

4

The Household Economy

The 'family' is a societal institution, the bedrock of society, but it is also an actor, a decision-maker. As an institution, it systematically patterns peoples' behaviour, expectations, and incentives. Parallel to the state and the market, it is part of an integrated regulatory infrastructure that defines what is rational and desirable, that facilitates normative compliance and social integration. As an institution, the family forms part of the 'cement of society', to borrow a phrase from Elster (1989).

As decision-maker, the family is a 'player' in the daily life of society. What one family decides to do may not make waves throughout society, but if a huge number of families line up behind a certain behaviour they may very well create institutional change, indeed social revolution. There is always the odd husband who abandons wife and children, but this will hardly have major societal repercussions. Massive repercussions will, how-ever, ensue, when most women decide to transform themselves from housewives into workers. As dual-earner households become the new norm, the family as an institution has changed—indeed, society has changed.

As modernization theory tells it, households and 'community' were, until the rise of urban industrial society, the pre-eminent providers of wel-fare (Parsons and Bales, 1955; Goode, 1963). It was this functional vac-uum that the welfare state supposedly filled (Wilensky and Lebeaux, 1958). This view remained uncontested in most welfare state research until the 1990s.[1]

Why did the family languish as an unexamined residual in welfare state research? In the first place, post-war modernization thinking was mainly interested in the general laws of evolutionary motion; less so in the specifics. In its stylized depiction of the great convergent forces of indus-trialism, we see the seminal demise of the extended family and the affir-mation of its latter-day, nuclearized and 'de-functionalized', successor. In this trans-historical process of convergence, the old world of local, stable, and dense networks gives way to complex bureaucracies, anonymous

[1] The lack of systematic attention to households is painfully evident in my own *Three Worlds of Welfare Capitalism*. It starts out by defining welfare regimes as the interaction of state, mar-ket, and family and subsequently pays hardly any notice to the latter.

markets, and global transactions. People become individualized, intensely mobile, and adaptable; they come to face a barrage of risks that cannot be internalized within the nuclear family. Functional adaptation, as depicted by modernization theory, implied a shift in risk pooling from localistic micro-solidarities to societal institutions such as trade unions, insurance companies, or the welfare state. The parallel to Durkheim's transition from mechanical to organic solidarity is evident.

It is not easy to get a solid grip on what, exactly, are the vanishing functions of 'community' and 'family' that these writers cite. The standard depiction of familial change is that its only real remaining functions are emotional integration (the 'haven in a heartless world'), social reproduction, and consumption. Basically, it is no longer a producer. But, is this true? The standard family may no longer be the main unit of production for the market, but it certainly furnishes non-monetarized goods and services. Similarly, little concretely is said about the decline of 'community'. What community? Is the reference to self-help organizations, such as friendly societies and mutualities? Localistic solidarities and charities, such as neighborliness and the Church? Or, perhaps, lingering feudal practices of conventional obligations and *noblesse oblige*?

The political economy paradigm, which so powerfully underpinned welfare state research in the 1980s, did little to resurrect interest in the family. Its analytical lens was fixed on the battle between state and market, and the family received mention only in so far as it was the nucleus of a class constituency or the beneficiary of distributive outcomes and de-commodification. True, with the realization that welfare states could not be reduced to a contest between capital and labour, some writers discovered the impact of Catholicism on European social policy (Wilensky, 1981; van Kersbergen, 1995). Still, this literature also was preoccupied with the political influence of religion, not with the actual welfare role assigned to the family in different welfare states.

The family has made a major comeback in recent years. One impulse comes from the burgeoning feminist critique of 'mainstream' male-centred welfare state theory. Even when this critique is predominantly interested in the gender relations that are produced or reproduced by social policy, it inevitably leads us to reconsider the family. Hence, when Orloff (1993) argues that 'de-commodification' inaccurately describes women's relationship to the welfare state, it is because women's work is often unpaid family labour. And, when Hernes (1987) speaks of a 'woman-friendly' welfare state, her yardstick is social policy which enhances women's independence and minimizes the tension between work and family responsibilities. Or, when others identify 'male bread-winner' policy models, the referent is family organization (Shaver and Bradshaw, 1993; Ostner and Lewis, 1995).

Two, the family is now problematized because, in fact, it has become problematic. Where stability and inertia reign, the sociological eye tends to glaze over. Hence, the standard post-war Parsonian nuclear family model invited scarce empirical attention because it appeared so institutionalized. Yet, both family structure and behaviour are now undergoing massive change. Demographers and social scientists are coining concepts such as the 'second demographic revolution' (van de Kaa, 1987), 'post-nuclear' or alternative 'atypical' family forms (Oppenheimer and Jensen, 1995). The stable one-earner family is no longer standard but atypical. Cohabitation and single-person households are growing. Childhood today more likely means growing up with parents who both work, or with a single parent. Being a child today also means having few, if any, siblings and a fair risk of seeing one's parents separate or divorce.

In the vanguards of change, North America and Scandinavia, the one-earner family became minoritarian already in the 1970s. In 1940, almost 70 per cent of American families were of this type; forty years later they accounted for 28 per cent (Reskin and Padavic, 1994: 145). In Sweden, the employed share of mothers with small children jumped from 38 per cent in 1963 to 82 per cent by 1983 (Hoem, 1995, Table 12.1). Mclanahan *et al.* (1995, Table 11.3) show that, today, the traditional female housewife role nowhere surpasses 30 per cent. Except in Scandinavia, where stable cohabitation is widespread, the propensity to marry has changed little; what has changed is the permanency of first marriages. In most countries divorce and separation rates have doubled over the past decades (Wagner, 1996).

Such turmoil signals an emerging welfare deficit: the family that was the model for post-war welfare state reformers is still the linchpin of policy even if it is becoming extinct. In this chapter I revisit welfare regimes through the analytical lens of the family. Several points will be made. The first is that we should not have taken modernization theory at face value. Even if the long historical wave has, in general, eroded households' role in welfare production, this is perhaps less salient than specific international variations. Some nations are characteristic for their advanced level of 'defamilialization' of welfare responsibilities; others for their sustained adherence to 'familialism'. In other words, some societies may have brought the idealized Parsonian family into being; others reproduce many of the features of the 'pre-industrial' household. Most welfare state theory provides little help in understanding such variation. The real problem begins with the association of the nuclear family with industrialism; it is simply wrong to assume that it lost its welfare functions with the advent of welfare states.

The second point is in address to prevailing, often feminist, arguments that models of welfare regimes that have been specified via a political economy perspective fail to hold up when subject to a gendered analysis. Alternative 'gendered' typologies do, in fact, often contradict 'political economy' typologies. But the contradiction may be spurious because different phenomena are being explained and compared. The objective of this chapter is not to debate with gender theories, but to understand the position of the (changing) family in the overall infrastructure of welfare production and consumption. What happens to our political economy models of welfare regimes when we insert the family? What are the effects of family change on welfare states and, ultimately, on postindustrial change? Since household-welfare production is largely—but far from exclusively—based on women's unpaid labour, gender differences in the family–welfare nexus must clearly be addressed.

HOUSEHOLDS AND WELFARE PRODUCTION

In *Politics*, Aristotle expressed a politically very uncorrect view when he held that the family is 'an association established by nature for the supply of man's everyday wants'. Modern-day feminists would likely substitute patriarchy for nature; economists, market for family. However that may be, our concern begins with a simple empirical question: to what extent, and under what conditions, does the family still remain a significant association for the supply of 'man's' welfare?

There is an abundance of concepts intended to capture the role of families in the welfare mix. Some speak of various 'male bread-winner' models in order to highlight the continued male bias in social policy (Shaver and Bradshaw, 1993; Orloff, 1993; Ostner and Lewis, 1995). Sainsbury (1994) makes a distinction between individual and bread-winner models of social policy. The former approach is more likely to enhance women's autonomy because it gives entitlements that are independent of husbands.[2] The 'bread-winner' approach is analytically attractive because the link to welfare state attributes is easy to trace. Employment-, or career-based entitlement systems, such as social insurance or occupational benefit plans, implicitly favour the male bread-winner. Because women's attachment to paid employment is generally more tenuous, in such systems their social entitlements tend to be derivative of the husband. As a consequence, when marriage becomes less stable, women's access to social protection may suffer—in particular if they are barred from a permanent employment relationship. Thus, single-mother families, or women with interrupted careers, will easily find themselves in a welfare gap (Gornick *et al.*, 1997). Individualized benefit systems—especially if they

---

[2] For an excellent and thorough review of this vast literature, see O'Connor (1996).

are citizenship-based—are more likely to grant women some modicum of economic independence. This is particularly the case if transfers are coupled to affordable child care. It hardly comes as a surprise that single-mother families in the Nordic countries display high activity and low poverty rates (McFate *et al.*, 1995). The bread-winner approach can, and has been, extended to the domain of services and, more generally, to the broader family-benefit package (Bradshaw and Ditch, 1995; Gornick *et al.*, 1997). In this case, what matters is the degree to which social policy frees women from the burden of family obligations; the extent to which motherhood is compatible with careers.

A 'male bread-winner' approach presents problems, however. This kind of household was perhaps once dominant, but it no longer is. In some countries, it is close to extinction. To manage this problem, one easily ends up in a classificatory debate. Moreover, 'male bread-winner' typologies are principally of interest if our focus is on gender relations. Since my intent is to examine the degree to which families absorb social risks, I prefer to speak of degrees of 'familialism' or 'de-familialization', as also does Saraceno (1996).

De-familialization does not imply 'anti-family'; on the contrary it refers to the degree to which households' welfare and caring responsibilities are relaxed—either via welfare state provision, or via market provision. A familialistic system, again not to be confused with 'pro-family', is one in which public policy assumes—indeed insists—that households must carry the principal responsibility for their members' welfare. A de-familializing regime is one which seeks to unburden the household and diminish individuals' welfare dependence on kinship. The concept of de-familialization parallels the concept of de-commodification; in fact, for women de-familialization is generally a precondition for their capacity to 'commodify themselves' (Orloff, 1993). Hence, de-familialization would indicate the degree to which social policy (or perhaps markets) render women autonomous to become 'commodified', or to set up independent households, in the first place.

Familialistic regimes are often influenced by Catholic social teachings and the principle of subsidiarity: limiting public interference to situations where primary social networks—read 'family'—fail (van Kersbergen, 1995). This is why familialism easily goes hand-in-hand with a very passive and undeveloped family policy. As others have noted, it seems paradoxical but active family policies are extraordinarily undeveloped in the most familialistic regimes, such as Italy and Spain (Guerrero and Naldini, 1996; Saraceno, 1996).

Measuring the Family–Welfare Nexus

How do we empirically measure 'familialism' and 'de-familialization'? It is generally easy to measure governments' role in welfare production and distribution—we know the laws, we can examine programme performance, we can identify who gets what, and the national accounts provide us with a wealth of macro-level information. It is harder to identify welfare in the market, although some systematic evidence is available on private individual or collective occupational insurance. The most difficult part is to measure what goes on behind the family walls.

Household self-servicing is not monetarized and hence it fails to appear in most national statistics. Indeed, the architects of modern economic accounting refused to include unpaid family services in national income. In fact, one might even argue that they diminish national income because, if done for free, domestic services 'crowd out' a potential market purchase (Bruyn-Hundt, 1996: 73–4). Time-budget data, although often of uncertain reliability, do allow some estimation of the relative intensity of family self-servicing.[3] Indirect measures, such as data on three-generational cohabitation (assuming that co-resident elderly are cared for by their children and vice versa), can also be helpful. Alternatively, familialism may be captured via welfare state (or market) non-provision, such as the inexistence of child care or service provision for the elderly. Such indirect indicators are admittedly ambiguous: two welfare states may be equally service-lean, one because caring is assigned to the family (as in Spain or Italy), the other because it is relegated to the market (as in the USA). The only real solution is to adopt an eclectic methodological approach.

A Historical Prelude

Historical data tell us that the link between family and welfare state is far less straightforward than depicted in most writings. The standard evolutionary model of a progressive nuclearization of the family in tandem with industrialization appears, first of all, to be simply invalid. Family historians such as Laslett and Wall (1972) or family sociologists such as Barbagli (1988) demonstrate that the timing is wrong: the nuclear family reigned (almost) everywhere already in the seventeenth and eighteenth centuries, that is one or two hundred years prior to modern industrialism. Moreover, it was as dominant in backward regions (such as Sicilia or Calabria) as in advanced centres (London or Paris). It is therefore wrong to assume that the advent of the nuclear family went hand-in-hand with a loss of its wel-

---

[3] It is also possible—albeit problematic—to monetarize household labour time and estimate its significance within a national accounts framework. For an overview, see Eisner (1988) and Bruyn-Hundt (1996)

fare functions. It is equally false to believe, as many do, that Japan's or Southern Europe's pronounced familialist bias reflects a society of extended families.[4]

If, then, individual risks and needs could not have been collectivized in extended families, how was pre-industrial social security organized? Of course, we know that pauperism, begging, or vagabondage was widespread. There were charities and almshouses for the poor, guilds and friendly societies for urban artisans, commercial trades, and professionals. Yet, the vast masses were rural, and their livelihood depended not on alms but on family labour, either independently or for landlords and latifundistas. And, rather like today, pre-industrial families were not the epitome of stability. Masnick and Bane (1980) have shown that an American child was as likely to grow up with only one parent in 1870 as in 1970. Even in conservative Spain, the percentage never-married women was lower in the 1970s and 1980s than at the turn of the century (Garrido, 1992: 24). Certainly, the causes of instability have changed. Divorce has replaced death as a leading cause of solo parenthood (except in Spain and Italy); individual choice has replaced compulsion in the case of never-married women. Regardless, the one-earner-plus-housewife family appears to have been an historical exception rather than an institution; a fleeting, mid-twentieth-century interlude.

Historical portraits show us that the pre-industrial welfare nexus was built on a labour intensive, three-generational social contract. Families were large and their members worked literally non-stop—about twice as much as today. Take the early time-budget data (1930) furnished by Barbagli (op. cit) for an agricultural worker family (husband, wife, one daughter (age 20), one son (age 14) in the province of Milano. In unison, they worked 13,500 annual hours of which paid work was less than half (6,430); unpaid home work was a full 7,080 hours. The mother's 4,380 annual hours were exclusively devoted to unpaid domestic duties, and the daughter helped with an additional 2,700 hours. This compares unfavourably with the father's 2,500 paid hours and zero domestic hours. It compares even more unfavourably with today. In the 1990s, an average wage-earner puts in 1,800 annual paid hours; an average housewife about 2,300.[5] Lebergott (1984, Table 38.1) arrives at an almost identical estimate for American women in 1900 (84 weekly, or 4,368 annual hours).

---

[4] Indeed, as Barbagli (1988) shows, Tuscany (the cradle of the Renaissance and a relatively rich and advanced region) is the one and only Italian region in which the extended family remained important. The real reason had mainly to do with the mode of agricultural production (family-based and labour intensive).

[5] Household technologies and out-of-home servicing have contributed to a drastic decline in average unpaid domestic work. Today the average Italian housewife spends 2,340 annual hours on domestic activities; her employed equivalent 1,820 hours (which is virtually identical to the average American woman) (Chiesi, 1993; own calculations from Bonke, 1995). Note, however,

Until recently, it was the norm that aged parents would reside with their children. Laslett and Wall (1972) suggest that 30–40 per cent of aged Britons in the eighteenth century lived with their offspring; Barbagli (op. cit) estimates that this was the case for 60 per cent of aged Italians in the nineteenth century (here we must remember that life expectancy increased). As late as the 1950s, between one-third and one-half of the elderly cohabited with their children in Finland, Norway, the UK, and the USA. In Japan, a very familialistic society, the rate was 80 per cent (OECD, 1994c, Table 13). This, of course, reflected a two-way generational interchange of welfare: the young would receive the house and, perhaps, a helping hand in caring for infants: the old were secured meals and care when needed.

Contemporary Household-Welfare Production

Welfare state writings often wrongly assume that families' welfare responsibilities were effectively displaced with the advent of the modern welfare state. But if we take a closer look at post-war decades, the assumption is essentially incorrect for *all* countries. If, instead, the reference is to the mature welfare state of today, it still remains incorrect for *most* countries. Granted, the spread of national health care helped reduce the burden on families to care for their sick members. Still, the post-war welfare state was largely an income-transfer system, only marginally dedicated to family servicing. In fact, Lord Beveridge and other builders of the post-war welfare state explicitly assumed that mothers would be housewives. Even where a more progressive family policy was pursued, as with the Myrdals in Sweden, it took decades before it was translated into practice—at least as far as services were concerned. The commitment of all post-war welfare states was narrowly confined to health care and income maintenance: via money transfers, social policy helped defray part of the additional costs of having children or aged to care for. And the benefit, being typically delivered to the male householder, could hardly be interpreted as an implicit housewife wage. Post-war welfare states did not absorb the family caring burden.

Nor were income supplements to families particularly generous. Due to lack of system maturation and to the rather modest level of benefits, the post-war welfare state (say in the 1950s) nowhere guaranteed pension adequacy and therewith widespread economic independence among the aged (Myles, 1984; Palme, 1990). Neither were child benefits especially luxuri-

that such comparisons need to be qualified. For one, it is well established that housewives' unpaid hours exceed the necessary labour time by far. There is also alternative evidence which suggests that full-time housewives work far less than employed men in terms of aggregate annual hours (Hakim, 1997: 48–52).

ous—with the notable exception of pro-natalist France (Gauthier, 1996; Wennemo, 1994). The first nations to undertake a major expansion of family services—in particular child care, residential homes, or home help for the aged—were Denmark and Sweden (beginning in the late 1960s), followed by Norway and Finland, Belgium, and France (beginning in the 1970s). As of today, these remain the only welfare states meaningfully committed to a de-familialization of servicing burdens. True, a host of nations have a long tradition of pre-school kindergartens (*maternelles*) for the 3–6-year olds. In Belgium, France, Germany, Italy, Spain (and, again, Scandinavia) coverage is close to universal. The service, however, often remains limited to mornings or a few days a week (again, except in Scandinavia).

Put differently, most welfare states are still income transfer biased, and only a handful pursue a *de facto* reduction of the family's welfare burden. Of course, household technologies enhance domestic labour productivity. Fewer children and, not to forget, the recently acquired economic independence of the aged, imply that the relative weight of caring has declined dramatically over the past half-century. And higher incomes, perhaps supplemented by transfers, should enhance families' capacity to purchase care and services in the market—a purchased or subsidized 'de-familialization', so to speak. But, as we shall discover, the market for household servicing does not thrive easily. Moreover, where the principle of subsidiarity reigns there is little encouragement of de-familialization via subsidies. This may be one reason why family benefits are so surprisingly meagre in Catholic Southern Europe. Service-lean welfare states are not necessarily transfer-generous to families.

The Market Alternative

Markets only rarely substitute for public services or family self-servicing. In the past, of course, well-off families could hire nannies and domestic servants because they were cheap. One hundred years ago, 30 per cent of American working women were domestic servants (United States Department of Commerce, 1976, Part I, D 182–232) and, in Italy, most affluent families had one or two domestics (Barbagli, op. cit: 230–1).

Moving forward into the industrial era, the market for family welfare remained quite buoyant. Census data from around 1930 indicate that between one-fourth and one-third of all working women were employed as household servants. Be it in aristocratic Britain or in egalitarian Denmark, domestic servants accounted for 12–13 per cent of the labour force and for 30, and 38 per cent of female employment respectively (calculated from ILO, 1943). The decline of this market coincides with the rise of the post-war male bread-winner family. By 1960, domestic servants accounted for

2–3 per cent of the labour force in most countries; by the 1980s they had virtually disappeared (Elfring, 1988).[6] In their place have emerged black-market labour (typically immigrants) and the service economy.

Households' capacity to compensate with market purchase depends on three important factors. The first is the famous Engel's Law, according to which rising real household income allows the margin available for non-essential consumption to increase. Yet, this effect may be cancelled out by a second factor: the relative price of services. The gist of Baumol's (1967) cost-disease problem is that long-term service productivity will lag behind goods production. Many services, like hairdressing, psychoanalysis, child-minding, teaching, or massage, are inherently incapable of raising productivity by much. You cannot teach or massage quicker without a quality loss. The problem lies in wage relativities. If hairdressers' earnings were to follow relative productivity, they would in the long haul end up indigent. The service would most likely vanish on the supply side. If, alternatively, their earnings follow pace with those in highly productive sectors, their service may price itself out of the market—the service would vanish on the demand side. A very similar effect results from a high tax wedge, which implies that the net, post-tax cost of hiring one person (say, a child-minder) begins to approach the net earnings of, say, the mother. In either case, it does not pay to substitute market services for family self-servicing.

The 'cost-disease' or 'tax-wedge' problem differs substantially across the advanced nations, mainly because of earnings profiles and the burden of fixed labour costs. Where the tax on labour is high and the wage structure rather egalitarian (as in most European economies), the relative cost of labour-intensive personal and social services is high. The result is limited demand. Where, instead, there is a large pool of low-wage workers (such as in the United States), labour-intensive and cost-sensitive market services become affordable. This is why the labour force in personal services is small (and shrinking) across Europe (typically 5–7 per cent) while, in the United States it is large (12 per cent) and stable (Elfring, 1988, Table V.3).

The cheaper the service, such as daycare or laundering, the greater the opportunity cost to families of doing unpaid domestic work, such as washing and ironing. Unless subsidized, the high cost of market services in Europe compels families to self-servicing. Since this easily inhibits women's careers, an alternative consequence is delayed and low fertility—the opportunity cost of having children—becomes, for women, very high.

Where servicing is cheaper, the market can 'work'. In the United States, public (and employer) child-care provision is essentially nil. But since the

---

[6] At least according to *official* statistics. There is no doubt that a large amount of domestic labourers continue to exist in the informal economy.

cost of (low-end) private care is about 6 per cent of average family income, it is affordable to the 'middle class'.[7] This may explain why supply seems to grow (but not perfectly) with demand: the number of child-care workers has doubled since 1980, surpassing half a million in 1994 (Reskin and Padavic, 1994: 153; Monthly Labor Review (August, 1995, Table 2). As always, the problem with markets is that they 'fail' for the most needy. Hence, the cost of private child care would amount to 23 per cent of income in poor households—who are especially pressed to maximize labour supply. The predictable result is a caring gap. More than 10 per cent of American children with employed mothers are left alone (Reskin and Padavic, op. cit).

This brings us to a third, fundamental factor. If households are rational decision-makers, their marginal propensity to purchase either 'fun' or 'chore' services, restaurants or cleaning, will certainly depend on the balance of income and cost (affordability) but it will also depend on time constraints (need). A hallmark of new, emerging family forms is that they suffer from a scarcity of time. As the conventional family disappears so does the supply of unpaid domestic labour; the new 'atypical' families, be they single-person or dual-earner households, may be income-rich but they also crave services because they lack time.[8]

Time, Work, and Services in the Household Economy

Following the pioneering work of Gershuny (1978; 1991) and, more recently, Bonke (1995, 1996) the servicing problem of families can be measured through time-budget data. If we begin with a general comparison across nations, there is a clear negative correlation between female employment rates and women's unpaid hours of domestic work. Where most women are employed, as in Denmark, Finland, the United States, and Canada, unpaid weekly hours are relatively low (less than 25 per week in Denmark, 30-5 hours in Canada, Britain, Sweden, and the USA); where they are not, women tend to work long domestic hours (39 in the Netherlands, 45 in Italy and Spain).[9] The statistical relationship is almost perfectly linear. Roughly speaking, each per cent increase in female

---

[7] Prices vary widely with quality and region. Licensed, full-day quality care for under-threes will normally cost $850–1000 a month. At 40 per cent of average production worker earnings, this is clearly beyond reach of most 'middle-class' families. The '6 per cent' average cited above reflects the fact that most American families make use of cheap informal care from unlicensed women.

[8] This argument, it will be recognized, is very similar to Staffan Linder's (1970) paradox of the harried leisure class.

[9] The high Italian figures reflects the fact that the share of employed women remains modest. Among employed Italian women, however, the weekly unpaid hours approximate the Danes (28 hours).

employment translates into a half-hour reduction in weekly domestic work.

The intensity of the trade-off depends on several factors: number and age of children, whether mothers work part-time or full-time, and whether husbands help. As Gershuny's (1991) data show, having a child under age 5 produces a 17–30 per cent increase in women's unpaid working time. A recent German study shows that mothers with a child under 3 spend yet an additional 30 per cent, or a total of 8.5 hours daily, in unpaid work (Bundesministerium für Familie, 1996, Table 5.4). French data show that having children increases unpaid work by roughly 50 per cent, but the effect is, surprisingly, rather invariant whether there are one, two, or three children (Roy, 1984, Fig. 1). Clearly, this implies severe constraints on how much paid employment is possible.[10]

One possible family strategy would be to augment husbands' involvement in domestic chores to compensate for wives' lack of time. If this actually did happen, the correlation would have been substantially weaker. But the male-substitution effect is not impressive. True, as (working) wives' domestic hours have declined over the years, men's domestic hours have increased somewhat—but hardly enough to compensate (Bonke, 1996; Bruyn-Hundt, 1996; Hakim, 1997). The German study (op. cit), like the British, shows that fathers of small children contribute an hour of care-giving a day; the French arrive at roughly two hours. The lack of an immediate substitution effect comes out more dramatically in cross-national comparisons. Take the extremes of female unpaid labour: at one end Spain and Italy, where women's unpaid hours average about 45 per week; at the other end the United States and Denmark, where women's unpaid hours are, respectively, 31 and 25. Regardless, male's unpaid hours are almost identical in all four countries: 9–10 in Italy and Spain, 12 in Denmark, and 14 in the USA.[11]

Lamentable as this may be, it is perfectly consistent with a standard neoclassical joint-decision model of household behaviour (Becker, 1981). Since males' earnings power is typically greater, the family as a whole would lose more if it were to reduce paid male hours for the benefit of domestic work. In fact, Sweden is the only country where men's domestic labour input (at 21 hours a week) is substantial. The tempting explanation is that Swedish female–male earnings differentials are unusually narrow.

---

[10] Recent British data bring this out. Child care accounts for 10 per cent (19 hours) of housewives' time but only 1 per cent (1 hour) of fully occupied males' time (Hakim, 1997: 52).

[11] The lack of a male-substitution effect is also evident from Gershuny's data. Only in Sweden (21 hours) do men appear to approximate female domestic-duty time. Japan is a unique outlier. Women's average domestic hours (33) are similar to Canada and Sweden; men's, however, run to a total of only 2.6 per week. Since the reliability of time-budget data—especially for cross-national comparison—is rather uncertain, these figures should be read with a grain of salt. Yet, they probably do portray national rankings quite well.

In any case, where neither market nor the welfare state offer an affordable or adequate alternative, households are compelled to produce their own personal and social welfare. And, if not even the family is capable of this, the result is very easily lack of welfare.

It is probably true, as Hakim (1997) argues, that housewives' unpaid domestic work is more time-consuming than is necessary. Everywhere, employed wives put in much fewer domestic hours, especially when they work full-time.[12] Full-time employed women put in a low of 16 unpaid weekly hours in Denmark, about 20–5 hours in Britain, Canada, Norway, and the United States, and 25–30 hours in Italy and France (INSEE, 1990).

It is now widely recognized that the compatibility of family obligations with paid female employment is vastly enhanced by access to care services (Gustafsson, 1995). This emerges also in the regression analyses shown in Table 4.1. As the results indicate, daycare is crucial for women's employment; males' contribution to domestic work makes no difference.[13] When we omit daycare from our model, the negative effect of women's unpaid labour time is stronger (B = -1.2 rather than $-.88$), but its impact none the less pales against the daycare variable.

Considering how daycare is measured, the results suggest that if a country—like Germany, the Netherlands, Italy, or Spain—were to increase the supply of daycare from present levels to a 20 per cent coverage (like France), the female employment gain would be in the neighbourhood of 10 percentage points! Similarly, were a country like Belgium or France to double their daycare coverage to Danish levels, also they could expect a 10 percentage point growth in female employment. Husbands' domestic hours would have to increase phenomenally in order to achieve similar results.[14]

Clearly, then, mothers' employment prospects (and the family economy) would be better served by daycare than by encouraging fathers to put in more unpaid hours. Policies that advocate more male participation within the household may appear egalitarian from a gender point of view, but they do not appear to be a 'win-win' strategy. Most households, we can

[12] Part-time employment, in fact, does not diminish domestic hours by much (except in the Netherlands). Compared to housewives, the reduction is in the order of 2–3 hours per week (INSEE, 1990, Fig. 1).

[13] The simple bivariate correlation between men's and women's unpaid domestic hours is predictably negative, but insignificant (–.12).

[14] The analyses in Table 4.1 are based on pooled time and cross-section country-means data on domestic hours, daycare coverage, and female employment rates. The daycare variable has been coded the following way: <10 per cent coverage of the under-3 age group = 0; coverage between 11–20 = 1; coverage 21+ per cent = 2. The hours data derive from United Nations (1995, Table 7) and Bonke (1995). Daycare coverage data derive from Anttonen and Sipila (1996, Table 1), Gornick *et al.* (1997, Table 2), Borchhorst (1993) and Socialstyrelsen (1991). Employment data derive from OECD's *Labour Force Statistics* (various years).

TABLE 4.1. *The impact of unpaid work and of daycare on women's employment*

	Women's employment rate	Women's employment rate
Constant	80.21 (8.49)	43.45 (10.53)
Women's unpaid hours	−0.88 (−3.39)	
Daycare coverage	7.06 (2.88)	10.41 (3.91)
Men's unpaid hours		0.51 (1.51)
Adjusted R²	*0.622*	*0.451*

Note: Estimates are based on Robust Regression (N = 27), with T-statistics in parentheses.

Sources: For hours, Bonke (1996). For daycare, see Table 4.2.

assume, would prefer to reduce the necessary unpaid hours for both partners if that were possible.

We might therefore turn the question upside-down: what allows a reduction of women's unpaid domestic hours? Again, our regression estimates suggest the obvious answer. Bivariate OLS regressions, now with women's unpaid hours as dependent variable, yield the following results: the impact of male unpaid hours is insignificant ($B = -.144$, with $t = -.55$; R-squared $= .01$); fertility increases women's non-paid hours, but not significantly ($B = .217$; $t = .45$; R-squared $= .01$). The key, again, is daycare coverage: ($B = -4.03$; $t = -2.23$; R-squared $= .18$). In other words, increasing daycare coverage from German to French (or, from French to Danish) levels would permit women to reduce their weekly unpaid working time by 4 hours.

THE FAMILY AND COMPARATIVE WELFARE REGIMES

What, then, is the relative contribution of the family to the overall welfare mix? How does this affect our understanding of comparative welfare regimes? A first step towards an answer is to begin, not with the family, but with the welfare state: to what degree have welfare states absorbed family-care burdens?

De-familialization through the Welfare State

Welfare state 'de-familialization' can be captured by four kinds of indicators: (1) overall servicing commitment (non-health family service expenditure as a percentage of GDP); (2) overall commitment to subsidizing child families (the combined value of family allowances and tax-deductions); (3) the diffusion of public child care (daycare for children less than 3 years); and (4) the supply of care to the aged (percentage of aged 65+ receiving home-help services). Table 4.2 presents summary data for the three standard welfare regimes but treats the Mediterranean countries and Japan separately in order to examine whether, as many claim, their degree of familialism merits a special regime typology.[15]

Examining familialism via welfare state provision gives a bimodal picture, with the Nordic welfare states occupying one extreme. In terms of *public* provision, the 'liberal', 'Continental', or Mediterranean-cum-

TABLE 4.2. *Comparative welfare state de-familialization*

	Public spending on family services (% GDP) 1992	Daycare coverage (public) (% <3) 1980s	Home-help coverage (% aged) 1990
Social democratic regimes	1.85	31.0	19.5
'Liberal' regimes	.21	1.9	4.3
Continental Europe[a]	.37	9.2	4.3
Southern Europe[b]	.09	4.7	1.3
Japan	.22	n.a.	1.0

[a] Austria, Belgium, France, Germany, and the Netherlands.
[b] Italy, Portugal, and Spain.

Sources: Col. 1 is calculated from OECD (1996a: detailed country tables). Note that the data for Australia have been adjusted downward since about half of the reported expenditures are on non-servicing activities. Col. 2 is from Anttonen and Sipila (1996, Table 1) and from Gornick *et al.* (1997), supplemented with OECD (1993: 30–6) for Austria and Canada. Col. 3 is from OECD (1996b, Table 3.6).

[15] Detailed country data are provided in Appendix Table 4A to this chapter.

Japanese systems differ only by accent.[16] Granted, on almost all counts Southern Europe and Japan display extremely low public provision but whether this merits a separate regime-badge can only be settled with additional data (below). Of course, a truly familialistic or de-familializing regime cannot be identified solely via welfare state indicators. We need to know also what role markets occupy *vis-à-vis* families. Let us turn first to families.

De-familialization within Households

The intensity of familial welfare responsibilities can be measured by the time spent on unpaid domestic obligations, or by the degree to which families absorb social burdens, such as taking in the aged or supporting adult children who, for reasons of unemployment, are unable to form independent households. Indeed, many countries still retain a legally defined familial obligation to assist needy adult children or parents. Such laws, not surprisingly, are especially diffused in Japan and the Continental European welfare states: Germany, Italy, Spain, and France (for parents only).[17] Nor are the 'burden' indicators straightforwardly unambiguous. For one, it is not known whether the aged who reside with their children do so out of necessity or for other reasons. We may also underestimate the real caring burden since the aged parents may very well live next door and still receive the exact same level of care. In fact, this seems to be the case. In the United States and Britain, very few aged live with their offspring, yet the lion's share of care for infirm elderly is provided by kin. Nursing home residents are disproportionally aged without close relatives. British data suggest that one adult in seven supply regular care (averaging 20 hours a week) to sick, disabled, or elderly people. In their seven-nation comparison, Lesemann and Martin find that Sweden constitutes the only case where public institutions play a major role (Lesemann and Martin, 1993: 14–15, 45, and ch. 5). Table 4.3 provides a rough comparative estimate of families' caring burden.

In Table 4.3, the familialism of Southern Europe and Japan comes across much more distinctly and, again, the Nordic welfare regimes confirm their status as uniquely de-familialized. The weight of caring responsibility appears to be quite similar, in any way we measure it, in the liberal and Continental European clusters.

[16] In any case, as can be seen in Appendix Table 4A, intra-regime cluster homogeneity is quite strong on all three dimensions.

[17] Similar legal obligations exist in 23 of the American states, although they are hardly if ever enforced. Whether enforcement is real in the other countries is not always certain. In the case of entitlement to unemployment assistance in Germany, the rule is clearly enforced. The Italian governmental commission on poverty notes that enforcement in the case of acute indigence is rare (Presidenza del Consiglio dei Ministri, 1993).

TABLE 4.3. *The intensity of family welfare provision*

	Percentage aged living with children (mid-1980s)	Unemployed youth living with parents as a share of total (1991–3)	Weekly unpaid hours, women (1985–90)
Liberal regimes:			
Canada	—	27	32.8
UK	16	35	30.0
USA	15	28	31.9
Social democratic regimes:			
Denmark	4	8	24.6
Norway	11	—	31.6
Sweden	5	—	34.2
Continental Europe:			
France	20	42[a]	36.0[a]
Germany	14	11	35.0
Netherlands	8	28	38.7
Southern Europe:			
Italy	39	81	45.4
Spain	37	63	45.8
Japan	65	—	33.1

[a] Estimated average from INSEE (1990, Fig. 1).

Source: Col. 1: OECD (1994c, Table 13); col. 2: for EU countries (except Germany) the Europanel, 1994 (Bison and Esping-Andersen, 1998) and OECD (1994a, Table 1.18); col. 3: Bonke (1995) and UN (1991, Table 7); German time-budget data are from Bundesministerium (1996, Table 4.8).

So far, Scandinavia remains the only truly distinct cluster. Both the liberal and the Continental European systems are characteristic for their service-passive welfare states; the latter, and especially Southern Europe (with Japan), do come across as more familialistic as regards the household caring burden. To adequately distinguish regimes, we also need information on private, market-based welfare services.

De-familialization through Markets

As noted, there is no guarantee that markets thrive where states are absent. High wage costs may render market services prohibitively expensive for most households; even modest costs may inhibit consumption among low-income populations. Unfortunately we have little comparative information on the price of private welfare services.[18] We do have price data on private (or semi-private) daycare for the under-3-year olds for a handful of cases. As we would expect, it is (or at least, can be) unusually cheap in the United States, and very expensive in Europe (a full-year place costs 20 per cent (or more) of average two-earner family incomes in Italy, 14 per cent in the Netherlands and France, and 12 per cent in Germany). Britain's de-regulatory strategy may have produced rising income inequalities, but this has not spilled over into child-care costs. A full-year place averages around 16 per cent of a two-earner income. Except for the United States, these costs compare very unfavourably with Scandinavian public system rates. In Denmark, the average family will spend 6–8 per cent out of its own pocket; in Sweden, 10 per cent—and supply of daycare is rather ample. It is obvious that most Italian, British, Dutch, and German families will be barred from the market unless family allowances effectively reduce the net price.[19]

We know very little about the allocation of care among pre-school children of working mothers, especially for the very familialistic Continental nations. A comparison across two liberal and two social democratic cases is still informative. Private-market care is virtually non-existent in Denmark and Sweden (8 and 6 per cent of all types of care, respectively), but also marginal in the UK (only 15 per cent). As one would expect, in the United States private daycare is pervasive (about 50 per cent of total). Care by kin covers about 30 per cent of need in Denmark, 50 per cent in the USA, and a full 83 per cent in Britain.[20] As far as Britain is concerned, one might speak of concomitant welfare state and market 'failure'. This scenario, we can safely assume, fits also Italy, the Netherlands, Germany, and Spain.

Subsidies and Disincentives

Of course, reliance on family is relaxed if welfare state transfers to households meaningfully defray the market price. There has in recent years

---

[18] The estimated annual cost of public daycare in Sweden is around SKr.60,000 (about $10,000). See Rosen (1996).

[19] Data on child-care costs are derived from a Swedish government survey (Socialstyrelsen, 1991), except for the United States (Reskin and Padavic, 1994) and Italy and Germany (own data collection). The cost is *per child* and the family income baseline is an average production worker income + 66 per cent (as the assumed average wives' income). *Source*: OECD, 1995*d*, Annex 4. Undoubtedly, price differences reflect quality. It is bound to make a difference whether care is in a licensed centre, run by certified pedagogues, or in the private home of a woman down the street.

[20] We can, however, safely assume that the lion's share of care in Germany, Italy, and Spain is by family. Private daycare centres are very rare in these countries. The extraordinarily high degree of reliance on family in Britain is consistent with other typically noted features of the British economy, such as the very low rate of single-mother employment. *Sources*: for the United States, US Department of Commerce, *Statistical Abstract of the United States* (1995: Table 650); For Britain, Ginsburg (1992), and, for Denmark, Socialstyrelsen (1991).

emerged an extensive literature on comparative family benefit packages (Shaver and Bradshaw, 1993; Bradshaw and Ditch, 1995; Wennemo, 1994; Gauthier, 1996; Gornick *et al.*, 1997). Leaving aside the more complex and sophisticated 'package' calculations developed by Bradshaw and his collaborators, the issue can be reduced to the combined value of child benefits and tax relief. The welfare state may not engage in direct provision but the 'cost-disease' might none the less disappear if public money transfers to families are generous.[21]

This is, however, only one part of the story because the positive effect of subsidies may easily be undone by a tax-system which penalizes wives' employment. The opportunity cost of wives' employment becomes high to the family if their earnings imply a heavy marginal tax on husbands' income, or if husbands' benefit entitlements (say, in the case of unemployment) are drastically reduced when wives work.

Examining familialism through this double 'incentive wedge' produces several major surprises.[22] Let us begin with subsidies to child families. Our most familialistic regimes are the very same in which the welfare state provides extraordinarily little aid to households, be it in terms of services or, as now, of cash. Family allowances to a two-child household averages less than 2 per cent of mean income in Southern Europe.[23] Only in Scandinavia and in Continental Europe do child benefits approach a significant share of income. If we calculate the *net* cost of child care (for two children), considering transfers and tax relief, it is clear that access is effectively blocked for most families in most countries. (See Table 4.4.) The effective cost for a family with two small children in daycare is contained in Scandinavia (direct public provision), in France (subsidized and publicly regulated), and the United States (cheap markets), but hardly elsewhere.

Surprisingly, Southern Europe seems less familiastic when we turn to the second dimension: the discouragement of wives' employment (for details, see Appendix Table 4B). Here the Continental European group is unusually familialistic, either via benefit or tax treatment (or, indeed, both). Austria, Germany, and the Netherlands stand out as powerfully dedicated to the conventional male bread-winner model. There is virtual neutrality in Scandinavia and Southern Europe.

There is, in other words, no clear evidence in favour of singling out Southern Europe (with Japan) as a special case of familialistic welfare

---

[21] In fact, this is what the Conservative British government in the 1980s sought to do for care of the disabled. This invalid-care allowance, however, is very modest, corresponding to less than a fifth of the price of private nursing care (Lesemann and Martin, 1993: 39–40).

[22] Detailed country data on child-benefit levels and tax-benefit system disincentives for working wives are presented in Appendix Table 4B.

[23] Here we should note, however, that meagre child allowances might simply reflect the practice of paying the male bread-winner a 'family wage', that is, a supplement in the wage bill.

TABLE 4.4. *The net, post-transfer/tax cost of child care for a family with average income* (two children under age 3, mid-1990s)

	Net cost as a percentage of average family income[a]
Denmark	10.9
Sweden	15.7
France[b]	9.4
Germany	19.4
Netherlands	23.2
Italy	39.3
UK	28.1
USA	10.6

[a] Average production worker income + 66 per cent (wife's assumed income).

[b] French data are adjusted for the FF2000 per month additional subsidy for daycare. Note also that the French figures reflect the situation prior to the introduction of an income-test.

Source: See Appendix Table 4B.

regimes. Direct family benefits are truly meagre but then most Continental European countries penalize the dual-earner family. As far as the family–welfare state nexus is concerned, it would be more appropriate to separate France and Belgium from the rest, as also Gornick *et al.* (1997) propose.

The second surprise emerges in the 'liberal' cluster. Family subsidies are not especially generous when we consider that it is assumed that families will have to fend for themselves in the market. In one sense, the United States offers a superior cost-subsidy mix. Even if child subsidies (via tax deductions) are low (at 2 per cent of income), so are (low-end) child-care costs. The gap between the subsidy and costs in Britain is huge. Some Anglo-Saxon nations also display a curiously strong 'male bread-winner' bias in the benefit (but not tax) treatment of two-earner couples. In brief, if we compare nations across different dimensions of familialism, two things stand out. One, the social democratic regime constitutes—yet once again—a distinct world of rather advanced de-familialization. Two, there is some evidence that a group of nations (the Mediterranean and Japan) are unusually familialistic. But whether this implies that they form a uniquely separate regime is less clear. On some dimensions, other Continental regimes (like Belgium, Germany, or the Netherlands) appear more familialistic.

When we endogenize the family in welfare regime comparisons, one fact stands out: the household is still a key source of welfare production. But, how key it is depends very much on welfare *states'* absorption of caring responsibilities: the more welfare state, the less familialism. A similarly linear quid pro quo does, however, not obtain for the family–market nexus. As we have seen, markets do not easily and automatically substitute for either welfare state passivity or for household self-servicing. The wrench in the machinery is not difficult to identify: the relative price of private services. The very high market costs that permeate Continental Europe add theirs to the entrapment of families in internationally heavy caring burdens. We found a fairly similar effect in 'liberal' Britain.

Of course, families' access to private care can be eased with public subsidies, but these rarely suffice. Oddly enough, family benefits tend to be quite low exactly where they seem to be needed most. In the USA's essentially unregulated labour markets, a Baumol-type cost-disease is supressed, at least for the 'middle class'. When service workers, be they cleaners, home-helpers, or child-minders, are paid at minimum or low wages, families are able to afford their services—as long as they, themselves, do not happen to be low-wage workers. Hence, under these conditions a fair degree of de-familialization is possible via market substitution.

Reliance on market solutions will almost invariably create inequalities because low-income households are barred from entry. Where neither state nor market 'works', as in Continental Europe, inequalities are equally likely. Yet, it will be an inequality of the 'top': high-income families will have little difficulty purchasing their way into the market; the vast majorities will be excluded.

FAMILIALISM AND THE LOW-FERTILITY EQUILIBRIUM

The great paradox of our times is that familialistic policy appears counter-productive to family formation. At the heart of Catholicism's subsidiarity principle lies the ideal of large, well-integrated, stable, and responsible families. Yet, as things stand today, two Catholic countries—Italy and Spain—boast the world's lowest fertility levels while the most de-familialized welfare regimes in Scandinavia rank among the highest in Europe. Indeed, the correlation between fertility and women's paid employment is now exactly the opposite of what one might expect. The higher the rate of female employment, the greater the level of fertility.

Fertility advocates are often driven by traditional, pro-natalist ideology. In fact, the historical association of pro-natalism with authoritarian or Fascist regimes has given policies of encouraging fertility a bad name. However, the long-term welfare state consequences of population ageing give a new urgency to nations' fertility performance. Basically, if contemporary welfare states discourage fertility, be it directly or indirectly, they will undercut their future financial viability.

In the 1960s, the average European pension scheme appeared viable because mean fertility rates stood at 2.6. Pension expenditures will roughly double in real terms by 2040 across the OECD. The burden of upholding existing guarantees will be extraordinarily heavy if the average European fertility rate remains, as now, at 1.5. The Swedes are clearly better-off if they can sustain their current rate of 2.1. Italy and Spain, with current levels below 1.3, but also Germany and Japan with 1.4, face a particularly dire future.

According to common wisdom, fertility and female careers are incompatible. Of course, the trade-off may have weakened over the years as households accumulate time-saving capital goods, have higher disposable incomes and, at least in some countries, have access to daycare. In addition, men's contribution to household work may not exactly have revolutionized, but it is undoubtedly greater than in the 1960s. What is more, access to part-time jobs has grown substantially.

All in all, we should therefore anticipate that the correlation between female activity and fertility rates is somewhat less negative than what once was the case. What comes as a surprise is that the relation has, literally, flip-flopped. In 1960, it was decidedly negative; today it is positive, as the following cross-sectional OLS regressions in Table 4.5. suggest (N = 19).

TABLE 4.5. *Women's employment levels and fertility* (OLS estimates, N = 19)

	Dependent variable	
	Fertility (1960)	Fertility (1992)
Constant	4.10 (8.22)	1.09 (3.55)
Women's employment rate	−0.03 (−2.48)	0.01 (2.13)
R^2	*0.265*	*0.210*

Why are female employment levels now positively related to fertility? Has, contrary to what feminists claim, the classical trade-off disappeared?

No, it has not, but the trade-off has changed in fundamental ways. In some contexts, female careers and children can become fairly compatible; in others, not. One, albeit not the only, explanation has to do with familialism: if women, for lack of alternatives, are constrained to put in long hours on domestic labour, clearly their ability to pursue careers is reduced. Compared to the 1960s, however, women today are dramatically more educated (indeed female educational attainment levels now tend to surpass male) and ever more women demand economic independence and permanent integration in working life. The trade-off that once pushed women into housewifery is now more likely to push them to reduce or even forgo births (Blossfeld, 1995). Blanchet and Pennec (1993) provide one method of estimating the intensity of the trade-off. For the EU nations, they calculate an 'incompatability coefficient' for three different levels of potential trade-off: up to 2 children combined with *any* employment; 2+ children combined with *any* employment; and 2+ children combined with *full-time* employment. In the first situation, it is clear that the Nordic approach is very effective. Denmark's incompatability score is almost zero, moderately high in Belgium, Portugal, and the UK, and very high in Ireland, Germany, France, and Italy. If we turn to the toughest combination, however, we discover that Spain, Portugal, and Greece are the best performers, while Denmark arrives somewhere in the middle, and France, the Netherlands, and Ireland, and the UK exhibit severe trade-offs.

How is it that our most familialistic regimes now seem to have cut the Gordian knot? One explanation offered by the authors is that these countries have a strong element of self-employment and family businesses that, in effect, constitute an alternative source of reconciliation. To this we should add that part-time jobs in these very same countries are virtually non-existent.

Low fertility may therefore be caused by welfare state familialism, but the actual incidence may vary across population groups and on the actual job-fertility choices. A low-fertility equilibrium may harden when combined with factors that impede family formation in the first place. Among these is massive and, especially long-term, youth unemployment. Of course, youth unemployment *per se* does not necessarily imply delayed family formation if, that is, the young have alternative means of income that would permit autonomy. The problem is that familialistic welfare states assume that economic support for children is a familial obligation. Hence, in Southern Europe young adults continue to live with their parents until and even beyond age 30. As we have seen, the proportion of 20–30-year old unemployed Italian youth that live with parents is 81 per cent.[24]

The relationship between changes in fertility and female employment will therefore be affected by a combination of forces; in a positive direction where daycare and family services are available, or where part-time

---

[24] Estimates from the 1994 Europanel. See Bison and Esping-Andersen, 1998.

employment is available; in a negative direction where youth unemployment is high (and the problem is internalized in the family). This comes out in cross-sectional OLS regression analysis of changes in fertility rates, 1970–92:[25]

$$\text{Fertility Change} = \quad a \quad + B(\text{WSservice}) + B(\text{Youth Unem})$$
$$78.66 \quad\quad 3.25 \quad\quad\quad -.932$$
$$(12.63) \quad\quad (2.81) \quad\quad\quad (-2.65)$$
$$(\text{Adjusted R-squared} = .550)$$

This model shows that the fertility effect of a 'service-biased' welfare state is quite strong and positive, while youth unemployment rates pull the other way. Arguably, increasing the service intensity of welfare states should help reduce unemployment.

CONCLUSION

As a preliminary conclusion, and to anticipate analyses to follow, the kind of family–welfare state nexus that underpinned the 'Golden Age', postwar welfare state has, in postindustrial society, turned negative. Contemporary welfare states can no longer count on the availability of housewives and full-time mothers. The more they do so, either by actively encouraging familialism or by passively refraining from providing an alternative, the more they diminish welfare at both the micro- and macro-level.

At the micro-level, familialism is now counter-productive to family formation and labour supply. This means low fertility, lower household incomes, and higher risks of poverty. As we shall subsequently see, the child poverty rate in single-earner families is 3–4 times higher than among dual-earner families. At the macro-level, it implies a waste of human capital (in so far as educated women's labour supply is suppressed). But, above all, familialism has become the Achilles' heel of the welfare state itself. Lower levels of paid female employment mean also a smaller tax base; and low fertility now threatens the basic financial viability of welfare states in the future.

[25] Women's employment rate creates severe multicolinearity problems when entered as an independent variable with others. We will therefore omit it. The bivariate regression of women's employment on fertility yields the following: $B = 1.064$ ($t = 6.09$) and R-squared $= .699$. The part-time work variable does not correlate particularly strongly with fertility (.45), and has been dropped from analyses. 'WSservice' measures the ratio of welfare state service to income maintenance expenditure.

APPENDIX

TABLE 4A. *Welfare state services to families*

	Family-service spending as a percentage of GDP	Public child-care coverage	Home-help coverage
Australia	0.15	2	7
Canada	0.08	4	2
Ireland	0.06	1	3
UK	0.48	2	9
USA	0.28	1	4
Denmark	1.98	48	22
Finland	1.53	22	24
Norway	1.31	12	16
Sweden	2.57	29	16
Austria	0.25	2	3
Belgium	0.10	20	6
France	0.37	20	7
Germany	0.54	3	2
Italy	0.08	5	1
Netherlands	0.57	2	8
Portugal	0.16	4	1
Spain	0.04	3	2
Japan	0.27	—	1

See Table 4.2 for notes and sources.

Varieties of Welfare Capitalism

TABLE 4B.   *Welfare state incentives and disincentives for working mothers*

	Child benefits as a percentage of AWI (couple)	Percentage benefit loss to unemployed if spouse works	Percentage extra marginal tax if wife works
Year	1990[a]	1991[b]	1992[c]
Australia	2.5	100	0
Canada	3.6	0	0
UK	3.9	39	0
USA	2.2	19	0
Denmark	3.1	3	6
Finland	11.4	4	0
Norway	8.0	0	0
Sweden	4.3	0	0
Austria	7.4	56	—
Belgium	10.2	10	9
France	5.6	0	3
Germany	4.6	10	5
Netherlands	4.8	0	14
Italy	0.7	—	0
Portugal	3.0	0	0
Spain	1.6	0	9
Japan	2.2	0	—

[a] Estimated family benefits + tax relief as a percentage of couple's income (one at 100 per cent average production worker income, the other at 66 per cent). *Source*: Recalculations from Gauthier (1996, Table 10.1) and OECD (1995c, Part I).

[b] *Source*: OECD (1995c, Table 8.1).

[c] Increment in husband's marginal tax rate if wife's income equals 66 per cent of husband's. *Source*: OECD (1995c).

5

Comparative Welfare Regimes Re-examined

Following Richard Titmuss' (1958) pioneering contribution, there have been intense efforts devoted to welfare state classification. Typologies can be useful for at least three reasons. One, they allow for greater analytical parsimony and help us see the forest rather than myriad trees. Two, if we can cluster various species according to similar crucial attributes, the analyst can more easily identify some underlying connecting logic of movement and maybe even causality. And three, typologies are helpful tools for generating and testing hypotheses.

Typologies are problematic because parsimony is bought at the expense of nuance, but especially because they are inherently static. They provide a snapshot of the world at one point in time and do not easily capture mutations or the birth of new species. Any typology of welfare regimes therefore remains valid only as long as history stands still.

Welfare state classifications mirror a particular epoch, in most cases the status quo of the 1970s and 1980s. The 'three worlds' typology of regimes that underpinned my earlier work (Esping-Andersen, 1990) has been questioned on numerous grounds, and some provide compelling arguments for a major reconsideration. It was a typology too narrowly based on income-maintenance programmes, too focused on only the state–market nexus, and too one-dimensionally built around the standard male production worker.

There are primarily two avenues of criticism that merit attention. One questions the simple triad, arguing that we should distinguish additional models—a 'fourth world' so to speak. Another questions the basic criteria which were employed in the construction of the typology.

But before we proceed, there is one point of potential confusion that must be clarified. The bases for typology construction that I am here (as before) examining, are welfare *regimes*, not welfare *states* nor individual social policies. 'Regimes' refers to the ways in which welfare production is allocated between state, market, and households. Some confusion may arise because the word 'regime' is often applied to all kinds of phenomena: 'poverty regimes', 'pension regimes', or 'male bread-winner regimes', just to mention a few. Some criticisms of 'the three worlds' are, in a sense, irrelevant because they are not addressing welfare regimes but individual programmes. Leibfried's (1992) argument that there is a distinct Mediterranean regime because social assistance in Southern Europe is unique may be well-taken. But here Leibfried misses the mark because he is studying a qualitatively different phenomenon. A similar problem pervades some feminist contributions, at least in so far as they have redefined the dependent variable. It is unquestionably relevant to compare 'breadwinner models', and it goes without saying that this has direct relevance for welfare regime comparisons but, again, a welfare regime typology does not stand or fall solely on one social policy dimension; and, again, 'breadwinner regimes' and 'welfare regimes' are two distinct dependent variables.

THE THREE WORLDS OF WELFARE CAPITALISM RE-EXAMINED

The private-public mix was the principal analytical axis that underpinned the 'three worlds' typology; the key defining dimensions were degree of decommodification and modes of stratification or, if you wish, solidarities (Esping-Andersen, 1990). The regime labels that represent this triad— liberal, conservative, and social democratic—derive from classical European political economy. They reflect the political and ideological thrust that was dominant in their historical evolution, climaxing with the mature welfare states in the 1970s and 1980s.

The typology, regardless of political origins, becomes static in the sense that it reflects the socio-economic conditions that prevailed then, namely an economy dominated by industrial mass production; a class structure in which the male, manual worker constituted the prototypical citizen; and a society in which the prototypical household was of the stable, one-earner kind. Below is a summary presentation of the three welfare regimes.[1]

The Liberal Welfare Regime

Liberal social policy can trace its roots back to nineteenth-century English political economy, to its notions of 'less eligibility' and 'self-help'. It harboured an unbounded faith in market sovereignty. Liberal welfare regimes in their contemporary form reflect a political commitment to minimize the

---

[1] Although the labels differ, the typology has considerable affinity to Titmuss' (1958) original distinction between residual, institutional, and 'industrial achievement' models. American readers should be warned that 'liberal' and 'conservative' are used throughout in their classical, European usage. Liberal therefore does not imply 'leftist', but rather a *laissez-faire*, neo-liberal view; conservative does not refer to 'whatever is not liberal', be it the Christian right or the Republican party, but to the European usage of the term.

state, to individualize risks, and to promote market solutions. As such, they disfavour citizens' entitlements.

Liberal social policy prevails in countries where socialist or Christian democratic movements were weak or *de facto* absent. As Castles (1993) has pointed out, there is a peculiar clustering of the Anglo-Saxon nations around the liberal model. But, as he adds, it is important to distinguish between those societies, like Australia and Britain, where the labour movement played a significant role in social policy formation and those, like the United States, where its role was peripheral. In the former 'lib-lab' case, to use Castles' terminology, the welfare state is more comprehensive and collectivist. Disregarding such variation for the moment, there are three core elements that characterize the liberal regime.

It is, firstly, residual in the sense that social guarantees are typically restricted to 'bad risks'. It adopts a narrow definition of who should be eligible. Liberal social policy is therefore very much the child of nineteenth-century poor relief, favouring means or income tests so as to ascertain desert and need. Accordingly, the relative weight of needs-based social assistance compared to rights programmes should constitute an excellent indicator of 'liberalism'. Indeed, international comparisons show that the Anglo-Saxon welfare states are extraordinarily biased towards targeted social assistance: Australia, New Zealand, the United States, and Canada in particular (Esping-Andersen, 1990, ch. 3). This is amply confirmed in later research (Gough *et al.*, 1997, Table 2): it is either dominant or at least a major element of the total social protection package in Australia, Canada, Ireland, New Zealand, the UK, and the USA; as a percentage of total social expenditures, it now accounts for close to 100 per cent in Australia and New Zealand; about 40 per cent in Ireland and the United States; and 20–30 per cent in Canada and the UK. The closest non-liberal runner-up is Germany with 12 per cent.[2]

Liberal policy is, secondly, residual in the sense that it adheres to a narrow conception of what risks should be considered 'social'. The United States is extremely residual because of its lack of national health care, sickness and maternity benefits, family allowances, and parental leave provisions. To address market failure in these areas, the approach is targeted aid to 'bad' risks: Medicaid benefits to the poor and Medicare to the aged, AFDC to lone mothers, and tax credits to low-income child families. Yet, if there is a strong tradition of selectivity there are also creeping elements of comprehensiveness. This is no more evident than in the emerging popularity of some form of negative income tax, an approach originally

[2] There are, to be sure, significant variations in how much targeting is built into social assistance programmes. As Castles (1996) and Myles (1996) show, the Canadian and Australian approach to targeting implies screening out the rich rather than, more narrowly, 'screening in' only the abject poor.

proposed by Milton Friedman and now being gradually extended in Australia, Canada, the UK, and the United States.

On one count, liberal and conservative policy are similarly residual, namely as regards family services. The reasons, however, are different. Liberals view servicing as a natural market activity, as an individual responsibility; conservatives insist that it be the prerogative of families.[3]

The third characteristic of liberalism is its encouragement of the market. Nowhere was this more pronounced than in America's promotion of 'welfare capitalism' during the 1920s or in the Thatcher era in Britain. Indeed, it was not until the New Deal in the 1930s that the United States introduced the first national social security programmes. As noted, the residual approach cultivates dualisms: the good risks can be self-reliant in the market; the bad ones become 'welfare dependents'. There are, of course, several ways of playing the market: individually (personal retirement accounts, life insurance, and the like), or collectively (group insurance or occupational welfare plans). What unites them both is that they generally benefit from substantial tax concessions.

Welfare regimes are quite polar in terms of the role of market provision: the ratio of private to public pensions is .5 in Australia, .7 in Canada, .4 in Japan, .3 in the United States, but in Continental Europe or in Scandinavia the ratio is of the order of 0.1 (or less).[4] In health care, however, the picture is less clear. Several European nations appear quite private (20 per cent of total in Germany, 36 per cent in Austria) because much of health care is run by 'third sector', non-profit associations. And some 'liberal' regimes, like Canada and Britain, have universal national health insurance. Private health care dominates in the United States (57 per cent of total), but here again non-profit firms (like Blue Cross-Blue Shield) play a decisive role.

Private welfare plans have traditionally been more collective than individual in Australia, Britain, and the United States, to a large degree because of collective bargaining traditions (Esping-Andersen, 1990, Table 4.2). Declining union membership and coverage appears, however, to contribute to an erosion of occupational plans and to promote greater individualism. This is especially evident in the United States where coverage under occupational pension plans has declined from about 50 per cent in 1970 to less than a third today.[5]

---

[3] This was examined in Chapter 4.

[4] Calculated from Esping-Andersen (1990, Table 4.3).

[5] The Australian model of a 'wage-earners welfare state', as Castles (1993, 1996) calls it, may be considered a special case of market-biased welfare—indeed Castles insists that Australia (with Britain) be classified as a liberal-labour model. What underpins the seemingly prototypically residual, needs-tested Australian welfare state is a tradition of *de facto* job and high-pay guarantees to the male bread-winner. Hence, welfare guarantees have been implanted in the labour market.

If we define the liberal model in terms of the weight of residualism (few rights and modest levels of de-commodification) and of markets, there is clear evidence of nation clustering. The two attributes are highly correlated. The liberal welfare regime cluster is, furthermore, almost invariably Anglo-Saxon: the United States, Canada, Australia, Ireland, New Zealand, and the UK.[6] If we take two key measures (means-tested assistance as a share of total social expenditure (early 1990s), and private pensions as a share of total pensions (1980s) and correlate them with a 'liberal' nation dummy, the association is strong and positive: +.68 for the assistance variable, and +.52 for the private pension variable. For both the social democratic and the conservative regimes, the correlations are negative (–.31 and –.41 for assistance; –.27 and –.29 for private pensions).[7] This can be presented in terms of logistic odds-ratios, as in Table 5.1.

Table 5.1 shows that the liberal regime is fairly well predicted by these two features, while the two others are clearly not. It also suggests that the social assistance bias is a more distinctive feature than are private pensions.

TABLE 5.1. *Logistic odds-ratios for social assistance and private pension dominance by welfare regime*

	Liberal regime	Social democratic regime	Conservative regime
Social assistance as a percentage of total	1.185**	0.855	0.922
Private pensions as a percentage of all	1.188*	0.925	0.924
Pseudo-R²	*0.681*	*0.088*	*0.215*

* Probability better than 0.05.
** Probability better than 0.01.

Sources: Esping-Andersen (1990, ch. 4) and Gough *et al.* (1997).

[6] Britain is a particularly interesting case since, in the 1950s, it would have been difficult to distinguish it from the Scandinavian. Here is a clear-cut case of typologies being undone by historical change, an issue to be addressed below.

[7] The social assistance data derive from Gough *et al.* (1997, Table 2), the private pension data from Esping-Andersen (1990, Table 4.3). The following nations are scored as 'liberal': Australia, Canada, Ireland, New Zealand, Switzerland, the UK, and the USA; social democratic include: Denmark, Finland, Norway, and Sweden; conservative, Austria, Belgium, France, Germany, Italy, Japan, the Netherlands. See below for a further elaboration.

The Social Democratic Welfare Regime

This regime is virtually synonymous with the Nordic countries. It is also an international latecomer. In Denmark, Norway, and Sweden, its cornerstones were laid with the advent of stable social democratic governance in the 1930s and 1940s; in Finland, twenty years later. Yet, cornerstones and mature form are not the same thing. There are good reasons why we should reserve the social democratic label for the period since the mid-1960s.

In fact, the historical roots of Nordic social policy were, with some minor exceptions, quite liberalistic (Kuhnle, 1981). The legacy, as in Britain, was nineteenth-century poor relief. This was gradually transformed into social assistance and then, from the 1940s through the 1960s, into modern entitlement programmes. None the less, universalism was embryonic in the Scandinavian welfare states already from early on. Denmark was a world pioneer when, in 1891, old age assistance (upon an income test) was extended to all aged. Sweden's 1913 pension insurance plan was, at least in spirit, meant to be universal.

Besides universalism, the social democratic welfare state is particularly committed to comprehensive risk coverage, generous benefit levels, and egalitarianism (Korpi, 1983; Esping-Andersen, 1990; Hicks *et al.*, 1989; Stephens, 1996). Most studies also concur that this particular package of attributes is very much the political child of decades of strong, even hegemonic, social democratic rule.[8]

That universalism is the cornerstone of social democratic risk pooling does not suffice to distinguish it as a unique regime. The social democratic 'peoples' pensions' or national health care are only marginally more universalistic than their post-war British or Dutch brethren. True, the Nordic countries have undoubtedly pushed the frontiers of universalism further than anywhere else. And, more importantly, rights are attached to individuals and are based on citizenship (whereas the British and Dutch pensions are contribution-based)—rather than on demonstrated need or on an employment relationship (Palme, 1990). And where the Nordic countries truly stand out in comparison to other tendentially universalistic systems (like the British) is their deliberate attempt to marginalize the role of needs-based assistance.

The social democratic regime is distinct also for its active and, in a sense, explicit effort to de-commodify welfare, to minimize or altogether abolish

[8] It is not difficult to trace the historical link between what social democratic leaders pursued in the name of socialist solidarity, and what eventually emerged, especially in Sweden. It is, however, possible that this historical 'correlation' is spurious in the sense that a culture of universalistic solidarities has its roots much further back in Scandinavian society (Baldwin, 1990; Esping-Andersen, 1992).

market dependency. While the UK (and also the Netherlands) has encouraged private welfare, especially in pensions and care services, the Nordic countries struggled deliberately to close off the market so as to maximize equality. When, in the 1950s, private occupational pensions began to mushroom so as to compensate for the rather meagre flat-rate public pensions, the Nordic countries (except Denmark) responded with a public second-tier system; Britain, in a similar situation, first vacillated and then eventually allowed the market to reign (Heclo, 1974; Pierson, 1994); the Netherlands encouraged company-based occupational pensions.

The closing off of private welfare is feasible only if benefits are adequate. There is no doubt that the Nordic social democracies boast very high income-replacement rates across the board. On various programme-specific or synthetic de-commodification indices, Sweden, Norway, and Denmark are the world's three highest scorers (Finland scores somewhat above the mean) (Esping-Andersen, 1990, Tables 2.1 and 2.2). More recent comparisons come to a very similar result (Ploug and Kvist, 1994). Yet, generous income replacement is not a uniquely 'social democratic' attribute. In fact, the Dutch and Belgian de-commodification scores are hardly inferior to the Danish. And, as to pensions, the largesse of Scandinavia pales in comparison to Italian and Greek benefits (Commission of the European Communities, 1993).

The point is that if we limit our study of de-commodification to standard income transfer programmes, the great regime divide is not so much social democracy versus the rest, but rather that the liberal regime provides uniquely modest benefits compared to either of the two other regimes. What, then, is uniquely social democratic is, firstly, the fusion of universalism with generosity and, secondly, its comprehensive socialization of risks.

By the early 1970s, most (non-liberal) welfare states had arrived at a fairly similar level of comprehensiveness as far as cash benefit programmes are concerned. It is at this point, however, that the social democratic regime comes into its own by complementing standard income protection with social services and generous income support for working women. Led by Denmark and Sweden in the late 1960s, the Nordic welfare states became 'servicing states'. On top of health services (where they hardly distinguish themselves from elsewhere) was built a huge and comprehensive infrastructure of services especially catering to family needs. As we saw in Chapter 4, care for children and the aged is especially privileged. The net outcome is that government employment now accounts for up to 30 per cent of the labour force, or more than double the OECD average.

The social democratic model and egalitarianism have become basically synonymous. To many, the egalitarian element is simply the practice of universalism: everybody enjoys the same rights and benefits, whether rich or poor. To others, it refers to the active promotion of well-being and life chances—perhaps no more evident than for women. Still others equate egalitarianism with redistribution and the elimination of poverty. As we shall see in subsequent chapters, they are all right.

Full employment has surely been a mainstay commitment in the social democratic model—but so it has elsewhere. What separates Scandinavia from most other nations is decreasingly low unemployment and, increasingly, maximum employment. As first Denmark, and now also Finland and Sweden, suffer from mass unemployment, the coincidence of full employment and social democracy appears shattered. This is, none the less, not as clear as it seems. For one, we should distinguish between actual performance and political commitment. As far as the latter is concerned, the coincidence remains. The Nordic countries' expansion of public employment since the 1960s may have been guided by egalitarian concerns, but it certainly was also a means of promoting employment. Current Nordic unemployment may not differ much from, say, the German or French, but it occurs on the backdrop of an employment rate of 75–80 per cent rather than 50–60 per cent—principally because full female participation was realized. The employment commitment is equally evident in active labour market policies, both in terms of resources spent and number of persons covered under various training, retraining, or employment promotion programmes.

Scandinavian welfare and employment policy has always been couched in terms of 'productivism', that is of maximizing the productive potential of the citizenry. Superficially this seems like an echo of what Americans call 'workfare'. In reality the two are different. Workfare in America implies that social benefits are conditional on accepting work whereas Nordic 'productivism' implies that the welfare *state* must guarantee that all people have the necessary resources and motivation to work (and that work is available).

The social democratic regime, then, is inevitably a state-dominated welfare nexus. But, the Nordic welfare states, and in particular the Swedish, are now experiencing hard times—to use Stephens *et al.*'s (1994) expression. For budgetary reasons, governments have reduced social benefits: lowering replacement rates, introducing waiting days for sickness benefits, shortening the duration of unemployment pay and, perhaps most ominously, introducing elements of targeting in the 'peoples' pensions'. While cuts at the margin hardly affect the essence of the social democratic regime, the implementation of an income test for pensions may do so since this implies a qualitative retreat from the principle of universalism: the notion of solidarity of risks is being rewritten.

Again, let us examine the validity of the regimes. Besides its strong accent on de-familialization (which will be examined below), two features of the social democratic regime stand out: universalism and the marginalization of private welfare. In Table 5.2 I present odds-ratios for the three regime types with the universalism and private pension scores from Esping-Andersen (1990, Table 3.1).

TABLE 5.2. *Logistic regressions (odds-ratios) of universalism and private pensions and welfare regime types*

	Social democratic regime	Conservative regime	Liberal regime
Universalism	1.321*	0.988	0.938
Private pensions	0.731	0.926	1.185*
Pseudo-R²	*0.651*	*0.078*	*0.350*
Chi-squared	*12.41*	*1.88*	*8.43*

* Probability = 0.1 or less. N = 18.

Source: Esping-Andersen (1990, Table 3.1).

Table 5.2. confirms more or less what we would expect. The odds that we will find universalism in the social democratic regime are comparably strong and significant. Vice versa, the odds of private welfare are low (however not significant) in the social democratic regime but, as we already have seen, positive and significant in the liberal. On these variables, the conservative regime is, simply, indistinct.

The Conservative Welfare Regime

Labelling the Continental European welfare states conservative may appear pejorative. The idea, however, is to signal the dominant political thrust behind their architecture. In most of Continental Europe, liberalism played a truly marginal role and, until after World War Two, the socialists typically found themselves excluded. Early social policy was often inspired by monarchical etatism (especially in Germany, Austria, and France), by traditional corporatism, or by Catholic social teachings. Leo XII's Papal Encyclical *Rerum Novarum* (1891) had a tremendous influence in Catholic-dominated countries. Moreover, the passage from origins to post-war welfare capitalism has, in this group of countries, been guided primarily by Christian democratic or conservative coalitions (in some cases with a Fascist interregnum).

The essence of a conservative regime lies in its blend of status segmentation and familialism. Most Continental European countries emulated

Imperial Germany's social insurance reforms and, like Bismarck, their original aims were far removed from any egalitarianism. The early social reformers were typically authoritarian (Rimlinger, 1971). In the post-war era, the imprint of social Catholicism and its doctrine of subsidiarity has been particularly strong in Southern Europe, the Netherlands and, to an extent, also in Belgium and Germany (van Kersbergen, 1995). French social policy has, in contrast, been guided primarily by a republican, anti-clerical spirit. France's (and Belgium's) membership in the conservative cluster is, as we shall discuss, problematic in that familialism is less dominant. Yet, both welfare systems display strong corporatist traits. There are several reasons why we might also include Japan in the conservative model. The powerful presence of Confucian teachings throughout Japanese social policy is a functional equivalent of Catholic familialism, and also Japanese social security is highly corporatist.[9]

The conservative imprint is most evident with regard to risk pooling (solidarity) and familialism. In both cases, the historical legacy was typically carried over in the making of the post-war welfare state. The etatist legacy remains strong in the privileged treatment of the public civil service, especially in Austria, Belgium, France, Germany, and Italy.[10] The civil service benefits not only from having its own scheme but also from vastly more luxurious eligibility and benefit rules.

Also, despite some attempts to consolidate the myriad occupational schemes, corporatist status divisions continue to permeate social security systems. Of course, the accent differs between individual schemes and countries. Germany is a case of modest corporativism in pensions (the principal distinction is between blue- and white-collar workers), while health insurance is a labyrinth of 1,200 separate regional, occupational, or company-based funds. Italy, in contrast, has a unified health programme while pensions are divided into more than 120 occupational plans (Castellino, 1976). Both France and Belgium combine fragmented pension systems with a national health insurance that is divided along broad occupational classes. Among the Continental European countries, only the Netherlands deviates markedly from the corporatist mould. Public pensions are organized more or less around the Beveridge principle of universal flat-rate benefits, and other programmes, such as health, education, and services generally, were 'pillared', that is, split along denominational and non-denominational lines (van Kersbergen, 1995).

---

[9] Japan deviates from this cluster only in terms of the large role of employer-provided occupational benefits.

[10] Government employee pensions account for 30 per cent of the total in Austria; 35 per cent in Belgium; 27 per cent in France and Italy; and 21 per cent in Germany. This is, on average, two or three times as high as in Scandinavia or in the Anglo-Saxon countries (calculated from Esping-Andersen, 1990, Table 4.3).

The accent on compulsory social insurance, complemented with more or less *ad hoc* residual schemes for strata without a 'normal' employment relationship, has meant that purely private market provision of welfare remains marginal. Granted, a significant part of health care is, in some countries non-state but this is chiefly due to the role played by non-profit, 'voluntary' associations, frequently affiliated with the Church (such as Caritas). As to pensions or other welfare provisions, both individual and collective occupational plans are generally of marginal importance, in some countries basically non-existing. A notable exception is, again, the Netherlands where (mandated) company pension schemes play a non-trivial role in the labour market.[11]

The third important attribute of conservatism is its familialism, especially in Southern Europe and Japan. As shown in Chapter 4, familialism is a composite of the male bread-winner bias of social protection and the centrality of the family as care-giver and ultimately responsible for its members' welfare (the subsidiarity principle). What unites Austria, Germany, Italy, and Spain is the continued legal prescription that parents (or children) be responsible for their children (or parents) in case of need. Social assistance, for example, will not be granted even to adults if their parents can support them. Besides legal obligation, there is a systematic disinclination to provide care services, and the more familialistic the welfare state, the less generous are family benefits. Family transfers are often regarded as redundant given the practice of a family wage. But, since the model assumes the standard male bread-winner family, provision for 'atypical' households, such as lone mothers, tends to be residual.

There is, then, a modicum of residualism in the conservative model that seemingly parallels the liberal. Yet, its target is very different: liberal residualism means picking up bad risks left behind by market failure; conservative residualism, in contrast, is primarily a response to family failure. In both cases, none the less, the approach favours social assistance over rights, such as the German Sozialhilfe, the Italian and Spanish social pension, or even the French RMI.

Again for different reasons, both conservative and liberal social policies inherently favour a passive approach to employment management. The liberal model simply prioritizes unregulated labour markets; the conservative, strong job protection for already employed adult, male householders. Active employment or training policies tend to be marginal in both

---

[11] Labour market pensions do play a role also in France, but their status should best be regarded as compulsory. Here Japan is of course deviant because so much of the entire welfare package is provided by employers within the context of lifetime employment. As in the USA, Japanese occupational welfare is mainly the privilege of core workers—about one-third of all. In the Japanese case, it is debatable whether this kind of private welfare conforms to market principles (Esping-Andersen, 1997a).

cases; the management of unemployment in a liberal regime is ideally a question of market clearing and wage flexibility; in a conservative regime, either a question of family support (as in the case of youth or female unemployment) or of induced labour supply reduction (discouraging married women's careers and favouring early retirement).

Let us now repeat our 'regime tests', this time focusing on alleged conservative regime attributes: corporatism, etatism, and familialism. See Table 5.3.

TABLE 5.3. *Logistic regressions* (*odds-ratios*) *of welfare regimes and corporatism, etatism, and welfare state de-familialization*

	Conservative regime	Social democratic regime	Liberal regime
Corporatism	4.18e + 17***	} Welfare state de-familialization perfectly predicted	} Corporatism and welfare state de-familialization perfectly predicted
Etatism	5.204		
Welfare state de-familialization	2.20e – 08***		
Pseudo-R²	*0.793*		
Chi-squared	*19.07*		

*** Probability = 0.001 or more. N = 18.

Sources: Corporatism and etatism variables from Esping-Andersen (1990, Table 3.1). See fn. 19 for an explanation of welfare state de-familialism.

In comparison with our earlier estimations, the conservative regime is very distinctive. The odds of corporatism and familialism are powerful indeed. It does not, however, stand out as especially etatist. The uniqueness of the conservative regime comes out even stronger when we recognize that the social democratic welfare states are, without exception, uniquely de-famililializing and that the liberal regimes all score low on corporatism.[12]

Based on the foregoing, we can outline the main attributes of the three regimes. See Table 5.4.

An alternative way to classify welfare regimes would be to pinpoint their dominant approach to managing social risks within labour markets, the state, and the family. As far as the labour market is concerned, we might simply distinguish between a regulatory and non-regulatory approach. For the state we could distinguish between residual, universal-

[12] Here, as in earlier analyses, we should bear in mind the small sample size (18) which impairs estimation. Under such conditions, we should probably attach less importance to the size of the odds and more to the signs (positive or negative).

TABLE 5.4. *A summary overview of regime characteristics*

	Liberal	Social democratic	Conservative
Role of:			
Family	Marginal	Marginal	Central
Market	Central	Marginal	Marginal
State	Marginal	Central	Subsidiary
Welfare state:			
Dominant mode of solidarity	Individual	Universal	Kinship Corporatism Etatism
Dominant locus of solidarity	Market	State	Family
Degree of decommodification	Minimal	Maximum	High (for bread-winner)
Modal Examples	USA	Sweden	Germany Italy

ist, and social insurance models. And with regard to the family, the vital difference is whether families are meant to be the primary locus of welfare (familialism) or not; i.e. whether welfare states grant the family social rights or not. Following this approach, we would arrive at the following schematic nation classification:[13]

A: LABOUR MARKET REGULATION

Little regulation: Australia, Canada, Denmark, New Zealand, Switzerland, the UK, and the United States.

Medium regulation: Japan, Ireland, the Netherlands, Finland, Norway, Sweden.

Strong regulation: France, Germany, Austria, Belgium, Italy, Portugal, and Spain.

B: WELFARE STATES

Residual: Australia, Canada, New Zealand, the United States (and, to a degree, the UK).

[13] Reflecting the situation in the early 1990s. Thus, Australia scores as non-regulated in labour markets while, twenty years ago, Australia would have scored as highly regulated. Similarly, Britain twenty years ago would have been easy to classify as a universalist welfare state while today, considering the strong push towards income testing over the past decades, it has moved closer to the residual category. The scoring for labour market and family is based on the discussion in Chapters 3 and 4.

Universalist: Denmark, Finland, Norway, Sweden, the Netherlands (and to a degree, the UK).
Social insurance: Austria, Belgium, France, Germany, Italy, Japan, and Spain.

C: FAMILIES
Familialist: Austria, Germany, Italy, Japan, the Netherlands, Portugal, Spain (and, less so, Belgium and France).
Non-familialist: Australia, Canada, Denmark, Finland, New Zealand, Norway, Sweden, the UK, and the United States.

We turn now to the question of whether a 'three worlds' typology remains robust and valid.

THE HISTORICAL AND COMPARATIVE ROBUSTNESS OF REGIME TYPOLOGIES

Since typologies refer to one time-point, we shall miss out on possibly decisive transmutations. And since they are, in a sense, ideal types there are bound to be ambiguous cases. Some critics have, for example, pointed out that the Netherlands and Britain, both in their own way, fit poorly in any of the three clusters.

It is also possible that the criteria employed to demarcate a regime may err: if alternative attributes were considered, the classification might break down or, at least, require additional regimes. For different reasons it has been argued that the Antipodes, East Asia, and Southern Europe all merit a 'fourth world'. It has also been argued that the entire typology is problematic because it is built on the experience of the standard male breadwinner; it is not gender-sensitive.

Getting the welfare regime typology straight matters not just for the historical record but also for further analytical progress. At the core of a welfare regime study lurks the presupposition that institutional configuration matters for how risks are absorbed and distributed, for social stratification and solidarities, and also for the operation of labour markets. Hence, regimes should display some degree of congruence and commonality in how they adapt to massive social and economic change. This is a major issue of this book and we need, therefore, to establish just how robust is the working typology.

If there are ambiguous cases in a typology, the question is how much they matter. The goodness-of-fit of the three-way regime typology has been tested utilizing several methodological techniques, including cluster analysis, Boolean algebra, factor analysis, and more conventional correlational analysis (Kangas, 1994; Ragin, 1994; Shalev, 1996). While these studies find that some countries fit more poorly than others (for different reasons, Belgium, France, Britain, and the Netherlands are frequently cited cases), there is also some support for the three clusters.

Britain is mainly a problem because the typology does not take into account mutation. Had we made our comparisons in the immediate post-war decades, we would almost certainly have put Britain and Scandinavia in the same cluster: both were built on universal, flat-rate benefit pro-grammes, national health care, and a vocal political commitment to full employment. Moving ahead into the 1970s and beyond, the two clearly part ways: Britain failed to uphold its full-employment commitment and to supplement modest flat-rate benefits with a guarantee of adequate income replacement (Heclo, 1974; Martin, 1973). Failure to keep up pro-moted a gradual privatization that was, no doubt, accelerated by con-certed de-regulation, more targeting, and privatization during the 1980s: sickness and maternity benefits were transferred to employers, council housing was sold off, the earnings-related pension (SERPS) was 'priva-tized' through opting-out, and both private pensions and health insurance have been nurtured via tax subsidies (Taylor-Gooby, 1996).[14] In a con-temporary comparison, then, Britain appears increasingly liberal. Britain is an example of regime-shifting or, perhaps, of stalled 'social democrati-zation'.[15]

The original 'three worlds' typology focused rather one-sidedly on income maintenance. Herein lie perhaps the ambiguities of the Dutch case. When we study income maintenance, the Netherlands appears 'social democratic' in the sense of strong universalism, comprehensive coverage, and generous 'de-commodifying' benefits (van Kersbergen, 1995). But when we include social service delivery—and when, more generally, we examine the role of the family—the Netherlands becomes squarely a mem-ber of the 'conservative', Continental European fold. Like Britain, this would not have been immediately obvious in the 1950s because then, also the Nordic welfare states were service-lean and transfer-biased. It is in its sustained inattention to social services that the Netherlands emerges as a prototypical example of Catholic familialism (Bussemaker and van Kersbergen, 1994; van Kersbergen, 1995; Gustafsson, 1994). What is more, the generosity of Dutch income maintenance is chiefly the expres-sion of a pervasive male bread-winner assumption.

[14] It is also telling that public residential care for the aged declined by 4 per cent, 1976–86, while private care grew by 363 per cent (Evers and Svetlik, 1991: 130).

[15] The bulk of the data used to identify regimes in my *Three Worlds* referred to *c.*1980. The true liberal nature of Britain's transformation only became fully visible later. It may be true that Britain and Sweden were rather alike in the 1950s, but this does not imply that Britain was then 'social democratic'. What I define as the essence of social democratic welfare regimes emerged in Scandinavia later.

The Dutch enigma, then, highlights the need to reconsider, once again, *what* must be compared and measured. Income-transfer programmes capture but one side of the welfare state. The real essence of the social democratic (or the conservative) welfare states lies not so much in their de-commodifying income-maintenance guarantees as in their approach to services and sponsoring women's careers. In any case, the Netherlands remains a Janus-headed welfare regime, combining both social democratic and conservative attributes.

The point here, as in other cases, is that we must weigh the relative importance of different, possibly conflicting attributes. No regime, let alone country, is pure. The United States epitomizes liberalism and, yet, the Social Security pension scheme has broad coverage and benefits that approach adequacy levels. Does this push the United States out of the liberal fold? No, because even if one programme deviates from the 'ideal type', the over-dominating character of the entire welfare package remains 'liberal'. Or consider Denmark which, like Britain, failed to implement a universal, second-tier pension system. Does this imply that Denmark, with Britain, is a failed social democratic model? On this count, again the answer is no. The benefits in the Danish 'peoples' pension', unlike the British, were systematically upgraded so as to uphold their universalistic appeal; and on virtually any other criteria, the Danish welfare state is prototypically 'social democratic'.[16]

There will always be slippery or ambiguous cases, and *one* programme does not define a regime. The real problem is how to deal with systematic deviants. The issue here is whether a three-way typology adequately exhausts the variance. If there are cases that follow a wholly different underlying logic, we would have to construct yet another, separate ideal-type—a fourth 'world of welfare capitalism'.

Three-plus Regimes?

There are in particular three cases that arguably call for an additional, fourth 'world': the Antipodes (Castles and Mitchell, 1993), the Mediterranean (Leibfried, 1992; Lessenich, 1995; Ferrera, 1996), and Japan (Jones, 1993; Rose and Shiratori, 1986). Assuming the validity of all three claims, we will find ourselves with a total of six models for a total of 18–20 nations. The desired explanatory parsimony would be sacrificed, and we might as well return to individual comparisons.

---

[16] Two very recent reforms may, however, very well push Denmark towards a more liberal fold. One, the peoples' pension has lost some of its 'rights' character with the introduction of an income test in 1996; two, legislation has just been passed to build a private (collectively negotiated) second-tier earnings-related labour market pension.

The Antipodean Fourth World

Castles and Mitchell (1993) and Castles (1996) argue persuasively in favour of a fourth, Australian or Antipodean, welfare regime (what they term the 'wage-earners' welfare state'). At first glance, Australia's and New Zealand's rather modest and targeted welfare *state* benefits conform to the residual, liberal model. All income maintenance schemes are now premissed on an income test, but 'Medicare' in Australia is essentially a rights programme. While needs-tested benefits are generally much lower than equivalent insurance benefits in other countries, they are also more 'needs-sensitive' than elsewhere. Thus, assistance benefits to child families are double those to single persons (Castles, 1996: 109). Moreover, the income ceiling for eligibility (in Australia, but less so in New Zealand) is drawn at middle incomes, not at a poverty line: assistance is more inclusive. Pensions are said to cover two-thirds of the aged; family benefits reach most middle-class families.[17]

The point that Castles and Mitchell make is that we err by focusing solely on state activity because in Australia (and once also New Zealand), strong and functionally equivalent welfare guarantees were implanted in the labour market via the wage arbitration system. What seems like an extreme case of a liberal, means-tested system when studying only state welfare is, in reality, something essentially social democratic with its emphasis on egalitarianism and wage-earner rights.

If valid, the argument is theoretically fundamental because it compels us to reconsider markets. In Australia, as the argument goes, the labour market is a welfare producer. Hence, it may be a fallacy to simply equate markets and liberalism. There is no doubt that the wage arbitration system in Australia implanted strong and egalitarian guarantees, at least as far as the male bread-winner was concerned. There was little need for a welfare state because male full employment was *de facto* 'full', because earnings differences were highly compressed, and because the employment relationship furnished general welfare guarantees, such as home-ownership and adequate pension income.

However, as Castles (1996) himself points out, these very same guarantees inevitably eroded when, during the 1980s, the Australian economy was liberalized; they were effectively eliminated in New Zealand. With unemployment rates hovering at 10 per cent, and with heightened wage inequalities, the 'wage-earners' welfare state' in the market is, almost by definition, being dismantled.

---

[17] For a period, old-age pensions became universal rights benefits, but are now again income-tested. For a general, comparative presentation of the Australian system, see also Saunders (1994).

It is possible that the Antipodean model provided a package of welfare guarantees that was essentially 'social democratic' in the 1960s and 1970s. Like Britain, however, the passage of time is pushing Australia—and certainly New Zealand—towards what appears as prototypical liberalism: minimal state and maximum market allocation of risks, and the market side of the coin appears increasingly genuinely market.

The Mediterranean Fourth World

It has been argued that the Mediterranean countries should be considered distinct from Continental Europe (Leibfried, 1992; Ferrera, 1996; Lessenich, 1995; and Castles, 1996). Ferrera's point has mainly to do with distributive practice—the pervasive use of social benefits, especially in Italy, for purposes of political clientelism. Invalid pensions and public jobs are notorious ways in which the Christian Democrats (but also socialists) maintained their grip on the electorate. A perverted use of welfare programmes and public bureaucracies may define the character of a polity, but it is difficult to see how it defines a welfare regime unless the entire system was from the very beginning specifically designed for the purpose of clientelism rather than social protection. Such an argument would be very hard to sustain.

Leibfried's (1992) call for a distinct Mediterranean regime is, as previously discussed, limited to one programme—social assistance. But even if social assistance practice is distinct, this hardly merits a distinct regime type. It would be a different matter if such deviance forms part and parcel of a broader complex of attributes. Does it? To an extent yes, because the extremely residual nature of Southern Europe's social assistance is but one face of its strong familialism. Unlike elsewhere, social assistance was never upgraded because of two assumptions: it is assumed (and legally prescribed) that families are the relevant locus of social aid; and it is assumed that families normally do not 'fail'. The acid test of a distinct Mediterranean model depends therefore on the issue of familialism, to which will shall return shortly.

The East Asian Fourth World

Japan, possibly with Korea and Taiwan, poses a particularly intriguing challenge to welfare regime typologies because it is such a unique version of capitalism to begin with: sustained full employment, highly regulated internal labour markets and industrial structure, compressed earnings, and a relatively egalitarian distribution of income, all overlaid by rather authoritarian employment practices, a conservative 'one-party' democracy, and 'corporatism without labour' (Pempel, 1989).[18]

---

[18] The following treatment is based on Esping-Andersen (1997a).

If we confine our examination to Japan, one aspect is immediately obvious: it blends vital regime attributes in a way which makes it either unique or hybrid. This, indeed, is the fundamental issue to be resolved. State welfare combines liberal residualism with conservative corporatism. Social insurance is, like in Europe, status-segmented along broad occupational lines. In part due to lack of system maturation (at least as far as pensions are concerned), insurance benefits are quite modest and attached with prohibitive eligibility criteria—this is especially the case in unemployment insurance. Levels of de-commodification are modest indeed.

The modesty of benefits reflects a certain in-built residualism. State benefits assume that the core (male) labour force will have private benefits via the employment relationship, but also ample family support. The former undoubtedly holds for the roughly one-third employees in the large corporate sector—but much less so for the rest of the labour force. Employer occupational welfare includes not merely standard health and pension coverage, but also a vast array of services from sports clubs to funeral services. And herein lies one important source of inequalities, not so much according to class or occupation, but because access and generosity depends on educational level and, of course, on whether one is employed by a large corporation or not. Japan's social assistance system is yet another example of liberalism: strictly means-tested and highly targeted as well as stigmatizing. The take-up rate is extremely low (below 30 per cent).

The welfare *state,* then, fuses conservative and liberal elements which is hardly surprising when we recall that the insurance component was inspired by German practice, and that assistance schemes were designed by the American occupation forces in the aftermath of World War Two. However, if we examine more closely the welfare *market* it would appear somewhat less than 'liberal'. Occupational welfare forms part of the consensual mode of labour regulation, but it also mirrors a conservative, paternalistic practice. It is none the less arguable that the market 'works': it provides (until now) a genuine employment guarantee and, for many, welfare benefits. The rather undeveloped and residual public welfare commitments could—like once in Australia—be ascribed to the fact that needs and risks are contained because the labour market functions so well.

In fact, several scholars maintain that Japan is an extremely highly developed 'welfare society' and that a large welfare *state* is therefore less pressing (Vogel, 1980). The state is not needed because the market and the family are sufficient. There is little doubt as to the importance of families in the overall Japanese welfare mix. Public social services, be it to the aged or children, are truly marginal because it is institutionally assumed that the family must carry the real responsibility. Thus, even today 65 per cent of the aged live with, and are cared for by their children—that is, the wife of the oldest son. The Confucian tradition of familial piety and loyalty has, like the Catholic subsidiarity principle in Europe, been the overpow-ering force behind Japanese welfare policy (Jones, 1993).

There is clearly nothing uniquely Japanese in any of these elements. It appears therefore a hybrid case. Yet, it is precisely this particular combi-nation of hybrid attributes that, some say, warrants a distinct regime label. True, Japan does manifest a mix of liberal and conservative traits and, unlike other 'mixed cases', they appear to form an internationally rather peculiar combination. Yet, the liberal side of the equation is less liberal than appearances suggest. There are also trends that point towards a strengthening of the conservative attributes. The corporatist social insur-ance system is now rapidly maturing and will, in the coming decades, dom-inate the pension mix. This, together with Japan's unusually accentuated familialism, makes a strong case for assigning Japan squarely to the con-servative regime.

In brief, it is inescapably true that Japan, like Australia and Southern Europe, manifests features that are not easily compatible with a simple trichotomy of welfare regimes. Yet, we must also ask ourselves what would be gained from adding a fourth, fifth, or sixth regime cluster? We would probably benefit from greater refinement, more nuance, and more preci-sion. Still, if we also value analytical parsimony, neither Japan nor the Antipodes warrant additional regimes. The peculiarities of these cases are variations within a distinct overall logic, not the foundations of a wholly different logic *per se*. The case for a unique Southern Europe regime depends ultimately on the centrality of families. This was the weak link in the original 'three worlds' model and therefore deserves special attention.

Families and Welfare Regimes

To what extent, then, does more systematic attention to the family alter our political economy of welfare regimes? Does it call for a fourth regime or even a radical rethinking of what constitutes a welfare regime in the first place?

Those who follow a more explicitly gender-based analysis often arrive at typologies that are at odds with the 'three worlds' model (for an overview, see O'Connor, 1996). A similar lack of fit emerges from some studies of the 'family benefit package' (Bradshaw and Ditch, 1995).

From the evidence presented in Chapter 4, there is much to be said for an additional Southern European regime (with Japan). Of course, in the final analysis it all comes down to the choice of indicators and measure-ment. The weight of the evidence in Chapter 4 addressed families (and not gender *per se*) and their role in welfare production (rather than family ben-efits provided by the welfare state). In fact, previous work on caring and servicing sometimes squares with the 'three worlds' typology (Kolberg and Uusitalo, 1992; Gustafsson, 1995), and sometimes not (Anttonen and Sipila, 1996; and Gornick *et al.*, 1997). Both Anttonen and Sipila, and Gornick *et al.* show that France and Belgium break ranks with the conservative regime, but only in this particular area.

Let us conduct a simple test of whether the conservative regime should be subdivided, whether a fourth 'Mediterranean' regime is warranted. If Southern Europe (Italy, Portugal, and Spain) together with Japan are qualitatively distinct from the remaining Continental European countries, this should show up on two dimensions of familialism: on welfare *state* policies towards families (welfare state de-familialization), and on the welfare burdens assumed by families themselves. Table 5.5 presents relative odds-ratios from multinomial logit regressions. The 'outcome' (dependent variables) to be predicted is 'high levels of welfare state servicing to families' (column 1) and 'high levels of intra-family caring burdens' (column 2). Each separate regime estimation includes a measure of women's employment rate (an indicator of underlying need for de-familialization, so to speak).

The prediction in column 1 is the degree to which welfare states furnish services to families; in column 2 whether traditional family behaviour prevails (share of aged living with their children combined with the 'male bread-winner bias' variable).[19] The evidence does not suggest any great

TABLE 5.5. *Multinomial logit regressions. The relative odds of high levels of welfare state family support and of low levels of family-caring burdens by welfare regime and women's employment levels*

	Outcome: high levels of welfare state servicing to families	Outcome: high levels of family welfare burdens
Southern Europe and Japan	5.86e – 19***	1.52e + 16***
Women's employment rate	0.91	0.43*
Chi-squared	*23.04*	*20.44*
Continental Europe *minus* Italy, Portugal, and Spain	Perfectly predicted	2.96e + 13***
Women's employment rate	5.34e – 17***	0.34*
Chi-squared	*42.05*	*18.24*

   * Probability = 0.10 or better.
 *** Probability = 0.001 or better.
N = 18.
See n. 19 for an explanation of variable measures.

[19] The welfare state de-familialism, and the household familialism variables have been recoded so as to develop synthetic indicators: Service spending has been coded 0 (if spending is

difference between our 'Mediterranean' subregime and the remainder of Continental Europe. The signs and relative odds are quite similar. In brief, the case for a fourth, uniquely familialistic, world of welfare capitalism is not very convincing when, as in this analysis, we focus on high levels of de-familialization. The difference does, however, become more accentuated when we relax our criteria. The correlations between regime type and various measures of familialism differ somewhat more between the two regime subdivisions when we measure familialism as continuous rather than categorical variables (as was done in Chapter 4). None the less, the signs of the correlations remain identical for the two subregimes.[20]

CONCLUSION

The comparisons undertaken in this chapter are certainly not the last word on the subject. The question of how to identify and classify welfare regimes will remain open because, as noted, researchers differ in terms of what attributes they consider vital and of how to measure them. The results presented here suggest that, as far as my choice of attributes and measurements is concerned, a simple 'three worlds' typology may suffice for most of the purposes that this book pursues. The final judgement is not yet in, and we shall in fact see that the distinctiveness of the Southern European countries does make its mark on issues such as postindustrial employment adaptation. It is to this that we now turn.

<.5 per cent), 1 (if spending is .5-1 per cent), 2 (if spending is 1 per cent+). Family benefit spending has been coded 0 (if less than 5 per cent), 1 (5–8 per cent), 2 (8+ per cent). Daycare coverage is coded 0 (for <10 per cent coverage), 1 (for 10–20 per cent coverage), and 2 for 21+ per cent coverage. Home-help coverage has been coded 0 (<8 per cent), 1 (9–16 per cent), and 2 (17+ per cent). Percentage aged living with children has been coded: 0 (30+ per cent), 1 (16–29 per cent), 2 (<16 per cent). The male bread-winner bias is a combination of the tax-benefit penalties of working wives and the loss of unemployment benefit if wives work. The coding is a simple dummy: 0 (if there is a significant penalty on either), 1 (if there is no significant penalty). For data sources, see Chapter 4.

[20] Bivariate correlations (not shown) indicate that the Southern European regime is considerably more familialistic than Continental Europe without the 'South', and this shows up also on consequences, such as women's employment levels.

PART II

THE NEW POLITICAL ECONOMY

A social trend is basically a projection from the past. Many of the early postindustrial theorists, such as Daniel Bell (1976), predicted a future in which most of what they deemed positive in the era of the 'democratic class struggle' would come to full fruition. Bell's vision was a coming society of professionals and technicians, one where 'situs' rather than class conflict would reign. This was a radical reinterpretation in so far as post-industrial society would do away with class altogether. Also Lipset has now embraced this position (Clark and Lipset, 1991; Clark, Lipset, and Rempel, 1993).

Today's visionaries find much less cause for optimism; their projections are most likely to range from the sombre to the outright gloomy. The sombre view insists that little of substance has changed (Wright, 1989; Erikson and Goldthorpe, 1992; and Hout et al., 1993); that the cleavages of the past remain pretty much intact. The gloom comes from those who see a new era of polarization. American or British observers see a world with a 'declining middle', job polarization, and a new underclass (Harrison and Bluestone, 1988; Jencks and Peterson, 1991; Levy, 1988; Burtless, 1990). Europeans, in contrast, see a two-thirds society with social exclusion, marginalization, and outsider classes (Van Parijs, 1987; Offe, 1985; Esping-Andersen, 1993; Brown and Crompton, 1994).[1]

What the new pessimists see, in brief, is the possibility of a resurgent proletarian underclass and, in its wake, a menacing set of new 'class correlates'. The transAtlantic difference of accent is clearly related to job performance: in North America labour market exclusion is less dramatic than is growing pay inequality, declining real wages, and a swelling army of the working poor. Europe's social safety net manages to stem the tide of inequality but its inferior job performance induces mass exclusion.

How do we understand the postindustrial employment problem? Is there indeed any problem? And, if new class configurations are emerging, what is driving them? Besides the radical optimists, such as Lipset et al., who basically deny that there is any problem worthy of discussion, the

[1] The specification of a 'one-third' outsider class in Europe today is surprisingly similar to Max Adler's (1933) analysis of the 1930s depression era.

reigning answers all fall back on the great 'equality–jobs' trade-off. According to mainstream analysis, exclusion in Europe and inequality in America are two sides of the same coin, namely the inevitable consequence of technology and the new global economy. What makes the difference is welfare statism and labour market regulation.

There are certainly powerful macroscopic forces at work which undercut the erstwhile harmony of jobs, equality, and growth and which, instead, catapult new social divisions. All nations are affected by the new global economy, by tertiarization, or by falling demand for low-skilled workers. Yet, it is evident that similar impulses do not produce similar results. How do we account for national variation in outcomes?

If globalization really were as important as some believe, comparative employment performance might have to do with nations' degree of external vulnerability. But then how do we account for the comparatively superior employment performance of very open economies like the Dutch, Austrian, Norwegian, and Danish?

There are of course other, and quite massive, forces at work. As servicing becomes the life-blood of our existence, privilege is bestowed upon the knowledge strata. Yet, there are huge areas of servicing which are labour intensive and low-skilled. The lower end of servicing society is where we must pin our hopes for mass-employment. Unfortunately, because of their sluggish productivity, low-end service jobs are threatened by a long-run 'cost-disease' problem. Tertiary employment is therefore likely to stagnate unless wages slide downwards. Taken together, globalization, new technologies, and the service economy seem to herald one inescapable necessity: less equality.

Regardless, the reigning view in much contemporary debate and research is that these same macroscopic changes are, in principle, positive. They may have pathological effects on employment or unemployment if societies are overly regulated and labour markets too rigid. The standard benchmark for the equality–jobs trade-off is a sclerotic Europe juxtaposed to a dynamic, unregulated America. But, Europe's employment performance is not uniformly inferior. Nickell (1997) has shown that 30 per cent of the European population resides in an economic environment with lower unemployment than in the United States. Some nations, such as Denmark, Austria, the Netherlands, and Norway combine relatively low unemployment or exclusion with an unusually generous welfare state, impressive levels of income equality, and very low poverty. Others, like Spain, can hardly be regarded as excessively committed to social citizenship or income redistribution and, yet, boast extremely high and chronic unemployment. Why is Britain's or Australia's employment performance, despite massive deregulation, less impressive than, say, the Dutch or Danish?

To begin answering such questions, we need to explore two sets of phenomena. Firstly, we must uncover what drives postindustrial employment. Global pressures may be massive everywhere, but this does not automatically imply identical outcomes. The great challenges of our times, be they international, technological, or demographic, coexist with and are, indeed, provoked by what happens within the four walls of our nations' families. Most contemporary debate is so enamoured with huge processes that it forgets the household.

Post-war households, helped by Marshall Aid, the welfare state, and rising real incomes, found themselves with money to spend. They went on a spending spree so as to make their lives better, and to approximate middle-class standards. Their appetite for refrigerators and cars was what, in the last instance, fuelled the post-war boom and full employment. Boom times in contemporary society will, in parallel fashion, depend on families' economic choices. In Golden Age capitalism, families could not themselves assemble refrigerators, let alone an automobile. The basic problem we face today is that households are perfectly capable of preparing their own dinner, tending to their own children, or washing their own car. Globalization may punish our low-skilled workers, but if families decide to lunch out they will stimulate various low-skilled jobs in restaurants. In brief, how does it all add up? What is the connection between global pressures, household behaviour, and employment? This is what I seek to explore in Chapter 6.

Families must survive and will try to make the best of things. They will naturally seize upon whatever opportunities that the welfare state or labour market makes available. If preciously little is available, they will seek alternative means for survival. Between the household and its economic circumstances we find a massive infrastructure of welfare state programmes and labour market regulations. National modes of managing structural change are radically different. This means that being unemployed, a lone mother, or a mid-career yuppie will differ if one happens to be Danish, Italian, or American. Institutions filter de-industrialization and pattern postindustrialization. Hence, this twin process may provoke mass unemployment and exclusion, but it may also generate jobs for all.

Neither outcome is pre-ordained by some higher order. It all depends on strategic political choice which, as we know well, is most often captive to the past, to the prevailing, dominant logic around us. The ghost of institutional path dependency is therefore our shepherd. It is the construction of welfare states, types of labour market regulation and, not to forget, national capacities for broad social pacts and interest concertation that will guide nations' adaptation to the service economy. This is the theme of Chapter 7.

The efforts to catalogue and understand the contemporary changes that underpin these chapters are, at bottom, guided by one central question, namely: if there are trade-offs can we identify which institutional conditions are more likely than others to yield positive welfare outcomes? What, in other words, are the preconditions for a win-win postindustrial welfare regime? What would such a regime look like?

6

The Structural Bases of Postindustrial Employment

INTRODUCTION

The currently popular contrast between sclerotic Europe and dynamic America is no doubt simplistic but, worse, it is also poor analytical practice. Does it make sense to compare 16-odd European nations with one single alternative, the United States? Western Europe combines distinctly different political economies, some small and highly 'open', others large and relatively protected from global trade competition. Some, as we saw in Chapter 2, have benefited from more fortunate timing in the dual process of agricultural and industrial decline than others. Some European labour markets are highly regulated and 'inflexible', others less so. And Europe combines polities and industrial relations systems with both superior and inferior capacity for managing conflicts through binding social pacts.

Regardless, there are compelling reasons why we should be heading towards a fundamental incompatibility between the cherished goal of equality and the equally cherished goal of full employment. And if this is so, we shall have left the epoch of the democratic class struggle and, possibly, regressed back to a world dominated by the 'social question' and social polarization.

These compelling reasons can be summarized under two labels. The first is globalization and technology, both of which undoubtedly enrich all nations. But in the process, they also accelerate industrial decline and contribute to unemployment. The second is tertiarization which favours those with human and social capital, but which also may stagnate because of low productivity. In any case, both reasons point in the same direction: the less-skilled are likely to become losers—be it as unemployed, or as low-paid workers. Let us, then, begin with a brief look at stylized employment trends.

TABLE 6.1. *Employment and unemployment performance in the advanced economies* (%)

	Job-growth, 1980–94	Unemployment change, 1983–93	Unemployment rate, 1996	Structural unemployment rate, 1990
Australia	33.0	1.0	8.2	8.6
Canada	24.0	–0.7	9.7	8.5
Ireland	1.5	1.7	11.9	16.0
New Zealand	24.0	2.9	6.1	7.3
UK	1.5	–1.5	8.2	8.4
USA	25.5	–2.7	5.4	5.8
Denmark	3.0	1.0	6.0	9.6
Finland	–10.5	12.2	15.7	8.0
Norway	9.0	2.5	4.9	4.2
Sweden	– 4.5	4.6	10.0	3.2
Austria	22.5	0.2	4.4	4.9
Belgium	3.0	–3.6	9.8	10.8
France	3.0	3.1	12.4	9.3
Germany	10.5	0.0	9.0	6.9
Italy	– 1.5	1.7	12.0	9.7
Netherlands	37.5	–5.6	6.3	7.0
Portugal	4.5	–2.4	7.3	4.9
Spain	1.5	5.8	22.2	19.8
Japan	18.0	–0.2	3.4	2.5

Sources: OECD, *Employment Outlook*, various issues; and Elmeskov (1998, Table 1).

JOBS AND UNEMPLOYMENT TRENDS ACROSS WELFARE REGIMES

It should not come as a surprise that the employment performance among the advanced nations is vastly more heterogeneous than convergent. If we take the long view, using rough general indicators such as aggregate job growth and unemployment, there is little doubt that post-war full employment with strong wage growth and earnings compression was less a Keynesian accomplishment than a combination of small cohorts, female housewifery, and impressive productivity gains. In the most advanced countries, this combination helped absorb the massive agrarian surpluses and war veterans. In some cases, the passage was less fortunate and de-ruralization coincided with de-industrialization.

None the less, net growth of service jobs has, as we saw in Chapter 2, generally offset losses in industry over the past decades. In fact, contrary to what is commonly believed, overall net job creation in the 1980s has not been uniformly inferior to the booming 1960s. By and large, those countries (especially the United States and Australia) that were dynamic in the 1960s remain so today. And those that were sluggish in the past (the UK, Belgium) still remain so. A few nations have suffered a dramatic change for the worse, mainly due to sudden shocks (Finland and Sweden in the 1990s); a few have improved markedly (like the Netherlands). Also, some comparably deregulated economies (notably the UK) perform less impressively than very regulated ones (Austria). See Table 6.1.

A similarly checkered pattern obtains for unemployment. We find modest and declining unemployment in some of the less-regulated, liberal economies (the United States) but not in others (Australia and Canada). And some supposedly 'rigid' labour markets (like the Austrian and Portuguese) do quite well.

The problem today, generally speaking, is not that the capacity to generate jobs has deteriorated compared to the 'Golden Age'. High and persistent unemployment must therefore find explanation elsewhere.

THE DILEMMAS OF GLOBALIZATION AND TECHNOLOGICAL CHANGE

Global trade and capital mobility are often seen as the culprits of deindustrialization. The Asian tigers can produce steel, scooters, stereos, or shoes much cheaper than Europe or North America. Even if their regimes are not authoritarian, unionism is weak and labour discipline arguably high. Regardless, they hold a massive competitive edge in terms of wage costs in mass-production industries as well as in many services. Lessskilled workers in advanced economies are no longer cushioned by Keynesianism or import protection. They must now compete in a global labour market.

The special vulnerability of the low-skilled is highlighted in Wood's (1995) study on the impact of imports from the 'South' on labour markets in the 'North'. He paints a fairly dramatic picture of worker displacement and downward wage pressures, in particular for the low-skilled. His findings are, however, widely contested. For one, the lion's share of European trade is *intra-European*. The share of total European Union trade with the outside world is, according to all estimates, less than 10 per cent of total—of which a large proportion is with North America, the Antipodes, or Eastern Europe. Hence, if there is any 'Third World' effect, it must be at the margin. This is more or less what the mainstream view concludes (OECD, 1994a).

It is, in the first place, questionable whether globalization really is something new, and if it indeed is altering our capacity to harmonize equality and full employment. Bairoch (1996) shows that the level of internationalization of trade, finance, and capital today is hardly greater than it was 80 years ago. In fact, it was the period of protectionism and mounting tariffs following World War One and the Great Depression which was anomalous. Moreover, the spurt in globalization over the past few decades has hardly altered the trade dependency of those small, open economies (like the Benelux or Nordic countries) that were *always* open.

With these qualifiers in mind, we might ask ourselves what has *de facto* changed to make equality and social protection problematic now, when once a strong welfare state was viewed as the precondition for successful international performance? It was precisely due to their extreme degree of international vulnerability that the small European economies spearheaded strong worker protection and welfare guarantees after World War Two. Global trade competition is not novel to Belgium or Denmark; it is to the large economies, such as the American or British, or the erstwhile protected ones, such as Australia. Perhaps the real problem is that the late-comers to globalization have chosen the 'low road-low wage' strategy of competition, thus forcing the hand of the vanguards?

Regardless, the facts point to technological change as the more potent source of falling demand for less-qualified workers. Employment lost due to trade competition from the 'South' (i.e. Asia or the Third World) is rather trivial in comparison with the volume of job loss due to 'structural change'. In a few countries (France and Japan), jobs gained from exporting to the 'South' actually outnumber those lost to import penetration. Only the UK and the USA, two countries traditionally dominated by comparatively low-skilled, mass-production industry, exhibit a substantial loss of domestic employment due to competition from Asia or elsewhere.[1]

The really powerful impulse, then, may come from rapid structural and technological change whether or not this was initially propelled by global trade. Whatever the root cause, the employment effect ends up being fairly similar: it raises the returns to education and reduces demand for lower-skilled and less-experienced workers. Hence the unfavourable labour market position of the unskilled in general, but also of youth and women to the extent that they lack experience and practical skills. In either case, therefore, we seem unable to dodge the evil choice between heightened pay and job inequalities, on one hand, or unemployment and exclusion, on the other hand.

---

[1] The ratio of jobs lost to competition from the 'South' to jobs lost due to structural change is, for the period 1970–85: .07 in Denmark; .04 in France; .06 in Germany; .01 in Japan and the Netherlands; .05 in the UK; and .08 in the USA (calculated from OECD, 1994*a*, i, Table 3.10).

Golden Age capitalism could absorb masses of low-skilled workers on simple assembly-line production, churning out mass-production goods for which there was massive demand. It is these kinds of jobs that are rapidly disappearing within the advanced economies and, as we know, virtually all *net* new job growth will have to come from services.

That simple, routine industrial jobs are vanishing must be considered a 'Paretian' welfare gain: the 'South' benefits from taking over simple mass production manufacturing, thus creating domestic jobs and wealth and paving the way for its own process of de-ruralization and, eventually, postindustrialization; the 'North' gains by eliminating its most unpleasant jobs, but only in so far as these are being substituted by more pleasant and better-paid jobs. The optimistic postindustrial theorists believed this to be the case. Current opinion is sceptical, and the data seem to confirm it. We must therefore examine more closely the workings of the service economy.

DILEMMAS OF THE NEW SERVICE ECONOMY

The decline of industrial employment began in earnest in the 1980s. Between 1979 and 1993, the OECD countries lost an (unweighted) average 22 per cent of their manufacturing jobs. Some countries (Belgium, France, Norway, Sweden, Spain, and the UK) have been hit especially hard, with a net loss between one-third and one-half.[2] Such magnitudes echo post-war de-ruralization. But today's equivalent to the assembly lines, namely low-end tertiary employment, has greater difficulty absorbing the joint impact of industrial job losses, women's rising labour supply, and the baby-boom cohorts. Why should this be so? In this chapter, I focus on three dilemmas. The first derives from a rarely recognized, inherent charactersitic of services themselves: the more we expand the tertiary labour market, the larger is the share of low-skilled services. The second comes from the well-known 'Baumol cost-disease' problem in services (Baumol, 1967). And the third derives from households' economic choices and, in particular, from women's choice to work for pay.

Today, almost all net job creation occurs in services but even with buoyant growth, their ability to absorb masses of redundant industrial workers cannot be taken for granted. Many, like business and health services, are skill-intensive, and the more routine and labour-intensive services (such as social care, waiting, or personal services generally) often require a modicum of social or cultural skills that a redundant steel worker

---

[2] In the more 'distribution-dominated' economies of Canada, the Netherlands, and the United States, manufacturing decline has been much more modest. Japan (and Denmark) actually experienced net manufacturing job growth. (*Source:* recalculations from OECD, *Historical Statistics*, 1995, Table 1.10).

is unlikely to possess. Labour-intensive services, be they in the public or private sector, are very female-dominated; not merely because they are easy-entry jobs, but also because they typically represent a marketized version of conventional domestic tasks. In any case, services and female participation have grown in tandem. To better understand contemporary employment dilemmas, we need to come to grips with the logic of services. First, what precisely is the service economy? Second, what drives it?

IDENTIFYING SERVICES

Following Gershuny (1978), services are distinct because businesses or households can, at least in principle, choose whether to purchase or, alternatively, satisfy their needs by self-servicing. A manufacturing company can elect to service its business-related activities in-house, as was once typical of the large corporation, or it can meet its needs, say accounting, software infrastructure, or design, through purchase. When firms shift from self-reliance to purchase, they simultaneously contribute to de-industrialization and tertiarization. By classificatory definition, they are moving jobs from 'industry' to 'services'. Our statistics will record a decline in manufacturing employment, and the relative size of the tertiary sector will have grown, but this does not necessarily mean that the net amount of business-servicing activity has increased.

Households also opt between servicing themselves or market purchase (if there is no public provision). Their demand for services falls into two broad classes: social reproduction needs (say, care of children or the aged), and activities related to personal care and 'fun' (say, hairdressing and laundry, or theatre and restaurants). Households create tertiary-sector employment when they out-service but, like businesses, not necessarily more work. Personal and social service jobs are usually the paid equivalent to domestic labour.

We therefore have severe measurement problems when we want to understand the service economy. Most methods of classification are *ad hoc* and a-theoretical. Early theorists, such as Clark (1940), defined services as the residual that remains once we have taken account of the primary sector and industry. More recent studies, such as Singelmann's (1978) and Elfring's (1988), argue in favour of more nuanced distinctions and, today, we typically classify services into four broad sectors: business, distributive, personal, and social services. Let us examine more closely the attributes of these four classes.

SERVICE SECTORS

Business (or producer) services include finance, insurance, real estate, and business-related professional services (such as accounting, consulting, marketing, engineering, or design), most of which employ a high quotient of technical, professional, and managerial jobs. Corporate 'downsizing', enhanced flexibility needs, and new technologies, all combine to create dynamism in this sector. Since the 1960s, its employment share has at least doubled and, in some cases, even tripled (Elfring, 1988: 108 ff.; Esping-Andersen, 1993: 37–8).

Distributive services include wholesale, retail, transportation, communications, and the like. They emerged as companions to mass consumption and mass transportation, and boomed therefore in the post-war decades. This was also what catalysed the first wave of female, white-collar employment. Although they account for quite a large share of total jobs (about 20 per cent), distributive services are now stagnant and are more likely to contract than grow in the future. They are thus unlikely to shape in any significant way emerging postindustrial employment trends.

Personal (or consumer) services are the modern equivalent of erstwhile servitude, of butlers, maids, cooks, gardeners, and other domestic help. But they also represent our growing quest for pleasure and purchased fun. In either case, they must usually compete with tasks that households, in principle, could do themselves: cleaning and laundering, repairing, entertaining, serving food and drinks, cutting hair, and preparing the jacuzzi.

The labour-intensive and low-skilled nature of personal services is, to a degree, offset by technology and household capital goods (such as washers, driers, or electric shoe-polishers). This makes household substitution more easy, but this depends in the end on opportunity cost. Hence, unless the service is affordable (i.e. labour costs are low), personal services will stagnate. This is what divides the United States and high-cost service economies such as the Swedish and German. In Britain and the United States, personal services account for 10–12 per cent of the labour force; in Germany and Sweden for 5–7 per cent (Elfring, 1988: 109; Esping-Andersen, 1993: 37–8).

Social services embrace health, education, and an array of care-giving activities (such as child-minding or home-help services). They have everywhere been hugely dynamic, initially due to the spread of mass education, later due to population ageing and intensified demand for health care. Here households are again the ultimate consumer, but except for a few countries (such as the United States) most social service growth has occurred in the public sector. The real divergence, however, has to do with non-health and non-education services. Here only the Nordic social democracies (with, perhaps, France and Belgium) have encouraged any significant expansion. This is the primary reason why Scandinavian welfare state employment (at about 30 per cent of total) is about twice as large as elsewhere (in most countries in the range of 15–20 per cent).

Social services are skill-intensive due to their large share of doctors, nurses, and teachers, but a notable feature is that the lower-skill bias increases as caring services grow. This, as we shall see, is why Denmark and Sweden actually outdo the United States in terms of the overall share of unskilled jobs in the economy.

SERVICE OCCUPATIONS

Apart from the pioneering work of Renner (1953) and, more recently, Bell (1976) and Goldthorpe (1982), little attention has been paid to occupational hierarchies in services. Since they were primarily concerned with the new knowledge class, the lower orders have been largely ignored. As in Braverman (1974) and Erikson and Goldthorpe (1992), they are simply lumped together with manual, industrial workers.

Such superimposition is not necessarily warranted. Even low-end service work is in typically less strict command hierarchies, it is less difficult to monitor, and orders will come more from customers than from bosses. Most servicing work is quite individualized. For heuristic reasons, it may therefore be useful to distinguish between the traditional skill and authority hierarchy of 'industrial society' and that of the servicing society.[3] In Table 6.2, I propose one such classification.

The two hierarchies exclude agricultural occupations and, more importantly, also the self-employed and entrepreneurs. Omitting self-employment may actually be problematic because, as we shall discover, it is becoming one means of gaining access to the labour market when the supply of 'regular' employment contracts is scarce. This classificatory exercise must be seen as an heuristic device.[4]

---

[3] The 'classes' in the industrial order are relatively unproblematic, but those in the servicing hierarchy need some clarification. Professionals are straightforward; semi-professionals refer to occupations such as social workers, nurses, technicians, and teachers. Skilled service workers embrace occupations for which a skill certification is required (hairdressers or nursing assistants, for example). Unskilled service workers are defined as those occupying jobs for which there are no particular skill requirements, tasks that, in principle, anyone could perform (cleaning, waiting, bell-hopping, car-parking, and so forth). For a detailed exposé, see Esping-Andersen (1993).

[4] There is none the less evidence that this classification scheme has validity. Salido (1996, ch. 3) has tested it both in terms of construct and criterion validity against the Treiman prestige scale, and also against a battery of hierarchy criteria such as autonomy, decision-making, and supervision, and the results are quite comforting.

TABLE 6.2. *Industrial and postindustrial occupational hierarchies*

The industrial hierarchy	The service hierarchy
Managers and executives	Professionals
Administrators, supervisors	Semi-professionals, technicians
Skilled manuals	Skilled service
Unskilled manuals	Unskilled service

LOUSY JOBS OR OUTSIDERS?

Our present preoccupation with the equality–jobs trade-off may have blinded us to a second dilemma, i.e. professionalization with exclusion or full employment with job polarization. The highly professionalized scenario depicted by postindustrial optimists can be attained only at the price of massive exclusion, while a massive growth of services is likely to produce a mass of 'lousy' jobs. We need therefore to gain a better picture of postindustrial job trends.

The postindustrial pessimists, like Braverman (1974), err on one count: tertiarization undoubtedly implies occupational upgrading. Over the 1980s, professional-technical jobs rose 3–4 times as fast as employment overall in Belgium, Germany, Sweden, and Japan, and an astounding 7 times as fast in France. Their relative growth was less spectacular in Canada and the United States (1.7 and 1.9, respectively), two nations with unusually strong aggregate service expansion.[5] Indications are that the professional bias is inversely related to service economy growth. This comes out in Table 6.3.

The statistical relationship is in fact quite strong: for each additional percentage point of service job growth, the professional ratio declines by –1.2 points.[6]

Since we must rely almost exclusively on services to furnish new jobs and thus reduce unemployment, the contours of postindustrial employment pose an unpleasant trade-off: we will come close to the professionalized world of Daniel Bell, but only when services are relatively stagnant. And this entails unemployment and labour market exclusion. Vice versa, we can minimize exclusion but here we must pay the price of accepting a less favourable, more 'proletarian' mix of service occupations. This comes

---

[5] The job-growth calculations are based on data from ILO, *Yearbook of Labour Statistics* (various years).

[6] Estimating the regression equation (using robust regression): Professional ratio = 5.377a – 1.235 (service growth). T-statistics for the constant = 14.87, and for service growth = –6.93. R-squared = .212 with F = 48.07.

TABLE 6.3. *Service growth and the professional-technical bias of job growth, 1980–1990*[a]

	Annual service growth	Ratio of professional to total growth
Australia	3.3	1.8
Canada	2.8	1.7
UK	2.1	2.8
USA	2.7	1.9
Denmark	0.8	2.0
Sweden	1.2	4.3
Austria	1.9	2.5
Belgium	1.4	3.8
France	1.6	7.3
Germany	1.8	3.1
Japan	1.2	3.8

[a] Years vary according to data availability.

Source: ILO, *Yearbook of Labour Statistics* (various years).

out quite clearly when we examine the occupational hierarchies in greater detail.

Table 6.4 divides the active population, c.mid-1980s, into our 'industrial' and 'postindustrial' hierarchy and, as somewhat of a residual, it provides an estimate of the excluded, 'outsider' population (here measured as a percentage of the working-age population). The three-way comparison between Germany, Sweden, and the United States is chosen because these nations are prototypical examples of our three welfare regimes—conservative, social democratic, and liberal, respectively. But they also represent three distinct employment trajectories: Germany stands as a best-case version of European jobless growth; Sweden is the epitome of the Nordic welfare state-led model of service expansion; and the United States is, *par excellence*, the leading example of unregulated, market-driven employment.

On some counts there is convergence. Manual workers decline, and the occupations that constituted the major source of post-war 'middle-class growth', such as managers, clerical, and sales jobs, are now stagnant. Today's growth is undisputably dominated by professionals and semi-professionals. This is all more or less consistent with the prognosis of Bell (1976). Accordingly, chances of upward class mobility in postindustrial societies will depend primarily on how much the skilled and professional

TABLE 6.4. *The distribution of occupations and the size of the outsider population* (percentage change, 1960–1980s, in parentheses)

	Germany 1985	Sweden 1985	United States 1988
'Industrial' society			
Unskilled manual	16.5 (–0)	12.4 (–42)	14.4 (–33)
Skilled manual	17.3 (–32)	15.2 (–18)	8.7 (–34)
Clerical and sales	29.6 (+30)	18.6 (+16)	28.3 (+21)
Managers[a]	4.5 (+36)	4.0 (–15)	9.1 (+17)
TOTAL	67.9 (–0)	50.2 (–18)	60.4 (– 8)
'Servicing' society			
Unskilled service	4.5 (–48)	16.9 (+78)	11.7 (– 0)
Skilled service	5.0 (+194)	4.4 (– 0)	6.6 (+57)
Professional-technical	17.3 (+121)	21.9 (+89)	18.1 (+56)
TOTAL	26.8 (+47)	43.2 (+70)	36.4 (+31)
'Outsider' society			
Not employed	35.2	16.7	29.5
Long-term unemployment[b]	46.3	5.0	5.6

[a] Includes also self-employed (non-professional).

[b] As a percentage of all unemployed (1990).

Note: The table excludes primary sector occupations.

Sources: Recomputations from Esping-Andersen (1993: Tables 2.3 and 2.4); and OECD (1992; 1994*a*).

service occupations grow. On the other hand, if the objective is full employment there will also be substantial growth of less-qualified service jobs, something that Daniel Bell did not envisage.

A postindustrial paradise would combine full employment with a slim but highly skilled industrial labour force in unison with a professionally dominated service economy. No country comes even close to this. In Germany, which often epitomizes skill-upgrading (see, for example, Kern and Schumann, 1984), skilled manual workers have actually disappeared faster than the unskilled—although from the 1980s onwards, this has reversed.[7] None the less, Germany's services are heavily professional and 'non-proletarian'. High labour costs crowd out private social services; low levels of female participation make them less demanded. One reason for Germany's lower female employment rates is the absence of public care

[7] As in Germany, the surprising lack of any unskilled bias in industrial slimming is evident elsewhere (Italy, in particular). As I shall discuss in Chapter 7, this may be due to the extraordinary degree of job protection afforded 'insiders', i.e. those already employed.

services. And, besides costs, one reason for Germany's stagnant personal services is that families engage in more self-servicing.

As a consequence, German postindustrialization provides no substantial employment outlet for either laid-off manual workers or less-qualified women. Instead, both these groups have been managed primarily through labour reduction strategies: early retirement or unemployment insurance for industrial workers, and discouragement of female careers. Germany may come closest to the postindustrial ideal as regards job structure, but this comes at the expense of employment exclusion.[8]

Sweden does conform to the industrial skill-upgrading thesis but suffers from strong polarization in the service occupations. The phenomenally high levels of female employment go hand-in-hand with huge numbers of (often low-skilled) public-sector jobs. And Sweden's formidable investment in retraining and active manpower programmes has, until the crash in the 1990s, helped recycle redundant industrial workers into alternative jobs. The combination of these two factors implies few labour market outsiders, be it in the form of early retirees, mass unemployment, or discouraged women.[9]

The United States, finally, exhibits skill polarization in both industry and services. It is an economy biased towards unqualified jobs. Deindustrialization has reduced manual employment equally between the skilled and unskilled; declining wages have helped maintain their relative share in industry and services. Of course, our data disguise the fact that, in absolute terms, the number of net new jobs has risen phenomenally. Hence, the absorption of immigrant masses, the huge growth in women's employment, and the relocation of redundant industrial workers were all made possible by the sheer volume of job growth.

The juxtaposition between Germany's more favourable skill mix, and the large share of unskilled servicing jobs in both Sweden and the United States highlights the basic dilemma: today, substantial employment expansion requires heavy growth in consumer and social services, both

---

[8] Germany scores rather well on some 'outsider' indices, such as youth unemployment. Had we instead examined Italy or Spain, arguably the two countries in Europe with the deepest insider-outsider divide, the rates of exclusion would have been dramatically higher. To cite some examples: the Italian not-employed rate is 46 per cent; the long-term unemployed are 68 per cent of total; youth constitute about 70 per cent of all unemployment, and average duration of unemployment is about three years.

[9] Overall female participation rates in Sweden and Denmark are around 80 per cent, whether or not they have small children. This is double the rate in Southern Europe and 30 percentage points higher than in Germany. About 45 per cent are part-time, although this is declining. In contrast to most other countries (except Italy), women's careers are lifelong. The recent collapse of the Swedish model may undo some of these accomplishments. Women's employment rate has fallen by 10 percentage points, 1990–4, and youth unemployment has skyrocketed. A creeping 'insider-outsider' scenario appears possible when we consider also the rise in long-term youth unemployment (OECD, 1995c, Tables A and Q). It is too early to say whether these trends are cyclical (the current recession) or long-term.

characteristic of a large unskilled quotient the more they grow—hence an apparent trade-off between either joblessness or a mass of inferior jobs.

The real issue lies in the correlates of class. It makes a notable difference whether inferior jobs provide inferior welfare. In Sweden, they are relatively well-paid and secure welfare state jobs; indeed, private sector 'Macjobs' hardly exist. While relative pay in Swedish welfare service jobs has been in modest decline, job security has not. A notable aspect of Sweden's gargantuan welfare spending cutbacks in the 1990s is that public employment is safeguarded. In the United States, the low-end service workers are mainly in the private sector, typically poorly paid and excluded from occupational welfare entitlements and basic job security. In Sweden, the concentration of women in low-end servicing jobs is extreme (women account for roughly 80 per cent of the total), while in America the bias is tendentially ethnic—Hispanics—rather than gender-based (Esping-Andersen, 1990; ch. 8).

In summary, there are undisputably forces that pull economies away from job homogeneity and wage equality, and towards polarization. It is therefore doubtful whether the great 'equality–jobs' trade-off overshadows everything else. It is, as we shall now see, more likely that trade-offs overlap.

THE COST-DISEASE AND SERVICE EXPANSION

Globalization, new technologies, and tertiarization all seem to produce heightened labour market polarization. The productivity lag within many services only helps reinforce this problem. As originally argued by Fourastiér, and subsequently formalized by Baumol (1967), services face a long-run 'cost-disease' problem. This will come about because, in the long haul, productivity grows on average much faster in manufacturing than in (most) services. As shown in Table 6.5, most services lag—sometimes dramatically—behind manufacturing.

There are three possible responses to the productivity gap. One would be to allow labour costs to adjust to productivity differentials—the market-clearing approach. The downside of unregulated wage adjustment is that this would push earnings in the more stagnant services towards zero. Many services, such as music concerts, psychotherapy, or aged care, are capable of almost no productivity enhancement (at least not without a quality loss), and they would therefore most likely disappear, simply because no one would be willing to perform them at earnings that correspond to relative productivity. The potential limits to the market-clearing strategy is poverty: aggregate service consumption may, on the one hand, be stimulated by low prices but if, on the other hand, this means that a

TABLE 6.5. *The growing productivity gap. Percentage change in the ratio of service-to-manufacturing productivity, 1983–1995, for select countries*[a]

	Ratio of restaurants to manufacture	Ratio of personal services to manufacture	Ratio of business services to manufacture	Ratio of social services to manufacture
United States	–7	–47	–55	–62
Denmark	–35	–30	–11	–2
Sweden	–82	–60	–71	–54
France	–56	–41	–38	+4
Netherlands	–40	–19	–38	–28

[a] Productivity is measured as GDP (in constant prices) per person employed.

Source: OECD Data File on Services Statistics on Value Added and Employment.

large population mass is employed at poverty-level wages, aggregate demand will suffer. Low wages can of course be offset by income supplements, as now Canada, Australia, and the United States do with various forms of negative income tax programmes.

The second and, in most countries, typical response has been to allow service earnings to follow general wage developments in the economy. This may matter little for engineering, product design, or financial consultancy, but it risks pricing out of the market labour-intensive, low value-added activities such as personal services, entertainment, or private daycare. Both the Nordic countries and Continental Europe have in common an institutional framework which has this effect: high wage costs across the board and a more compressed earnings distribution. Hence, personal services grow very sluggishly, if at all, and many services become almost extinct. To illustrate the problem, let us examine a prototypical labour-intensive service: laundries.

As we see in Table 6.6, time-saving household goods (washing-machines) are almost universal everywhere. What varies is the cost of out-servicing and, therefore, laundry jobs. Laundries literally clutter American streets because they are cheap. They are almost impossible to find in Copenhagen and Stockholm because they are priced out of the market.

In a service-led economy, this kind of cost-disease translates easily into jobless growth. But there is, of course, a third possible solution, namely to subsidize services—either directly via government production, or indirectly via subsidies to consumers. All advanced nations have to a greater or lesser degree adopted the subsidy strategy, especially for vital collective goods such as health and education, or for culturally valued goods such as opera and theatre. The European nations stress direct public provision, the

TABLE 6.6. *The cost-disease illustrated by laundry servicing. The comparative cost of washing and ironing one man's shirt, employment, and self-service equipment, mid-1990s*

	Cost ($US) 1996	Working-age population per laundry worker[a]	Washing-machines[b]
Denmark	5.20	3,500	74
Sweden	4.25	727	87
France	4.50		
Germany (West)	3.70	667	88
Italy	3.25	n.a.	96
Spain	3.90	905	87
UK	2.20	750	87
USA	1.50	391	75

[a] Data for the UK are 1993; for the USA, Spain, and Sweden, 1990; for Germany, 1987.

[b] Percentage households equipped with a washing-machine, 1991.

Sources: Employment: United States Statistical Abstract, 1995, Table 668; *Sveriges Statistiska Aarsbok*, 1993, Table 204; German Census of 1987, Part 2, Fachserie 1, Haft 10; Government Statistical Office, *Employment Gazette, Historical Supplement*, no. 4, October 1994; Ministero de Economia y Hacienda, *Prospectiva de las Occupaciones y la Formacion en la Espana de los Noventa*, 1991, App. Table 2. Washing-machines: United States Statistical Abstract, 1995,Table 1376. Prices: own data collection in Italy, Spain, and the United States, and special thanks to Francis Castles, Kevin Farnsworth, Joakim Palme, Jon Kvist, Karl Ulrich Mayer, John Myles, Kari Salminen, and Lucy Roberts for help on price and employment figures.

United States favours tax-subsidized private provision. The uniqueness of Scandinavia lies in government's huge role in furnishing labour-intensive, and otherwise unaffordable, care services to families. Hence, Scandinavian tertiarization is uniquely biased towards welfare state jobs and away from market services. In the United States, the lion's share of caring services is marketized while, in Continental Europe, it is basically familialized.[10] The limits of subsidization are a question of political economy: of the balance of political power and citizens' willingness to be taxed.

The cost-disease problem and the tension between professionalized or more polarized employment growth are clearly closely related. Where the

[10] Hence private sector 'social and community' related services account (1994) for 12.2 per cent of total employment in the USA, compared to 1.4 per cent in Denmark and 3.2 per cent in France (calculated from OECD Data File on Services Statistics on Value Added and Employment).

cost-disease in services is severe, and public servicing is scarce, the size of the 'outsider classes' is likely to be large; where it is countered by low-wage labour markets or by public-service provision, exclusion will be less of a problem than growing occupational polarization. It is this nexus which defines the varying employment scenarios within the three principal welfare regimes.

THE MICRO-FOUNDATIONS OF POSTINDUSTRIAL EMPLOYMENT

As we leave behind us the era of mass production, there is one thing that has not changed. The household still remains the *sine qua non* of how much, and what kind of, employment will grow. How much families save, consume, or produce affects the probability that their members will find themselves employed or unemployed.

Household market purchase is subordinate to three principal factors: levels of income, relative prices, and time constraints.[11] As we know from Engel's Law, our propensity to buy non-essentials, like services, will rise with disposable income. The phenomenal rise in real incomes in the postwar decades allowed us initially to satisfy demand for manufactured household goods, like cars and washing-machines. Subsequently, an increasing share went to servicing less essential needs like entertainment or foreign travel. One obstacle to tertiary sector growth today is that real incomes rise much slower. In the United States, real earnings have been stagnant—even declining for many—since the late 1970s.

But also the distribution of riches matters greatly. A very skewed income distribution may result in a 'Latin American' consumption scenario: a narrow, hyper-serviced élite being waited upon by a mass of impoverished servants. At the other extreme, a very egalitarian income distribution, as in Sweden, may very well impede mass consumption of market services because equal wages mean that service costs will be high.

Rising incomes might also push demand in the direction of 'positional' services, that is, services that are bought for their status value. Following the argument of Hirsh (1977), the 'democratization' of consumption means that traditional status-enhancing goods, like automobiles or cellular phones, eventually lose their prestige value. Hence, as mass consumption spreads so will demand for 'positional' goods (Armani suits or Porsches) and services (haircuts from 'Chez Pierre', rather than the local barbershop).

Secondly, household demand is sensititve to price relativities (the Baumol cost-disease problem). Often the lure of Third-World travel lies in

---

[11] The following argumentation lies close to the work of Gershuny (1978).

the amazing amount of servicing that our 'tourist dollar' can buy. Price relativities in services are intimately linked to wage differentials and, as we have seen, high wages in low-productivity services might price them out of the market.

Of course, where a service is consumed for its 'positional' value the logic of relative prices is altered, and may even operate in reverse. It is possible that status-seeking clients choose 'Chez Pierre' precisely because he is expensive. The status-hungry may follow outrageous pricing practices as their main signal.

Aside from the more esoteric world of positional goods, the cost-disease problem should be most acute in low-skilled, labour-intensive services that compete head-on with household self-servicing. And herein lies a fundamental misunderstanding in much contemporary economics. It is too often assumed that, since they are largely protected from international competition, services can provide a safe haven of employment—service workers do not compete with, say, Malaysians (except in the case of mass-immigration). True, in most economies the lion's share of services are sheltered from global competition. However, they face an even more ferocious competitor, namely family self-servicing. And, as Gershuny (1978) has stressed, this competition stiffens as households acquire time-saving household machinery (washing-machines, dishwashers, or microwave ovens). Yet, as we saw, Americans are massive consumers of laundries, Europeans wash and iron at home.

The problem is that the marginal cost of services such as laundry, day-care, or home-help services to the elderly affects not only women's ability to pursue careers, but also society's welfare–employment nexus. As women's educational attainment increasingly matches (and surpasses) males', the social cost of housewifery is lost human capital, productive potential, *and* jobs. The high costs of out-servicing in Europe compels families to self-servicing which translates into fewer market services.[12]

Here we come to the third, fundamental condition, namely households' time constraints. The emerging 'postindustrial' household types, be they single person, single parent, or dual-earner households, have one thing in common: a scarcity of time, great difficulties in harmonizing paid employment with family obligations, domestic duties, and leisure.

The trade-off between the burden of domestic unpaid work and paid employment can be quite severe. Since it is unrealistic to expect a major relaxation of this trade-off through male substitution (husbands do not generally compensate significantly with more unpaid work to offset wives'

[12] The contrast between America and Europe suggests that Gershuny (1978) may not be correct when he concludes that households will opt for capital goods (washers rather than laundries) and thus not contribute to service employment.

declining hours), the solution must come from outside the household itself. This means either the market or the state.

The employment potential of new household forms comes out in consumer expenditure data. In a pioneering study, Stigler (1956: 88) suggested that restaurant employment should rise with the rate of women's labour force participation. Today, the dual-earner family norm is much stronger and, in some countries, almost universal. Accordingly, this should show up not only in family consumption behaviour, but ultimately also in service-sector job growth.

Table 6.7 compares the spending behaviour of 'atypical' and conventional one-earner families in two countries: strongly familialistic Italy, where female employment rates are low (although those who do work are almost invariably on a full-time basis); and the United States, where female employment is very high and familialism is weak. Of course, the greater service demand among two-earner couples is partially an added-income effect. However, the massive leap in out-servicing that occurs in the Italian data between couples without children and those with suggests that family structure has an important independent effect. Clearly, time constraints and servicing needs augment sharply when children are present in the household. The comparatively low figures for single-person households is partially due to the high share of single elderly whose incomes and demand for personal services tend to be low. In Italy, non-aged single-person households spend 170.5 per cent more than single-earner couples on personal services.

TABLE 6.7. *Difference in expenditures on restaurants, hotels, and personal services by household type*[a]

	Italy 1994	United States 1990
Single person	95.5	91.5
Two-earner couple	125.5	137.5
Two-earner child family[b]	180.0	n.a.

[a] One-earner couples = 100.
[b] Compared to one-earner child families.

Note: The two countries are not fully comparable, at least as far as multi-person units are concerned. The Italian, but not the American, data are adjusted for family size (using the square-root of number of members). American expenditures include only 'eating out'.

Sources: Calculations on 1994 Italian Consumer Expenditure survey; Statistical Abstract of the United States, 1995, table 692.

THE NEW KEYNESIAN HOUSEHOLD

Families or, more precisely, time-strapped households, are therefore a potential counterweight to the forces that repress labour-intensive services. But this all depends on the nexus of disposable income, relative prices, and time. There exist, unfortunately, no ready-made data that allow us to examine whether, and how, these variables really have an employment effect. As a second best, I propose to examine this kind of 'postindustrial Keynesianism' in two steps. In the first, I estimate (on a cross-sectional basis) the relative effect of demand (household expenditure on servicing) given relative prices (measured by degree of wage inequality). In the second, I estimate the service-job creation elasticities of married women's (mothers') employment growth.

The first step, then, consists of estimating how much household spending and relative costs affect employment levels in personal services (including restaurants, bars, and hotels):[13]

$$\text{jobs} = -2.514a + .160 \text{ (household spending)} + 3.098 \text{ (wage inequality)}$$
$$(-2.82) \qquad\qquad (2.20) \qquad\qquad\qquad (6.97)$$

This is quite a strong model (with almost 90 per cent of variance explained), but from an egalitarian point of view it provides pessimistic results. As is evident, the impact of wage differences is substantially stronger (this variable accounts for two-thirds of total variance explained).

The rise in women's—and especially married women's—employment is what creates severe domestic time constraints (and also higher disposable incomes), and this may offset or, at least, reduce the importance of servicing costs. We turn therefore to the second step in the analysis, in this case time-series analyses on the service-employment impact of changes in married women's employment.

I present three parallel analyses, for France, the United States, and Spain.[14] This nation selection allows us to compare one example of strong wage inequality and cheap services (the USA) with two where wages are much less unequal, and with one in which labour costs are very high (France). It also highlights international differences in married women's labour force attachment: very high levels of female employment (the USA), very low (Spain), and medium-level (France). The results,

---

[13] Cross-sectional, robust OLS regression estimation with N = 17 and adjusted R-squared = .865. Data source: OECD, *National Accounts, Detailed Tables* (1995), as well as national accounts data from individual OECD countries (the following OECD countries are omitted: Greece, Ireland, Japan, Korea, Mexico, and Turkey).

[14] I would like to thank Luis Toharia for providing me with the Spanish EPA data set.

TABLE 6.8. *Time constraints and personal-service jobs. The impact of married women's employment on job growth in services. Cochrane–Orcutt time-series estimates*[a]

	France 1982–97[b]	Spain 1977–97[b]	United States 1960–95[b]
Intercept	–57.192	42.343***	2.351***
Women's employment	0.151***	0.590***	0.378***
Rho	0.209	–0.270	0.237
Durbin–Watson	1.616	2.188	2.077
R²	*0.793*	*0.429*	*0.248*

*** Indicates significant at 0.001 level or better.

[a] The dependent variable is lagged (t – 1). For France and Spain, we measure all married women; for the United States, all women with children under age 6.

[b] For the United States, the data are percentage-differenced; for France and Spain, absolute numbers. Note that service employment in the United States is more inclusive than in France and Spain since it includes also marketed social services.

Sources: France and Spain: Annual Labour Force Surveys. The United States: Current Population Survey.

presented in Table 6.8, are to be read as indicative. These are all very reduced-form models, which accounts for the low levels of variance explained.[15]

Despite some statistical shortcomings, the results in Table 6.8 do lend support to the basic idea that working women and two-earner households create service jobs because they need to purchase 'time'. The job-creation elasticities are probably exaggerated, and would almost certainly decline if we could include additional relevant variables (such as relative servicing prices). Regardless, the signs of the coefficients are all positive and significance levels are strong. It is also worth noting that the statistical pattern is quite similar even for a comparison across such different countries.[16]

It is of course true that women's, and especially mothers', capacity to become employed in the first place depends on whether they can access affordable child care. The kinds of intensely service-consuming house-

---

[15] Even with Cochrane–Orcutt iterations, there remain problems of autocorrelation, as witnessed by the Durbin–Watson statistics (France), and in some cases the model fit is quite poor (R-squared is low). This is almost inevitable in such simple models.

[16] For Spain, I tested also a 'reverse' model, namely the impact of non-working wives. In this case, the coefficient turns strongly negative (–1.526), significant at the .001 level. And conducting separate estimates for only hotel and restaurant employment yields fairly similar results. For the USA only it is possible to control for changes in family real income. This does not change the outcome. The income variable is non-significant (B = .084 with t = 1.31), and the elasticity of mothers' employment remains basically unchanged (now B = .358 with t = 3.18). In this comparison at least, the 'time-constraint' effect seems to outweigh by far the 'income' effect.

holds that we need for job growth presuppose the existence of what they, themselves, are likely to create, namely services. This may seem like a paradox, but in reality we have uncovered little that is new. The logic appears quite similar to Say's time-old 'law' which says that supply begets its own demand.

CONCLUSIONS

Job growth in services is, accordingly, caught between rival forces. There are, on the one hand, the constraints that come from the inherent features of tertiarization or globalization and, on the other hand, the potential catalyst that comes from changing family life. If changing household forms can have positive employment effects, our focus should logically turn to which conditions would help maximize just such an effect. Women with careers are likely to reduce fertility, unless the tension between job and children is eased. If, then, access to child care is one constraint, society may find itself locked into a low-fertility equilibrium as seems to be the case in Southern Europe. And this will affect long-term job and growth prospects because, after all, aggregate demand depends on the size and growth of our population. Hence an ample social service infrastructure is one precondition for service-job growth.

The alternative scenario is that women are discouraged from economic activity. In this case, of course, a beneficial job spiral is blunted. The service economy may flourish with more inequality but also with two-earner households. In either case, we face institutional constraints. Some welfare regimes, and some modes of regulating labour markets and the distribution of welfare constrain or ease more than others. It is to this that we turn in the next chapter.

7

Managing Divergent Employment Dilemmas

THE REGULATORY FRAMEWORK OF LABOUR MARKETS

The macroscopic changes that were examined in Chapter 6 are unlikely to affect all nations similarly. Job loss through de-industrialization, for example, will be more massive where existing industries are uncompetitive (like in Britain or Spain) and less devastating elsewhere—perhaps because firms are more adaptable (as in much Danish, Italian, or German industry), but possibly also because wage costs decline (as in the United States). De-industrialization may cause heavy unemployment or it may not, depending on skill and production structure, and also on how labour markets are managed. Most of Europe has, for example, transformed mass lay-offs into early retirement.

This all goes to say that similar root causes will have radically divergent outcomes. There is no such thing as one postindustrial model because nations' institutional make-up differs, and so do also their choices of how to manage change.

INDUSTRIAL RELATIONS

In Chapter 2 emerged a fair degree of regime clustering in terms of industrial-relations arrangements. 'Liberal' welfare states, especially since the late 1970s–early 1980s, exhibit low levels of union coverage, centralization, and co-ordination (Australia being the sole exception). The Nordic social democracies score generally high on all three measures, although there has been some decline in both centralization and co-ordination since the 1980s, especially in Sweden. Continental Europe presents, however, a more mixed picture. Coverage rates are generally high, but there are important variations in centralization and co-ordination. At one end, we find Austria, Germany, and the Netherlands with strong 'neo-corporatism'; at the other end, France and Spain with a weaker capacity for co-ordinated collective action. In between lie Belgium and Italy.

It is now firmly recognized that collective-bargaining systems matter greatly for economic performance, from securing low-inflation growth to minimizing unemployment, from skill formation to wage-setting. The point of departure is collective-choice theory. Following the early work of Mancur Olson (1982), Cameron (1984), and Crouch (1985), the problem is that rent-seeking interests, when powerfully organized, can obtain egoistic gains which will harm the broader collectivity: militant unions may win impressive real-wage gains for their members, the insiders, but this will probably worsen the position of the unemployed, the outsiders.

[handwritten margin notes: Unions help insiders; But hurt the outsiders (unemployed)]

There are two alternatives to this scenario, the first being feeble organizations—in which case the free market is likely to operate. The second alternative is comprehensive, 'universalistic' organizations, compelled to represent the broader community and therefore more apt to seek consensual solutions through co-ordinated bargaining. If unions are strong, but incapable of co-ordination, they will likely impose externalities on others, while their comprehensive equivalents are compelled to internalize whatever negative by-products may arise from their actions. In short, the worst-case scenario occurs where organizations are strong but neither centralized nor capable of co-ordination. Economic performance is likely to be superior when either 'markets' or 'neo-corporatism' prevail. This is the essence behind Lindbeck and Snower's (1988) insider-outsider theory, and the so-called 'hump-shaped' curve hypothesis of macro-economic performance (Calmfors and Driffill, 1988; Layard *et al.*, 1991; OECD, 1997*b*).

Applying such insights to the problem at hand, industrial relations should matter for how nations cope with an eventual jobs–equality trade-off. Where our 'worst-case scenario' obtains, we should more likely find a deep divide between privileged insiders and a mass of outsiders; where unionism is ineffectual, we would expect rising wage inequalities; and where neo-corporatism prevails, we should find lower unemployment with equality.

For the most recent decades there is evidence that national differences in trade union evolution has substantial effects on inequalities. Thus, Freeman and Katz (1995) suggest that the deepening wage inequalities in America and Great Britain can, in part, be attributed to union decline. When the Netherlands is held up as the contemporary success model, it is because strong co-ordinated bargaining has brought about an impressive decline in unemployment without more inequality or any dramatic roll-back of social protection (Visser and Hemerijck, 1997). And, as Bentolila and Dolado (1994) suggest, Spain's seeming incapacity to eradicate mass unemployment has its roots in the monopolistic power of the insiders.

Although there has been a decline of centralization and co-ordination in some countries, this cannot possibly explain why there may be a growing equality–jobs dilemma, only why some nations fare better or worse in terms of managing it. Sweden constitutes an obvious test-case since rising wage differentials and, since 1990, European-level unemployment seem to coincide with a decay of co-ordination and centralization. To be sure, the drift towards more wage inequality must be seen on the backdrop of unusually egalitarian wages; Sweden still boasts one of the world's most compressed wage structures. And the collapse of full employment after 1990 certainly has multiple causes.

LABOUR MARKET REGULATION

From Chapter 2 we also know that nations differ with regard to levels of labour market regulation. The package of regulations can be regarded as the labour market equivalent to social citizenship rights. Indeed, the historical timing of either is quite similar, since both welfare states and existing systems of employment protection all matured in the late 1960s and early 1970s—generally spurred by worker militancy and union bargaining power (Buechteman, 1993).

The neo-liberal position is that labour markets, as a result, have become too rigid and that this is especially harmful in times that call for maximum and swift adaptation. Their diagnosis is Eurosclerosis, their remedy is to flexibilize (Giersch, 1985; Lindbeck, 1992; Siebert, 1997).

Models of employment regulation have a close affinity to our welfare regime types, but in ways which at first appear paradoxical. Not surprisingly, liberal regimes combine weak, decentralized industrial relations with weak employment regulation. A hallmark of virtually all Continental European, but especially the Mediterranean, labour markets is their very strict levels of employment protection, high wage costs, and rather compressed wage structures. While the liberal regimes systematically score low on the labour market 'rigidity' index, the opposite is the case for the conservative regimes. Italy, Spain, France, Germany, and Austria exhibit extraordinary high levels of strictness.

The apparent paradox arrives when we examine the Nordic countries and the Netherlands. These are countries with a long legacy of powerful unions and, in the former case, also social democratic governance. Although these countries boast high levels of wage equality and welfare state benefits, their labour markets are generally quite flexible by international standards. Why?

The paradox dissolves when we recognize that nations apply different methods in the same pursuit of worker security. To maximize adaptation to rapidly changing external markets, the small and very 'open' Nordic-cum-Dutch countries opted for a combination of high labour market flexibility with strong social guarantees to the individual worker—partly in the form of very generous social protection; and partly in the form of active labour market measures (in Scandinavia) or pensions (the Netherlands). In Continental Europe, the same aims were pursued through the extension of powerful job guarantees for those in employment. This strategy is akin to the Japanese model in so far as it pursues a *de facto* lifetime employment guarantee.

It is not difficult to identify the reasons behind these rival strategic choices: pervasive familialism and low levels of female employment mean that family members must rely on both the wage and the accumulated pension rights of the male bread-winner. Here is, then, a political economy in which the welfare of virtually all is wedded to the career of the household head, and this means that the premium on lifetime job security becomes high indeed. Compare this to the less familialistic and more individualistic logic of the social democratic regime where, since the 1960s, the dual-earner household has rapidly become universal. Scandinavia's triple accent on generous income guarantees, active labour market policy, and staggering welfare state employment growth, was meant to minimize individual insecurity while maximizing flexible employment adaptation. In fact, the Swedish Rehn–Meidner model deliberately sought to accelerate employment decline in uncompetitive industries so as to reallocate labour in the most dynamic sectors.

We must not forget that these models of labour market regulation were, like their welfare state brethren, built to cater to the kind of economy that then prevailed. High unemployment benefits, wages, and labour costs together with job protection may not have adverse effects in a predominantly industrial setting with full employment and rapidly rising real earnings. The problem is that the setting has changed: it is now services which must produce any net job growth, demand for less-skilled workers has diminished, female labour supply has exploded and, as we have just seen, high labour costs can be problematic at the lower end of the service economy. To what extent, then, are nations' management of the postindustrial transition determined by their institutional infrastructure?

THE DILEMMAS OF FLEXIBILIZATION

To most contemporary economists, the crux of our employment problem is that labour markets are too inflexible. There are, firstly, potential rigidities that spring from welfare state guarantees (the reservation wage), not only because they may create negative work incentives and prolong unemployment duration, but also because generous welfare states raise the wage floor and labour costs. A second source of rigidity can come from wage-setting behaviour. And the third refers to legislated or *de facto* job protection, including costs of hiring, the burden of severance compensation, difficulties of dismissing workers, restrictions on hiring casual workers, seniority clauses, and so forth.[1] According to the argument, rigidities impair labour market adaptation and will result in mass unemployment and exclusion, especially among workers in low demand. There may, in brief, develop a deep abyss between the protected and privileged insiders and the unemployable outsiders.[2]

THE WELFARE STATE AND THE RESERVATION WAGE

The idea that social guarantees induce idleness is as old as capitalism itself. Social benefits experienced a substantial upgrading during the 1960s and 1970s, but most countries have, in the more troubled 1980s and 1990s, initiated some—usually marginal—downward adjustments of unemployment pay (typically in the order of 10 percentage points) or of benefit duration.[3] Such cuts have, however, often been accompanied by new forms of social protection, such as the development of various social minima for the unemployed (unemployment assistance in Germany and Sweden; the RMI and its equivalent in Belgium, France, and Spain). Most contemporary research fails to find any major effect from benefit levels, but there is evidence that the duration of eligibility prolongs unemployment (Layard *et al.*, 1991; Scarpetta, 1996; Nickell, 1997).

The effect of welfare state guarantees on labour demand may, in fact, be of greater importance in so far as they raise the wage floor. This can price the less-productive workers out of the market (Alogoskoufis *et al.*, 1995; Nickell, 1997). What is clear is that welfare state generosity cannot explain *levels* of unemployment; at most, it affects *who* happens to be unemployed.

Even this is debatable. From simple cross-section regression estimates for 18 OECD nations, none among four different measures of 'decommodification' (be they net or gross unemployment benefits or benefit-duration measures) are significant in predicting either relative youth, female, or unskilled worker unemployment rates.[4] Although this appears to contradict other findings, that is not really the case. There exists, as far

[1] For a general overview, see Alogoskoufis *et al.* (1995); Bean (1994); Bertola (1990); Blank (1994); and OECD, *The OECD Jobs Study*, Part II, ch. 6 (1994*a*). The OECD study has also developed a synthetic index of strictness based on various existing country rankings (op. cit. Table 6.7) that will be used in subsequent statistical analyses.

[2] The insider-outsider theory was first developed by Lindbeck and Snower (1988). For a general discussion of the issues, see Layard, Nickell, and Jackson (1991); Atkinson and Mogensen (1993); Freeman (1993); and Blank (1994).

[3] See, for example, Ploug and Kvist (1994). Average European unemployment replacement rates, in the mid-1990s, lie around 70–80 per cent in Belgium, Denmark, and the Netherlands, and around 40–50 per cent elsewhere except for the UK (24 per cent) and Italy (about 30 per cent) (Bison and Esping-Andersen, 1998).

[4] I therefore omit the analyses from the text.

as I know, no study which manages to demonstrate any powerful effect. The ambivalent findings that permeate the literature suggest that, if any significant effect is found, it is probably not very robust: small measurement differences (such as year selected, countries included, or how benefit levels are estimated) make a big difference.

There are also substantive reasons why welfare benefits have only minor effects. As we know, Scandinavian social protection standards are unusually high, and it is in these very same countries that measures in favour of employment (re-) activation are most developed. Hence average unemployment duration is much shorter than in other European countries (9 months compared to 30 months in Continental Europe, and a low of 6 months in the liberal regime cluster).[5] Indeed, moving to the other extreme, in Italy a genuine system of unemployment benefits does not even exist, and the lion's share of unemployed Italians (youth) can make absolutely no claim on the welfare state. Yet, average Italian unemployment duration is 36 months.[6] This surprising lack of programme development can best be explained by the fact that worker dismissals are virtually unknown.

WAGE REGULATION

Wage regulation is, like welfare state benefits, a Janus-headed animal. Wage relativities may influence who is unemployed; long-term real wage growth may affect aggregate unemployment rates. If the wage structure is too compressed, and the minimum too high, the less-productive segments of the workforce are priced out of the market (Dolado *et al.*, 1996: OECD, 1994*a* and 1996*b*). Hence, wage structure should influence the composition, but not the levels of unemployment.

There is considerable disagreement in the literature on the wage effect. On one hand, the comparative job performance of the United States and most of Europe seems superficially related to differences in wage distribution. The minimum for both youth and adults is higher in Europe (around 50–60 per cent of average wages for adults; 40–50 per cent for youth) than in America (35–40 per cent in either case, depending on year). But one thing is official minima, another is practice. The proportion of workers actually receiving low wages (defined as less than two-thirds of median) is 23 per cent in the USA and 20 per cent in Britain, and much lower in

[5] Denmark's unlimited-duration unemployment benefits have been shown to retard job search in the past, but after the 1994–6 reforms, most unemployed are 'activated' within 6 or even 3 months (Pedersen and Smith, 1997).

[6] Unemployment duration data are from OECD (1994*a*) and refer to 1991. Italy's Cassa Integrazione serves as a surrogate but only for already employed workers laid off temporarily. They do not figure in unemployment statistics.

Europe (the range is from 5 per cent in Sweden to 13 per cent in Italy) (OECD, 1996*b*, Table 3.3; Dolado *et al.*, 1996).[7]

On the other hand, the purportedly negative impact of the minimum wage is highly disputed. Card and Krueger's (1995) famous study of the MacDonalds sector shows, in fact, that raising the minimum brings about more employment. None the less, most studies find that minimum wages mainly influence the employment opportunities of youth and low-skilled workers (Wood, 1994; Bertola and Ichino, 1995; Dolado *et al.*, 1996; and Nickell, 1997).

Earnings differences may be important if the profile of labour demand is changing. A defining characteristic of postindustrial economies is that the premium on education and skills is rising. Vice versa, the penalty on little education, redundant skills, and lack of experience is increasing (Burtless, 1990; Freeman, 1993; Freeman and Katz, 1995; OECD, 1994*a*). Herein lies a major break with the past, when low-skilled construction and factory workers were in strong demand and, aided by powerful trade unions, could command high earnings. The low-skilled worker and youth epitomize the contemporary equality–jobs dilemma.

The inexperienced and less-skilled should, accordingly, be especially at risk of exclusion in protected, high-wage labour markets while, in deregulated markets their chief risk should be low pay. It is generally true that the unskilled suffer from higher unemployment rates; for youth the risk is even worse. Drèze and Snessens (1994) show a dramatic deterioration in the unskilled/skilled employment ratio in France and Germany among both blue-collar and white-collar workers. In contrast, almost all American studies show a similarly dramatic deterioration in the relative pay of youth and the unskilled (see especially Freeman and Katz, 1995).

Yet, the link between unemployment and wages becomes more ambiguous when we broaden our comparison. As shown in Table 7.1, the unskilled actually fare relatively worse in the 'low-wage' deregulated countries and better in 'sclerotic' Europe.

The trade-off is accordingly more multifaceted. For one thing, the relative risk of unemployment will depend on the existing stock of low-skilled workers. De-industrialization in some countries (notably Australia and the UK, but also Sweden, Italy, and the Netherlands) occurred on the backdrop of an unusually large stock of low-skilled workers, but in others not (OECD, 1996*b*, Table 4.1). Yet, there is no significant correlation between 'stock' and unemployment, mainly because of policy. In Scandinavia, the less-skilled are likely to receive retraining; since they are frequently women, they are likely to find employment in low-end welfare

---

[7] Wage minima for particular groups, such as apprentices or youth, may be much lower. Real wage costs to the employer may also be reduced because of subsidies, such as for youth training contracts in France and Italy.

TABLE 7.1. *Low wages, and the relative risk of unemployment among the less-skilled, youth, and women, 1990s*

	Incidence of low pay[a]	Unskilled relative unemployment[b]	Youth relative unemployment[c]	Female relative unemployment[d]
Anglo-Saxon group[e]	48.3	1.6	2.6	1.3
Nordic group[f]	22.9	1.4	3.0	1.4
Continental Europe[g]	36.4	1.3	5.7	3.8

[a] Percentage of full-time young workers (under 25) earning less than two-thirds the median in c. 1994–5 (*Source*: OECD, 1996b, Table 3.2).

[b] Ratio of low-skilled to total unemployment, 1992 (*Source*: OECD, *Education at a Glance* (1995a, Table R21(A)).

[c] Ratio of youth to adult male unemployment, 1994 (*Source*: OECD, *Employment Outlook* (1995b, Table B).

[d] Ratio of female to adult male unemployment, 1994 (*Source*: OECD, *Employment Outlook* (1995b, Table B).

[e] Australia, Canada, New Zealand, the UK, and the United States.

[f] Denmark, Finland, Norway, and Sweden (except for earnings, which includes only Finland and Sweden).

[g] Austria, Belgium, France, Germany, Italy, the Netherlands, Portugal, and Spain.

state servicing jobs. In Continental Europe, their risk of unemployment is suppressed because of early retirement and strong job protection: either they are insiders or they disappear entirely from unemployment statistics.

In fact, where the insiders enjoy powerful protection, those who have not yet gained a foothold in the labour market will face barriers to entry. This is surely what explains the preponderance of youth and female unemployment in Continental and, especially, Southern Europe. Protecting the male bread-winner means exclusion of his wife, sons, and daughters. In other words, wage structure may influence the composition, but probably not levels of unemployment.

If our concern is with levels, the wage-effect should mainly come from long-term movements in real earnings. One of the fundamental facts cited again and again in the current debate is that European (including British) real wages have continued to rise, while in North America they have stagnated and even fallen. This is said to account for European jobless growth and, at the same time, for the American (and Dutch) job miracle (OECD, 1994a; Visser and Hemerijck, 1997).

In reality wages have everywhere stopped growing at the kinds of rates that prevailed in the Golden Age. During the 1980s, real manufacturing wages declined in the Anglo-Saxon countries, and in Europe they grew by a modest one-fifth of the rate that prevailed in the 1960s.[8] Still, it may very well be that national differences in real wage development lie behind variations in unemployment levels. In fact, this is where 'neo-corporatism' should really matter: centralized, nation-wide and co-ordinated bargaining constitutes the basic precondition for full employment through sustained wage moderation (Soskice, 1990; Rowthorne, 1992; Calmfors, 1993). Do industrial relations matter then?

The evidence is, once again, mixed. The OECD (1997b, Table 3.B.1) finds that real earnings growth is negatively, albeit modestly, correlated with union centralization and co-ordinated bargaining. I fail to find any significant correlation for real wage growth, 1979–93. When it comes to explain unemployment *levels*, the evidence is once again unclear. The OECD study (op. cit) finds that union centralization and co-ordination (I.R.) do reduce unemployment. However, re-estimating the relationship and including also real-wage growth, 1979–93, and economic 'openness' yields (almost) significant results in only one case, namely for the level of structural unemployment (Y):[9]

$$Y = 8.661a + 1.785 \ (\text{Wage growth}) + 6.270 \ (\text{Trade}) - .980 \ (\text{I.R})$$
$$\ \ \ \ \ (3.40) \ \ \ \ \ \ \ \ \ \ \ (1.77) \ \ \ \ \ \ \ \ \ \ \ \ (1.12) \ \ \ \ \ \ \ \ \ (-1.95)$$

In other words, the 'neo-liberal' case against regulation is, so far, hardly overwhelming.[10] Most of the debate has, however, centred on the third type of labour market rigidities, namely employment protection.

EMPLOYMENT PROTECTION

The principal rigidities that come from job protection include rules regarding hirings, dismissals, non-regular employment contracts, and so forth. Since most such measures serve to protect workers from becoming unemployed why, then, should they matter? The link is, in fact, indirect. The argument is that strict worker protection means high firing costs and obstacles to assuming more flexible labour. Hence, there will be few lay-offs during downturns but also few hirings during upturns. This should of

[8] Calculated from OECD, *Historical Statistics* (1995).

[9] Estimates are based on robust regression, with R-squared = .277. T-statistics are shown in parentheses. Data on structural unemployment are from Elmeskov (1998), on wage growth and trade from OECD, *Historical Statistics, 1960–1995* (OECD, 1997), and industrial relations data are from OECD (1997b).

[10] Since the basic theory behind the centralization-cum-co-ordination argument predicts a 'hump-shaped' curve, our estimations should have included a quadratic term of the variable. In fact, separate analyses (not shown) indicate that the models improve somewhat, but the neo-corporatism effect remains, none the less, non-significant.

course equal things out. Yet, as the argument goes, parity will obtain only in the short run. In the longer haul it means that firms will prefer to give extra hours to its existing, possibly shrinking, labour force rather than hire new staff. Hence, once again we should expect a deepening abyss between the insiders and the outsiders, and the size of the excluded should grow. In other words, strict employment protection will push the rate of structural unemployment upwards (Buechtemann, 1993; Bentolila and Bertola, 1990; Blank, 1994; Alogoskoufis *et al.*, 1995; and OECD, 1994*a*, Part II).

Formal 'rigidities', whether legislated or not, will possibly engender countervailing flexibilities. In Japan, these are rather formalized (the female labour force and older workers often employed on a franchise basis). Early retirement is the European equivalent to instititonalized flexibilization. Informal flexibilities, especially prevalent in Southern Europe, mainly take the form of informal (or black-economy) employment and, increasingly, self-employment.

THE REGULATORY INFRASTRUCTURE AND THE MANAGEMENT OF INDUSTRIAL DECLINE

As has been argued before, the welfare state has become an indispensable participant in contemporary labour markets. This is especially evident in the use of pension schemes in managing de-industrialization (Kohli *et al.*, 1993; Kolberg, 1992).

To be sure, the use of social policies for labour market purposes is nothing new. In the broadest sense possible, we can trace the very origins of social policy to (authoritarian) governments' attempt to manage the social conflicts of early industrialization (Rimlinger, 1971). And social policies—like the G.I. bill—were surely not unimportant in securing a smooth process of de-ruralization. The difference today lies partly in the sheer scale of welfare state intervention and, partly, in its recast role. In many countries, the welfare state seems to have *de facto* replaced the 'invisible hand'.

This is certainly clear with regard to national modes of managing industrial labour force redundancies. The Nordic countries in general, and Denmark and Sweden in particular, have favoured what Swedish social democrats fondly call the 'productivistic' approach. The stress is on re-employment through retraining and reactivation programmes rather than parking excess workers on income maintenance. With the exception of Finland, the result is internationally low levels of early retirement and high rates of participation in general, and among women and older workers in particular. Scandinavia's high average retirement age is especially noteworthy when we consider that pension benefits are very generous.

The liberal, deregulated Anglo-Saxon countries arrive at a fairly similar outcome, but by different means. Early retirement is less pervasive, in part because the modesty of public pension benefits constitutes a disincentive unless topped-up with an employer plan—which, as we know, applies mainly to workers in the 'primary' economy. A second reason has to do with comparatively weak worker protection and union power. Unlike in Europe, employers who embark upon industrial downsizing are likely to face fewer obstacles and lower costs. Hence, redundant workers are more likely to be either unemployed or re-employed—in the United States often at lower wages (Levy, 1988: 93).[11] Indeed, deregulation and low wages may be one reason why, in absolute numbers, American manufacturing employment has remained stable since the 1970s. The real annual earnings of a full-time, year-round adult male factory-worker dropped by more than $1,000 from 1979 to 1987; the least-skilled workers experienced a real earnings loss of almost $3,000 (McKinley *et al.*, 1990, Table 1). The legislated minimum wage was about 50 per cent of average manufacturing wages in 1970; 44 per cent in 1980; and down to only 35 per cent in 1990 (Statistical Abstract of the United States, 1995, Table 681).[12] In brief, many industrial jobs were saved by wage erosion.

Continental European countries boast unusually generous pension benefits and, considering pervasive worker protection, strong unions, and very weakly developed active labour market policies, it is hardly surprising that early retirement policies became the main—if not exclusive—means to facilitate industrial restructuring (Kohli *et al.*, 1993). Here the activity rate of older (55–64) males is now typically below 50 per cent and, in some countries (Belgium, Italy, and the Netherlands), well below 40 per cent. In contrast, the Scandinavian rate remains around 65 per cent, and the Anglo-Saxon average at about 60 per cent (OECD, 1995*b*).

These national differences reflect the institutional nexus of our three 'regimes'. Where employment regulation prohibits mass redundancies, the welfare state can, as in Scandinavia, facilitate mobility via active measures; or, as in Continental Europe, via passive income maintenance. Where institutional blockage is less solid, as in the 'liberal' group, the 'invisible hand' of the market comes to dominate.

---

[11] The average unemployment rate of older males (1993) is 9.8 per cent in the Anglo-Saxon group, 6.2 per cent in the Nordic, and 5.3 per cent in the Continental European. Finland and Germany have been excluded since unemployment insurance is the normal pathway to early retirement (*Source*: OECD, 1996*b*: Annex Table B).

[12] Among young workers, the real pay decline has been $2,000. As McKinley *et al.* (1990) show, the decline in average earnings is not so much caused by sectoral shifts in the labour force (e.g. moving from manufacturing to services), as it is by declining unionism and changing pay practice *within* industry. Of all displaced workers in the first half of the 1980s, only one-third was re-employed at similar or better wages than before (Levy, 1988: 93).

Yet, this seemingly tight institutional fit is arguably spurious. While early retirement may be presented as a policy to contain unemployment among older workers and to create openings for the young, this may not be the only or even main objective. In fact, it is almost universally recognized that the youth employment dividend of early retirement is trivial. In Graebner's (1980) now classical formulation, easing out older workers is also a means to raise productivity, and hence profits. But how would this account for such large national variations? Here Sala-i-Martin (1992) offers an intriguing reformulation, namely that early retirement is especially attractive when, in periods of rapid technological change (like in the past decades), there is a huge skills gap between older and younger workers. It is, in other words, a means to clear the market of suboptimal skills.

Under such circumstances, early retirement may be an especially attractive option in countries where unskilled workers predominate, or in economies where 'labour market rigidities' prohibit redundancies and labour mobility. As we know, the unskilled bias in unemployment is much heavier in the liberal regimes. This same risk group may simply have been retired out, or re-employed, elsewhere.

The uniqueness of the Continental European model is not so much labour market regulation as such, but rather the absence of any acceptable alternatives to early retirement. Here, families become crucial. An alternative to throwing families into poverty because of lay-offs is to retire the main bread-winner, a policy that will enjoy backing from both unions and the median voter, especially if the only option is deregulation and wage decline. A similar national coalition against change is less likely to emerge in Scandinavia, in part because the cost of mobility and retraining is socialized, in part because families are less dependent on one member's contribution.

We can test this argument. If it has substance, we should expect that early retirement rates are mainly related to 'welfare regime', to the strictness of unemployment protection (measured with the synthetic index discussed earlier), and to the prevalence of one-earner families (measured as rates of female employment), controlling for the incidence of unemployment among the unskilled. Unfortunately, a full statistical estimation is made impossible by the strong collinearity between welfare state type and female employment rates (for conservative welfare states, the $r = -.787$: for the social democratic welfare states, $r = .688$). We will therefore perform seperate regression tests. In Table 7.2 we examine the impact of unskilled unemployment levels and the welfare state effect on early retirement.

Recourse to early retirement is clearly a peculiarly Continental European strategy, predominant where few women work, and where worker protection is very strict. The Sala-i-Martin effect, namely clearing labour markets of low-skilled, older workers to make room for young

TABLE 7.2. *Explaining early retirement* (robust regressions)

	Model 1	Model 2	Model 3	Model 4	Model 5
R^2	0.392	0.020	0.060	0.293	0.189
Constant	29.80***	49.59***	42.86***	109.52***	5.88
Low-skilled unemployment rate	1.10	0.16	0.95	0.67**	2.43***
Conservative regime	16.82**				
Social democratic regime		−12.67			
Liberal regime			−10.89		
Female rate of employment				−1.17***	
Rigidity measure					1.77***

** Probability significant at 0.01 level.
*** Probability significant at 0.001 level.

Sources: OECD, *Education at a Glance* (OECD, 1995a), OECD, *Employment Outlook* (OECD, 1996b), and OECD, *Historical Statistics* (OECD, 1995c).

blood, does not manifest itself within our regimes, but it does become important in the last two estimations—when held together with women's employment and, in particular, with labour market rigidities.[13]

The effect of female employment and of job protection is noteworthy (−1.17 and 1.77, respectively). This implies that for each percentage rise in women's employment we would have a similarly smaller rate of early retirement. As a thought experiment, let us imagine that German women were employed at Swedish levels (79 instead of 53 per cent in 1990). This should, ignoring all other possible factors (which are many in light of the modest R-squared), produce an inactivity rate among the 55–64-year old males of only 22 per cent rather than the actual 42 per cent. An even more dramatic reduction would ensue from more flexibility. In any case, the two phenomena are, as we know, part of the same story.

MANAGING THE EQUALITY–JOBS TRADE-OFF

Together with falling or stagnant real wages, the Anglo-Saxon nations have experienced a rather sharp increase in earnings inequality since the

[13] It could be (rightly) argued that unemployment among the unskilled is a misleading variable since the rate, in the first place, might be affected by early retirement. However, analogous regressions were estimated with alternative measures such as the existing stock of low-skilled workers as a percentage of the labour force or the relative risk of unemployment among the low-skilled relative to the total labour force. The results obtained remain basically identical.

late 1970s. This is not true for either Continental Europe or Scandinavia.[14] Moreover, the incidence of low earnings in the Anglo-Saxon economies is especially high among the least employable: youth and low-skilled workers. In the Anglo-Saxon group almost half (48.3 per cent) full-time employed youth (aged 20–5) earn less than two-thirds the median compared to a third (33.7 per cent) in Continental Europe, and only 19 per cent in Sweden (calculated from OECD, 1996*b*, Table 3.2). From Table 7.3 it appears that the link between jobs and wages holds up.

TABLE 7.3. *The equality–jobs trade-off*

	Rigidity index[a]	Wage inequality[b]	Real wage growth[c]	Employment growth[d]
Liberal regimes[e]	3.4	0.53	–0.10	1.4
Continental Europe[f]	16.4	0.70	1.20	0.6
Scandinavia[g]	9.8	0.74	1.00	0.8

[a] Average OECD ranking, taken from col. 5 in OECD (1994*a*, Part II, Table 6.7).

[b] The ratio of lowest decile to fifth decile earnings, latest data (OECD, 1993, Table 5.2). (New Zealand and Finland are excluded from these calculations.)

[c] Annual average real wage growth in manufacturing, 1979–89 (OECD, *Historical Statistics*, 1995, Table 9.2).

[d] Annual average percentage growth of employment, 1979–89 (OECD, *Historical Statistics*, 1995, Table 1.6).

[e] Australia, Canada, New Zealand, UK, and USA.

[f] Austria, Belgium, France, Germany, Italy, and the Netherlands.

[g] Denmark, Finland, Norway, and Sweden.

As we can see, the more deregulated Anglo-Saxon labour markets suffer from wage stagnation and more inequality, but then enjoy twice as much job growth as the highly regulated and more egalitarian Continental European nations. Yet, when we probe a little deeper we discover that the simple correlation ($r = -.180$ for 17 nations) between employment and real wage growth in the 1980s is actually insignificant. This is also the case for the association between wage inequalities and job growth ($r = .372$ for 14 nations).[15]

[14] Sweden is a partial exception since wage inequalities have risen somewhat during the 1980s (the ratio of the median to the lowest decile rose from 1.30 to 1.34 between 1979 and 1994). Yet, when we consider the extremely egalitarian point of departure, the Swedish wage structure still remains the world's most egalitarian (OECD, 1996*b*, Table 3.1).

[15] Data on employment and real wage growth are from OECD, *Historical Statistics* (1995), while data on earnings inequality are from OECD (1996*b*, Table 3.2). Note that our wage inequality measure is the incidence of low-paid employment among full-time workers. Low pay is defined as less than two-thirds median earnings. Many believe that it is real growth of total labour costs that matter. Still, if we re-estimate the model with labour costs the conclusion remains the same. The correlation with employment growth is slightly higher, yet not significant (–.40).

The argument that employment protection impairs job growth is somewhat easier to sustain. Although the correlation is not impressive ($r = -.497$), it is statistically significant ($t = 2.20$) and accounts for 25 per cent of the cross-national variation in employment growth during the 1980s. The elasticity of job growth with respect to our rigidity measure ($B = -.063$) appears rather modest but, ignoring all other factors, a substantial effort at deregulation would, in some countries, yield a more impressive employment performance. Vice versa, were highly deregulated economies to embrace greater job-protection policies, their relative performance would suffer. The effect of this hypothetical situation is presented in Table 7.4 which estimates the potential loss or gain in job growth that can be attributed to labour market 'rigidities'.[16]

TABLE 7.4. *Labour market protection, actual job growth, and regression-estimated hypothetical deviation from actual job growth during the 1980s*

	Protection score	Actual growth	Hypothetical growth deviation[a]
Australia	4	2.4	−0.4
Canada	3	1.8	−0.4
New Zealand	2	0.1	−0.5
UK	7	0.5	−0.2
USA	1	1.7	−0.6
Denmark	5	0.7	−0.3
Finland	10	0.9	0.0
Norway	11	0.8	+0.1
Sweden	13	0.7	+0.2
Austria	16	0.9	+1.0
Belgium	17	0.1	+0.5
France	14	0.1	+0.3
Germany	15	0.8	+0.3
Italy	21	0.4	+0.7
Netherlands	9	1.6	−0.1
Spain	20	0.2	+0.4
Japan	8	1.1	−0.1

[a] The gain or loss in employment growth that would have occurred had a country's level of protection been equal to the mean (9.9).

[16] The estimated loss/gain equals: $(P +/- \text{mean}P \times (.063) +/- A)$, where P is protection score and A is actual employment growth.

Put differently, if the United States were to have a level of job protection equal to the mean, its growth performance during the 1980s would have been 1.1 per cent per year rather than the actual 1.7 per cent. Or, if Italy had reduced its level of protection to the Finnish level, job growth would have been a respectable 1.1 per cent per year. Overall, if all nations had shared the same mean rigidity score, differences in job performance would have been much narrower. The hypothetical rate for the Anglo-Saxon group would have been 1.2; for the Nordic group, 0.8; and for the Continental European group, 1.3 per cent.

THE HUMP-SHAPED CURVE

The statistical association between 'rigidities' and jobs has, so far, been defined in strictly monotonic, linear terms (an extra dose of protection means an extra dose of unemployment).[17] However, if institutional differences play a role, and especially if collective action theory is right, the world should not behave linearly. A straightforward test of this hypothesis is to introduce a quadratic measure of rigidities. If such a specification is better at explaining employment outcomes, this may be because of differences in collective action. Tables 7.5–7.7 examine the impact of rigidities, first linearly in Model 1, then non-linearly in Model 2 and, finally, in Model 3, I include the union centralization-co-ordination variable to see whether this might account for non-linearity in Model 2.[18] I examine three relevant types of employment outcomes: aggregate employment growth and the *level* of structural unemployment; the bias of unemployment (youth, unskilled, and female unemployment as a ratio of adult male unemployment); and relative probabilities of leaving unemployment (the ratio of youth and female to adult male exits).[19]

When we look at general patterns of employment or unemployment performance, the purported negative influence of labour market 'rigidities' is not especially evident. They have a weak impact on overall job growth, and none on service growth or on structural unemployment rates. The single most interesting finding here is that rigidities predict the incidence of (non-agricultural) self-employment very strongly. The variance explained is surprisingly high, and the coefficients are systematically significant.

The hump-shaped curve effect of bargaining structure is not especially evident. The squared model (2) is significant, but weak, in the case of

[17] In fact, to my knowledge all existing econometric studies approach the issue as monotonically linear.

[18] The co-ordination-centralization measure is a simple average of rankings from OECD (1997*b*, Table 3.3.).

[19] The unemployment ratios can be interpreted as indices of an insider-outsider situation: the higher the ratio, the more exclusion of youth, women, or the unskilled compared to prime age adult workers.

TABLE 7.5. *Rigidities, bargaining structure, and employment outcomes*

	Model 1	Model 2	Model 3
	B(RIG)	B(RIG)+B(RIG)^2	B(RIG)+B(CORP)
Employment change 1983–93	–0.07**	–0.19 +0.01	–0.07** +0.03
R^2	0.200	0.233	0.171
Market service growth, 1979–90	–0.04	–0.35** +0.01**	–0.02 +0.07
R^2	0.03	0.153	0.064
Self-employment rate	0.41**	0.98 + 0.06**	0.51** +0.41**
R^2	0.335	0.515	0.461
Structural unemployment	0.01	–0.37 +0.02	0.15 +0.26
R^2	0.076	0.015	0.136

** Probability significant at 0.01 level or better.

Notes: All estimations are robust regressions. RIG = OECD synthetic rigidity index. CORP = centralization–co-ordination measure.

Sources: OECD, *Historical Statistics* (OECD, 1995); OECD, *OECD Jobs Study*, Part II. (OECD, 1994*a*, Table 6.8); and Elmeskov (1998).

services growth, and is strong in the case of self-employment. But in neither case does bargaining structure help explain non-linearity.

Following up on earlier dicussions, we would have predicted that 'rigidities' have a greater and more direct influence on *who* is the victim of unemployment. Employment protection is primarily an instrument of safeguarding the position of already employed insiders, and this may create outsiders and perpetuate their exclusion. This is basically what comes out in Table 7.6. Rigidities have a strong and positive effect on relative youth and female unemployment. The effect on relative unskilled unemployment is, however, negative and significant. Why?

The answer, again, is that strictness of job protection shelters those already employed, even the low-skilled. Vice versa, where labour market flexibility prevails, those most likely to find themselves made redundant are the unskilled. Hence, relative low-skilled unemployment is high in deregulated, and low in regulated, labour markets.

The hump-shaped curve hypothesis finds some confirmation in Table 7.6. as far as the unskilled and women are concerned. But, once again, bargaining structure is not what causes it.

In Table 7.7 we turn to flows out of unemployment. Since, as before, rigidities cement the privilged status of insiders, they should logically also reinforce exclusion among the outsiders—meaning inferior chances of leaving unemployment. The evidence confirms this: labour market regula-

TABLE 7.6. *Rigidities, bargaining structure, and the unemployment bias*

	Model 1	Model 2	Model 3
	B(RIG)	B(RIG)+ B(RIG)^2	B(RIG)+B(CORP)
Low-skilled/all unemployment	–0.02**	0.03 –0.01**	–0.02** +0.00
R^2	0.370	0.286	0.287
Youth/adult male unemployment	0.13**	–0.17 +0.02	0.18** +0.09
R^2	0.363	0.562	0.489
Female/adult male unemployment	0.13**	–0.19 +0.02**	0.14** –0.04
R^2	0.465	0.673	0.523

Notes: for estimation procedure, see Table 7.5.
Source: OECD (1995*b*).

tion is a quite potent explanation of exclusion, that is, of low chances of exit both in general, and for young unemployed in particular. In the former case, the quadratic form is significant but, surprisingly, bargaining structure still remains wholly unimportant.

In brief, labour market regulation harms women and youth, but it hardly plays any role in overall job or unemployment performance. Where labour markets are quite rigid, it would seem that one major response is to dodge the regulatory system through self-employment.

Although the association between rigidities and outcomes is occasionally 'hump-shaped', the great mystery is why bargaining structure plays absolutely no role. None of the obvious rival explanations hold up. One such might be that some nations have experienced a decline in union centralization or co-ordination capacities over the 1980s. Yet, this does not help resolve the issue because the results remain identical when we compare bargaining structure for 1980 and 1990, or when we measure change between 1980 and 1990.[20]

Another alternative candidate is that nations are affected unequally by global trade. Yet, 'economic openness' is systematically insignificant in all the models tested. Still another is that differences in employment performance may be caused by sheer demographics. High unemployment may be the result of excessively rapid labour supply growth—either because of large birth cohorts or of rapidly rising female labour supply. Yet, also demographic variables remain systematically insignificant.

---

[20] OECD (1997*b*, Table 3.8). Research does find some effects of bargaining structure on employment performance, but the correlations are quite weak.

NATIONAL IDIOSYNCRASIES AND WELFARE REGIMES

There is, in other words, no clear answer that can be culled from the existing literature. In fact, the most recent writings conclude that the Eurosclerosis thesis has preciously little empirical support (Nickell, 1997). It would appear that comparative employment performance must be explained by national idiosyncrasies.[21]

Put less tautologically, what the kinds of statistical analyses carried out here (and in most studies) cannot capture is the interwoven institutional fabric that underpins any political economy. Welfare state programmes and regulatory mechanisms are, in each nation, inserted within a particular societal framework; visible rigidities may be offset by informal flexibilities and vice versa; individuals may react very differently to an identical welfare or regulatory programme, depending on who he or she is, in what kind of labour market he or she operates, or in which society he or she resides.

We cannot capture such complexity via quantitative research, and it is even doubtful whether a qualitative study could do substantially better. Still, there is a distant, second-best solution. Throughout this book, I have developed the analysis around distinct regimes which, I argue, encapsulate a set of distinct institutional characteristics. They are 'ideal types' in the sense that no individual nation fits the bill perfectly. But a similarity of 'logic', of basic attributes, among societies suggests a considerable degree of clustering around our ideal typical models.

One way to capture the interwoven complexity of national institutional arrangements is, therefore, to explore the impact of 'regimes' on key labour market performance indicators. In Table 7.8 I provide such an attempt, bearing in mind that this is little more than a heuristic means of capturing 'idiosyncrasies'. Parameter estimates are included only when significant.

The results from Table 7.8 are suggestive. There is above all a distinct orthogonality between Continental Europe, on the one hand, and social democratic and liberal regimes, on the other hand. The Continental European welfare regimes stand out for their strong female unemployment bias and low exit probabilities from unemployment. Within this cluster, the Mediterranean group is unique in its youth unemployment bias and in the strength of self-employment.

The social democratic regime shines in terms of its ability to maximize outflows from unemployment and it actively discourages self-

---

[21] The same conclusion emerges in a recent EU study on the relationship between unemployment and labour market regulation (Regini, 1998).

TABLE 7.7. *Rigidities, bargaining structure, and probabilities of leaving unemployment*

	Model 1	Model 2	Model 3
	B(RIG)	B(RIG) + B(RIG)^2	B(RIG)+B(CORP)
Rate of exit from unemployment, all	−0.94**	−3.40**+0.11**	−0.88** +0.35
R^2	*0.399*	*0.491*	*0.359*
Rate of exit from unemployment, youth	−1.31**	−3.35* +0.09	−1.30** +0.13
R^2	*0.400*	*0.364*	*0.321*

Notes: Unemployment exits are measured as the monthly probability of leaving unemployment. Otherwise see Table 7.5.

Source: OECD, *Economic Outlook* (OECD, 1994*b*, Dec.).

TABLE 7.8. *Regimes and employment performance* (coefficients from robust regression estimates)

	Conservative regime[a]	Mediterranean regime[b]	Social democratic regime[c]	Liberal regime[d]
Structural unemployment	n.s.	n.s.	n.s.	n.s.
Employment growth	n.s.	n.s.	n.s.	n.s.
Self-employment	n.s.	7.899***	−4.217*	n.s.
Ratio of female/male unemployment	1.739***	1.388**	n.s.	−1.123*
Ratio of youth/adult male unemployment	n.s.	2.907***	n.s.	n.s.
Youth exit from unemployment	−13.985***	n.s.	16.542***	n.s.
Exit from unemployment, all	−8.669***	n.s.	10.554***	n.s.

   * Probability significant at 0.05 level.
  ** Probability significant at 0.01 level.
 *** Probability significant at 0.001 level.
n.s. = variable insignificant.

[a] Austria, Belgium, France, Germany, Italy, Japan, Netherlands, Portugal, and Spain.
[b] Italy, Portugal, and Spain.
[c] Denmark, Finland, Norway, and Sweden.
[d] Australia, Canada, Ireland, UK, and USA.

employment.[22] The liberal regime, finally, is indistinct except for its positive effect on women's unemployment.

CONCLUSIONS

There exists a considerable gap between reigning theory (deregulation will create jobs) and evidence (rigidities seem to matter only selectively). Of course, there are strong reasons for why theory might become progressively more credible, be it for reasons of technological progress, global trade, or a creeping cost-disease in services. In this scenario, strong welfare guarantees that once did little harm will increasingly prove fatal. However, is historical progress really moving us along an axis of ever-intensifying trade-offs?

This is a question that I leave to futurists or, preferably, future generation social scientists. I can, for the moment, cite one piece of evidence that suggests the need for sceptical second thoughts: we have seen that job growth and real wage growth are basically uncorrelated in the 1980s and 1990s. But, calculating the same correlations for the golden 1960s, presumably an epoch in which wages and jobs grew in harmonious concert, it turns out that the trade-off, then, was actually worse than today (r = −.468). In fact, four out of eight Continental European economies (Austria, Germany, Italy, and the Netherlands) show stronger job growth in the 1980s than in the 1960s. Vice versa, all 'liberal' nations, except the UK, enjoyed stronger employment growth in the 'egalitarian' 1960s than in the 'deregulated' 1980s. And Britain's net job growth over the past decades, at .5 per cent per annum, is not spectacular; it is actually lower than the EU average.

Because the data produce such confusing results, it is tempting to conclude that 'general laws' matter less than national idiosyncrasies. National economies are pulled and pushed by factors that have a certain resiliency, an overpowering internal logic in the way they combine into a whole. In the analytical framework that I prefer, the gist of resilient logics is to be found in institutional path dependencies. These derive from the prevailing nexus between households, welfare state, and labour markets.

It is this nexus which differentiates welfare regimes. Rereading the evidence through a regime lens may, in fact, influence one's conclusions. Let us then re-examine what we have learned. The first thing that strikes the eye is that the liberal regime—with lean-welfare states, comparatively

[22] In all previous analyses, active labour market policies had no statistically significant impact. This finding is, of course, premised on aggregate cross-sectional analyses, and does not preclude that in *some* countries they do matter. Layard *et al.* (1991) do in fact identify a positive impact for the 1980s. For at least Denmark and Sweden, there is little doubt that active measures do diminish unemployment, in particular among youth.

highly deregulated labour markets, and more inegalitarian earnings—does not present itself as a particularly superior arrangement to minimize unemployment and maximize jobs. In fact, it may not be deregulation that makes the difference as much as merely being the United States of America. As I noted in the beginning of this chapter, the argument that rigidities block employment progress is typically based on this one single case. The USA does of course enjoy low employment and impressive job growth, and long-term unemployment is modest. But such is not the case in Canada, Australia, or the UK. The United States is internationally unique with regard to just about any variable we might entertain, not just with regard to 'flexibility'. Hence, advocates of the American way would have to sell the European peoples not just flexibility, but also a racial divide, the world's largest integrated economy, massive immigration, and an incarceration rate that is about ten times the European average.

The equality–jobs trade-off theory does gain some credibility if our attention is limited to the 'conservative', Continental European regimes. These do seem to nurture outsiders and exclusion, particularly among youth and women and, we may surmise, this is why in Southern Europe self-employment has been growing at a rapid pace in the past decade. Whether this is solely attributable to strict employment regulation is a mute question. Indeed, we might question where 'rigidities' fit in the causal order: is it overly rigid worker protection that causes the insider-outsider divide, or is it the perceived necessity to protect the main bread-winner against labour market risks that compels these countries to maximize regulation in the first place? It is tempting to conclude the latter: strong familialism and low levels of female employment imply that the male bread-winner needs employment security—he must, so to speak, be made into an 'insider'. If this turns into a self-reinforcing spiral in which evermore privileged insiders produce evermore excluded outsiders, the welfare effects may hardly be noticeable, precisely because the outsiders will share in the dividends that accrue to the insider.

As we shall see in the next chapter, income inequalities and poverty rates have changed little in Europe, not even where unemployment is high and chronic. This is because the oustiders can normally draw on generous welfare state benefits (Northern Europe) or on the steady, high incomes of the male bread-winner (Southern Europe). Families in Continental and especially in Southern Europe must absorb the social risks that, in Scandinavia, are collectivized in the welfare state. This means they can ill afford that unemployment hits the main—and usually only—income earner. And this means that median voters and their collective voice will continue to prefer strong employment security over uncertainty. A hallmark of familialistic political economies is that the common good matters less than family welfare.

The variations in employment performance that we have examined in this chapter find their mirror image in welfare performance. The social democratic regime developed relatively flexible labour markets, but with strong and universalistic social guarantees, thus granting households security and welfare even when the labour market is in turmoil. The conservative regime, with some exceptions, favoured the opposite, minimizing labour market turmoil, and then delegating most welfare responsibilities to families. The liberal regime cannot fall back on familial welfare obligations in its quest for deregulation, and it is concommitantly unwilling to allow the welfare state to step into the welfare void. Hence, greater precarity, inequality, and poverty emerge whether or not high employment and low unemployment ensue. Let us then turn to the issue of how new social risks are managed in latter day welfare capitalism.

PART III

WELFARE CAPITALISM RECAST?

8

New Social Risks in Old Welfare States

INTRODUCTION

The idea of a 'mature' welfare state has several distinct connotations. In the first place, it refers to the move from basic, minimal protection (which characterized the 1950s) to a much more ambitious promise of benefit adequacy and universal coverage; income-maintenance systems matured in this sense around the late 1960s and early 1970s. In the second place, we can now, with the aid of hindsight, regard the welfare state of the 1970s as mature basically because few, if any, major changes have occurred since (it ceased to mature even further). In the third place, not only did the welfare *state* stabilize, but so also did the more embracing welfare regime. The division of welfare between public, private, and family had become consolidated. Altogether, the welfare state flowered at the very same moment that 'Golden Age' capitalism began to wilt.

Most pundits, be they foes or friends, believe that the welfare state now faces an irreversible crisis. It was sustainable as long as there was strong growth and full employment—hardly a hallmark of present-day capitalism. Indeed, in addition to its proclaimed unsustainability, many also claim that the welfare state has become a millstone around our necks, the principal impediment to urgently needed economic readjustment and brisk job growth: it upholds rigidities where flexibility is needed, and the rights of social citizenship stifle our incentives to work and save. But is the crisis real? Is the welfare state incompatible with postindustrial society?

A paradox of our times is the more that welfare states seem unsustainable, the greater are the demands for social protection. Of course, the paradox resolves itself easily when we keep in mind the distinction between welfare state and regime. As we saw in the opening pages of this book, the core symptoms of the contemporary welfare state crisis were all exogenous, shocks on the system coming principally from the labour market and from declining family stability. When we have simultaneous welfare 'failure' in these two institutions, it is only to be expected that growing pressures will be brought to bear on the third pillar of welfare production—the welfare *state*. It would therefore be much more fruitful to analyse the crisis as pertaining to welfare regimes.

If, as I argue, the essence of the problem lies in a growing disjuncture between existing institutional arrangements and emerging risk profiles, the bottom-line analytical question is how, and under which conditions, welfare regimes are being recast to respond to the new—let us call them postindustrial—economic realities. I believe that we have established quite firmly that welfare regimes vary sharply. The Nordic has proceeded along a distinct path of de-familialization over the past decades; the liberal Anglo-Saxon has, if anything, reinforced markets at the expense of the state. In contrast, the Continental European—and especially the Mediterranean familialistic—models have undergone very little regime alterations. If welfare regimes, then, are moving along different paths of adjustment, it is hard to believe that the so-called crisis is universal.

On some dimensions there is no doubt a modicum of convergence across nations. Existing social protection systems were built in an era with a radically different risk profile than today. The populations of late-century capitalism find themselves everywhere barraged with new and possibly ever more intense social risks. Labour markets demand flexibility and create insecurity; youth and women find it difficult even to get started on a career; older, experienced males find themselves unwanted and often face the choice between unemployment or early retirement; inadequate skills and education are now very likely to guarantee inferior life chances; more and more people are likely to spend years with low pay or, indeed, no pay; unstable working lives are, in turn, a threat to income security in old age. In the United States, people may have jobs but then more than 15 per cent full-time, full-year workers earn wages that fall below the official poverty line. Across the European Union there are more than 15 million unemployed, and some seemingly for ages. In Germany, the average unemployed can expect to remain so for 14 months, in France for 23, in Italy for 39, and in Spain for a terrible 42 months (OECD, 1994b). It is hard to believe that this will not jeopardize a person's life chances. It certainly will tax families' ability to provide social integration.

Families, always a vital source of social support when markets 'fail', are themselves failing. Marital unions are less stable, and children therefore experience heightened risks of poverty. Falling household incomes, in particular among the young or low-skilled, imply the need to augment family labour supply. Yet, the cost of purchasing care for children and the elderly is often prohibitive, especially for those who need it most. Resource inequalities between household types are undoubtedly growing and we face the menacing spectre that access to social and cultural capital is polarizing between 'winner' and 'loser' families. In this case, current inequalities will evolve into a future abyss.

THE PUZZLE OF PUBLIC OPINION

The welfare state will probably always be contested terrain to the extent that it de-commodifies social needs, redistributes the costs of risks, and attempts to construct collective rather than individualized or familial solidarities. So far it has survived one crisis after another, in part because it adapted itself to each; in part because moods and demands change. In fact, the general mood today is as supportive as ever. According to public opinion data, Scandinavians, Americans, Brits, and Continental Europeans all show great appreciation for their welfare state. A significant percentage everywhere desires more, not less, welfare statism. The quest for improvements, even if this means more taxation, is particularly evident in Britain (Taylor-Gooby, 1996).

There certainly is also grumbling. Thirty or forty per cent of Europeans are dissatisfied with the quality of health care, climbing to 70–80 per cent in Southern Europe (Ferrera, 1996). Still, the majority systematically disagrees that 'social security is too costly for society, and that benefits should be reduced and contributions lowered'. Where, as in Italy, the pension system is unusually generous, indeed bloated, there is actually a majority ready to accept reductions. Otherwise, pension system supporters outnumber the critics by a large margin; in the UK, by a full 60 percentage points! (Ferrera, op. cit., Table 11). In Scandinavia, not surprisingly, public backing of the welfare state is high and stable. In Denmark, those in favour of 'sustaining existing social reforms' are as majoritarian today as they were in 1969.[1]

But not all elements of the welfare state are equally popular. Targeted programmes enjoy much less popularity than do universal benefits (Taylor-Gooby, 1996). This may explain why the Nordic (and European) welfare states are so much more enshrined than is, say, the American. Leftists, rightists, and the median voter all uphold the edifice because all benefit from it directly and personally. In fact, the more comprehensive and universal, the larger is the population whose entire life-course calculus is premissed on social entitlements.

There are, however, signs of an impending head-on collision when we disaggregate both voters and the welfare state. This comes out dramatically from Danish data (Andersen, 1995, Table 4). Support for pensions, health, and various benefits for the aged is overwhelming and homogeneous across all age groups. Since we all eventually age, there is basically no difference between an 18-year old and those already in retirement. But when we turn to youth programmes, such as family benefits, child care,

[1] There was a 'dip' in welfare state support in 1973, but it was back to normal again by 1977 (Andersen, 1995, Fig. 1).

unemployment support, or education, the generations clash: massive support from the younger cohorts, very little if any from the aged.

A new, assymetric 'chrono-politics' appears to be displacing the old political frontlines when it comes to welfare state support. Not only is the median voter ageing, but as the necessity of financial cuts mounts, the need for trade-offs mounts. Backed by the major interest organizations, trade unions in particular, pensioner interests are easy to defend even if this implies underfunding 'youth' programmes. The catch is that an erosion of social entitlements will threaten not only the losers but, more importantly, also the winners. And the winners are much more able to call upon the political weight of their organizations.

There is therefore a ready-made alliance in favour of saving the existing welfare state edifice, whether or not it is financially sustainable or even 'doing the right things'. And herein lies the Achilles' heel of the welfare state's vast popularity. If the alliance against reform represents the traditional, rather than emerging, risk structure, a successful defence of the status quo becomes problematic. The welfare state may then be servicing the insiders, the A-team. And the more it is upheld, the less is its capacity to address the risks of the outsiders, the B-team. If postindustrial society is altering the structure of social risks, the real crisis of the welfare state may be that it enjoys too much popularity.

THE TROJAN HORSE OF THE WELFARE STATE

The exogenous shocks to the welfare state can be likened to the sacking of Troy. Presented as a gift, a handsome and apparently innocent wooden horse, packed with dangerous warriors, managed to get inside the impenetrable walls of the city. In no time, Troy was sacked and its citizens enslaved. The warriors inside the Trojan horse of our times are globalization, ageing, and family instability; a simultaneous market and family failure.

Troy, i.e. the post-war welfare state, was built to cater to the risk structure of its times. Its prototypical client was an unskilled or semi-skilled industrial worker, what the OECD calls the 'average production worker'. The main *class risks* were defined in reference to the old, pre-war 'Arbeiterfrage', the workers question. Whether the approach was universalistic, targeted, or corporativistic, the great accomplishment of the welfare state was that it bridged (more or less) the class divide, incorporating (more or less) the working class as social citizens. With the welfare state new cross-class solidarities were forged.

The prevailing family was integral to the post-war risk structure. Social policy both assumed, and actively encouraged, the male bread-winner, female housewife norm. The perceived risks had less to do with divorce or lone motherhood, and more with the possibility that the bread-winner would lose his capacity to furnish an adequate family wage. Hence the accent on income maintenance and job protection. Social services or 'women friendly' programmes, such as parental leave and daycare, were very undeveloped because women were assumed to withdraw from employment at childbirth.

The risk structure was patterned also by the Keynesian optimism of sustained full employment and the guarantee that even unskilled workers would obtain stable, well-paid jobs. Indeed, all the leading welfare state architects of the epoch—from Lord Beveridge in Britain to Gustav Moller in Sweden and F. D. Roosevelt in the United States—were adamant that jobs and families, and not the welfare state, should be the real pillars of welfare. Their ideal was a regime with little need for the welfare state because families and labour markets functioned optimally.

Life-course risks were understood pretty much in Rowntree's terms: the problem of a cycle of want and plenty; the special risks of poverty in large child families and in old age. Policy therefore privileged family allowances and pensions. Otherwise, it assumed that the 'average production worker' would proceed along an orderly, standardized life course: obligatory schooling until, say, age 16; 45–50 years of stable employment; retirement at age 65 or 70. Average life expectancy in the 1950s was 8–10 fewer years than today. This kind of life course was fundamental for the financial equilibrium of the welfare state: one could assume that most workers would contribute at least 40 years to defray perhaps 7 years' retirement benefits (plus an additional 4–5 years widow's pension). One could also assume that unemployment would be rare and quite brief. When the economy is dynamic, it is difficult to imagine widespread entrapment in poverty, unemployment, or social exclusion.

Intergenerational risks, finally, were largely defined away. Echoing the 'democratic class struggle' thesis, it was believed that prosperity and education would eradicate the vestiges of ascription. Growth and prosperity might not do away with the working class, but it allowed working class families to embrace middle-class lifestyles, and their offspring to attain white-collar careers. As Levy (1988) argues, each new cohort did better than its parents. Compulsory education was meant to be the great leveller of human capital which, in turn, was believed to be the key to equal opportunity. The prevalent response to extreme disadvantage was targeted promotion of opportunity. Hence emerged typically income-tested educational grants to children from poor families so as to boost access to higher education, or social work on behalf of problem families. In brief, life chances and class origins appeared decoupled.

Now at century's end, this admittedly stylized risk portrait appears almost unrecognizable. We discover new classes of losers everywhere; there is the 'two-thirds', or the 'two-speed' society; there are new marginal strata, like the B-team, welfare mothers, 'RMIstes', or the new underclass. These implicitly herald the arrival of a bundle of new social risks, and signal the possibility that many may find themselves sidelined and even trapped in some kind of underprivilege. The old pluralist hope that we shall all blend into one satisfied middle class has been replaced with fears of polarization and closure.

The Trojan horse is the carrier of a new risk package which is doubly distinctive. It is first of all clear that risks have shifted towards younger, adult ages because neither the labour market nor the family can be counted upon to guarantee welfare as once was the case. Indeed, both are now catalysts of risks. It is, secondly, equally evident that new risks in large measure must find their solution in access to social services. Two-earner households may embody women's desire for careers, but they may also be a response to declining male earnings, a last-ditch effort to maintain their accustomed middle-class lifestyle. Like single mothers, their ability to work (and escape poverty) depends on the availability of care services.

NEW RISKS, NEW INEQUALITIES

How contemporary welfare regimes deal with the Trojan horse depends on their response to both the employment problem and the new demographics of ageing and family behaviour. We can identify clear differences in strategy, differences that largely mirror past institutional legacies and welfare regime adaptations over the past decades.

MANAGING THE LABOUR MARKET

The new 'equality–jobs' trade-off has generated two distinct strategic responses (Soskice, 1994; Freeman, 1994; and Blank, 1994). In what Soskice calls 'un-coordinated' economies (largely the Anglo-Saxon, liberal regimes), deregulation through wage flexibility, declining trade unionism, and weakened employee protection has predominated. As markets have been encouraged to 'clear', inequalities have risen. According to Soskice (op. cit), this model also risks finding itself in a 'low-skill equilibrium'. The absence of active public training programmes is compounded by lack of employer incentives because of the availability of a mass of low-cost, substitutable workers. In contrast, 'co-ordinated' economies have opted for a high-wage, quality production strategy that privileges a core of skilled, stable, mainly male workers at the expense of the 'outsiders'. In the latter model, which represents most European Community member countries, early retirement and welfare guarantees have helped downsize the workforce and absorb excess labour. The underlying premiss is that the budgetary burden of early retirement can be covered by the resulting productivity dividend.

This contrast is of course quite stylized. The European countries with a long tradition of worker protection have, to varying degrees, introduced flexibility measures since the 1980s. Almost all countries have made it easier to hire workers on temporary contracts, rules regarding part-time work have been eased, and the cost of employing youth workers has been *de facto* lowered (either with subsidies or by lowering social contributions).[2] As Blank (1994) and Regini (1998) conclude, partial deregulation reforms hardly alter the basic workings of the system.

Take the most widespread deregulation measure, temporary contracts. In Germany, despite great fears to the contrary, they are not widely used and, in any case, they usually conclude in a permanent employment relationship (Buechtemann, 1993). The underlying reason is that the entire German labour market is organized around the formal (dual) apprenticeship system. In Italy, it is true, the lion's share of youth hirings are now on a fixed-term basis, primarily with subsidized 'training contracts'. About half eventually result in a permanent contract, and it is evident (as in the German case) that flexibility here mainly serves as a cost-advantageous screening device, not as an incentive to add additional workers to the payroll. Employers' quest for flexibility remains, as always, focused on hours adjustment among their permanent staff (Adam and Canziani, 1998). Spain represents the single most dramatic case of liberalized temporary contracts. Since the mid-1980s, almost all new hirings are fixed-term. Unlike in Germany and Italy, however, only a very small fraction (10–15 per cent) eventually move into a permanent job (Bentolila and Dolado, 1994; Toharia, 1997; Adam and Canziani, 1998). The consequence has been to actually strengthen and deepen the existing gulf that separates insiders and outsiders. Firms use their prime-age, male permanent workers as their dependable and trained core workforce; the heavily youth and female fixed-term employees, in contrast, serve to achieve numerical flexibility (people instead of hours). Since the latter are easily substitutable there is very little incentive to invest in training. Partial deregulation in Continental Europe has, by and large, meant the preservation of traditional protection standards within the prime-age, insider workforce.

This bipolar contrast ignores the Scandinavian 'third way', until recently regarded as a model 'win-win' strategy, since full employment went hand-in-hand with an unusually high level of equality.[3] The distinctiveness of this

---

[2] For an overview, see Buechtemann (1993) and OECD (1994*a*).

[3] Denmark, of course, has suffered from fairly high unemployment rates since the mid-1970s. Until 1991–2, Finland, Norway, and Sweden succeeded in maintaining *de facto* full employment.

approach lies in a combination of policies and institutions. The institutional precondition has been strong, nation-wide consensual wage bargaining which, until recently, helped control the inflationary pressures of wage equality and full employment.[4] The main policy principle has been to permit a rather extensive degree of labour market flexibility while guaranteeing the welfare of individual workers through generous income maintenance and active labour market programmes. Welfare state employment constituted, until the mid-1980s in Denmark and Sweden, the principal means to absorb the huge growth of female employment, and to offset job stagnation or decline in the private sector. Since the early 1970s, public employment accounts for roughly 80 per cent of net new job growth in Denmark and Sweden. Active labour market policies have been important in recycling redundant industrial workers and minimizing youth unemployment, either via training or sheltered (mainly public) jobs. Active labour market spending, at 1–2 per cent of GDP through most of the 1980s in Denmark, Finland, and Sweden, is two or three times the OECD average (OECD, 1996*b*). Participation in active measures may, to a degree, imply camouflaged unemployment. None the less, the Nordic countries' active investment in employment is what accounts for their doubly impressive employment record: the world's highest employment/population ratios and, until the 1990s, low unemployment. The contrast becomes even sharper when we compare older workers (55–64), whose activity rate in most Continental European countries has declined to roughly 40–50 per cent but remains at 60–70 per cent in Scandinavia. Similarly, the activity rate of single mothers in Denmark and Sweden hovers around 80 per cent, compared to 50 per cent in Germany, 30 in the UK, and 45 per cent in the United States.[5]

Why, then, has the Scandinavian 'third way' stranded? Does the arrival of mass unemployment everywhere except in Norway (with its ample oil revenues) give credence to the argument that there is no way to dodge the 'equality–jobs' trade-off; that some are bound to lose? To arrive at an answer we must omit Norway which, with abundant oil revenues, is able to finance itself out of the dilemma. Beyond chance effects (such as the collapse of the COMECON market for Finnish exports), there are a number of explanations which all, unfortunately, confirm the argument. The first has to do with the all-important consensual bargaining infrastructure: since the early 1980s, the system of nation-wide concertation has decentralized; the capacity to strike mutually binding, long-term consensual

---

[4] The successful performance of the Netherlands since the mid-1980s is, similarly, ascribed to the capacity of the social partners to hold back real wage growth (Netherlands Ministry of Social Affairs, 1996). Dutch real wage growth paralleled the United States, Australia, and New Zealand by being negative through the 1980s and early 1990s.

[5] These calculations are based on second wave (1985–7) Luxemburg Income Study data files.

deals has weakened considerably (Pontusson, 1992; Swensson, 1989; Stephens, 1996). In Sweden, one of the most visible effects has been increased wage and income inequalities (Bjorklund and Freeman, 1994).

The second explanation is more fundamental, a true Achilles' heel in the system itself. What the Nordic countries attempted was, in a way, to 'cheat' the Baumol cost-disease problem through direct public-service provision—which now accounts for a full one-third of total employment. In a compressed wage structure, like the Nordic, the long-run lag in public-service productivity implies that the relative cost rises; the burden of sustaining this tax-financed sector becomes ever heavier. One solution might be to widen the wage gap between public- and private-sector workers, but in a thoroughly unionized labour market this is very difficult to accomplish. Thus, even if these countries were capable of sustaining long-range wage moderation across the board, the problem remains that public services put an ever-growing, direct and indirect, cost burden on the labour market.

'Equality and jobs' therefore end up being at loggerheads regardless of strategic response. Still, strategic choice produces different outcomes and therefore also a different set of winners and losers. The Continental European model of privileging the core workforce in the context of jobless growth means the fortification of an insider-outsider divide: the high wages and job security enjoyed by (chiefly male) insiders, in effect, are also what causes the exclusion of their sons, daughters, and wives. As we have seen, Germany is the only Continental European country where unemployment is not concentrated among youth. Otherwise, most of the unemployed are female or young, and the duration of unemployment is exceedingly long. This is then the most likely B-team clientele, and lengthy spells of unemployment are the most probable source of entrapment. Flow-data for 1989–90 show that a small minority of those who were unemployed in 1989 had found employment a year later: 23 per cent in Belgium, 36 in France and Germany. This compares very unfavourably with Denmark's superior performance (65 per cent) (European Commission, 1993).

The labour-reduction strategy is primarily based on low female labour supply and early retirement. Both contribute to raising labour costs and reproducing rigidities. Pressures for high wages and fixed labour costs come from the rising financial requirements of pension systems and also from families' dependence on one earner. The need to sustain male breadwinners' job protection is similarly over-determined by early retirement and familial dependencies. Rather than the traditional 40–50 years' uninterupted employment, European workers now start their career much later (longer education and often very long unemployment) and retire early. It is difficult to assume more than 30–5 contribution years, and this means that any disruption of a career would have catastrophic consequences for their welfare calculus. And with family dependency on the single-income earner, the risk of job-insecurity is multiplied throughout society.[6] Hence, median voter support for the existing privileges of insiders becomes virtually hegemonic.

A similar scenario obtains neither in liberal nor in social democratic regimes. The liberal deregulatory 'low-wage' strategy may assure substantial labour market flexibility, but it also creates more poverty and income inequality which is easily compounded by the logic of deregulation itself: if wages, especially at the lower end, decline this will engender poverty traps unless also guaranteed social minima follow suit. A hallmark of American and Antipodean (but not British) adjustment policy is that more people earn low wages and that low-wage workers have lost terrain.[7] But (non-pension) income maintenance benefits have eroded also in the UK. Both poverty rates and income polarization have therefore risen over the past decades. During the 1980s, the lowest decile earners have, relative to the median, lost 8 percentage points in Australia, 11 in Canada, 13 in New Zealand, 23 in the UK, and 29 in the USA (recalculations from OECD, 1996*b*, Table 3.1). The liberal, deregulatory strategy is less likely to create entrapment in unemployment—in fact, average duration is generally low—but low-wage entrapment is a real possibility. Recent data on earnings mobility show that the likelihood of moving out of the lowest wage quintile between 1986–91 is much lower in the USA than in any of the European countries: for males, only 38 per cent of Americans escape low-wage employment compared to 55 per cent Germans, 61 per cent Italians, and 64 per cent Swedes. More or less the same pattern holds also for American youth workers, indicating that low-wage employment is not only a youthful stop-gap experience (OECD, 1996*b*, Table 3.9).[8]

Since the end of the Scandinavian 'third way' is so recent, at least in Finland and Sweden, it is difficult to identify trends and consequences. If we judge by Danish experience and recent distributional developments in Sweden, there appear to be no clear losers. There is certainly more unemployment in Finland and Sweden, especially among youth. And the share of long-term unemployed has risen—although nowhere near Continental European levels. One remarkable feature of Scandinavian unemployment is that it is much more 'democratically' spread than elsewhere: there is less

---

[6] As we have seen, Southern European youth unemployment is almost exclusively absorbed within the family.

[7] The minimum wage as a percentage of average earnings is 39 per cent in the USA and 40 per cent in the UK. In most European countries it hovers between 50 and 60 per cent (Dolado *et al.*, 1996: Table 1).

[8] Note, however, that there is little low-wage entrapment in the UK (65 per cent move up).

of a gender and age bias.[9] This can be attributed to active labour market policy efforts to reactivate especially the young (OECD, 1995*b*). A second remarkable feature is that the welfare state appears stronger than market forces even when, as in Denmark, heavy unemployment has been a constant feature over the past decades. This comes out in all studies of income and welfare distribution: whether unemployment rises or wages become more unequal, this has no noticeable effect on final household income or welfare standards. On the basis of 10 welfare resource components, the Swedish Level of Living studies conclude that equality has actually risen, even during the more troubled 1980s and early 1990s (Fritzell and Lundberg, 1994). A similar conclusion derives from the Danish Level of Living studies, comparing the 1970s and 1980s (Hansen, 1995), and from more recent studies that focus especially on the weakest population groups (Ingerslev and Pedersen, 1996; Velfaerdskommissionen, 1995). For Denmark, the only Nordic country with a long experience of unemployment, evidence suggests that very few—mainly the completely unskilled—remain entrapped in marginality for long (Bjorn, 1995). Being all longitudinal, panel-type data, they also suggest that there are no major groups that show any significant degree of entrapment, be it in social exclusion or poverty. In fact, as we shall see, unusually high-risk groups, such as lone mothers, do not have poverty rates that are appreciably higher than the average.

LABOUR MARKET RISKS AND WELFARE REGIMES

In order to fully evaluate emerging risks, we need more than 'static' poverty or unemployment headcounts for any given year. We also need to examine trends and, above all, the 'dynamics' of deprivation and entrapment. Table 8.1 presents recent 'static' data on exclusion, focusing on relative youth and unskilled worker unemployment, low-wage and poverty risks. Table 8.2, in turn, examines unemployment and poverty trends among the same groups over the past 10–15 years. Finally, Table 8.3 presents available 'dynamic' data on duration and on chances of mobility out of unemployment, low-wage employment, and poverty.

Within our 'static' comparison, it is above all clear that risks of exclusion or poverty fall disproportionally on the shoulders of the young. Yet, the profile of the losers varies significantly across our welfare regimes.[10] In

[9] A female bias may be evolving in Sweden, not so much in unemployment as in declining participation. The female participation rate has dropped from 83 per cent 1990 to 76 per cent in 1996. Male rates have, however, also seen a drop (from 88 to 82 per cent) (OECD, 1997*b*, Table B).

[10] Table 8.1 (and subsequent tables) include only countries for which we have adequate and comparable data).

TABLE 8.1. *'Static' headcount indices of exclusion and inequality, early mid-1990s*

	Youth–adult unemployment ratio[a]	Low-skilled–all unemployment ratio[b]	Percentage low-wage workers[c]	Poverty rate in young child families[d]
Australia	2.2	1.0	14	14
Canada	1.9	1.4	24	14
UK	2.1	1.4	21	25
USA	2.8	2.1	26	27
Denmark	1.8	1.7	9	5
Sweden	2.2	0.9	5	3
Belgium	2.4	1.0	7	2
France	2.4	1.2	14	—
Germany (West)	1.0	1.7	13	7
Italy	3.7	1.1	12	—
Netherlands	2.0	1.2	14	10

[a] 1995. Youth is below age 30; adult is 30–64. *Source*: OECD (1997*b*).

[b] 1992. Unskilled is defined as less than secondary educational attainment. *Source*: OECD (1995*a*).

[c] 1993–4. Low wages are defined as less than two-thirds of median. *Source*: OECD (1996*b*, Table 3.2).

[d] Latest year in LIS data base, *c*.1990–2. Poverty is defined as less than 50 per cent of median, adjusted household income (new OECD equivalence scale). *Source*: data calculated from Luxemburg Income Study data files. Special thanks to Koen Vleminckx for his generous help.

Continental European countries (except Germany), the youth bias of unemployment is exceptionally high. In the Anglo-Saxon nations, unemployment tends also to be biased but here we must bear in mind lower overall levels of unemployment. These countries do, however, stand out for their systematically very high low-wage and poverty rates. The Nordic performance gives credence to the argument that, so far at least, it is a regime which is rather effective in minimizing social risks among the young.

If, as so many believe, we face an inherent and evermore intensifying jobs–equality trade-off, this should become evident in trend data. Table 8.2 suggests a less than clear-cut picture. In most countries, the relative youth bias in unemployment is actually declining while that for the unskilled is rising.[11] In other words, there is a general redistribution of victimization under way as far as unemployment is concerned. However, trends in unemployment bias seem basically unrelated to trends in poverty,

[11] The sharp jump in the youth bias in Sweden reflects the dramatic deterioration in overall unemployment since 1991.

TABLE 8.2. *Trends in employment and poverty* (%)

	Change in youth unemployment, 1983–94	Change in low-skilled unemployment males, 1980–94	Change in child–family poverty rates, 1980–90s
Australia	−9	+101	+12
Canada	−16	+37	−2
UK	−18	+24	+80
USA	−27	+24	+31
Denmark	−46	+90	−10
Sweden	+101	+220	−42
Belgium	−9	—	+4
France	+40	+150	+30
Germany	−25	+100	+120
Netherlands	−46	—	+31

Source: OECD (1997*b*) and Luxemburg Income Study (waves *c.*1980 and *c.*1990).

which is rising in both liberal regimes and in Continental Europe, but declining in the Nordic countries.

If we are concerned with the formation of an outsider class, or a B-team, 'headcounts' may reveal very little. The issue is akin to Schumpeter's (1964) use of the omnibus as an analogy for class formation: the bus may always be full of people but if they are never the same, there is no closure, no social class. Put differently, if the experience of low income or unemployment is sporadic it is unlikely to have lasting negative consequences for life chances; if those who are counted as poor or unemployed in any given moment soon disappear from the statistics, it is hardly likely that outsider classes are being formed. The young may be poor simply because they have just climbed aboard the bus and will then get off at the next stop. What do we know about longer-term entrapment? Does the omnibus systematically fail to unload some of its passengers?

Unravelling the risks of entrapment is exceedingly difficult because we need longitudinal-panel or life-history data, and such exist for only a handful of countries. It is additionally difficult because of the 'right-censoring' problem: we can only monitor people up until the latest survey year, and therefore we do not know their future. If we observe that someone has been chronically unemployed or poor over, say, the past five years we cannot automatically conclude that there is entrapment. Still, it is very probable that extended periods of exclusion or low income will have

long-term consequences and, indeed, affect life chances negatively.[12]
Indeed, it is possible that long spells of unemployment will produce a self-
reinforcing downward spiral of skill deterioration *and* impoverishment.
We know, for example, that household poverty risks among the long-term
unemployed virtually double compared with those who have been unemployed less than six months.[13] Table 8.3 presents available data on transitions and entrapment.

The 'equality–jobs' trade-off changes considerably when viewed in
dynamic terms, as done in Table 8.3. It may very well be that deregulated

TABLE 8.3. *Transitions and entrapment*

	Exit from unemployment[a]	Average duration of low-paid employment[b]	Exit from poverty[c]	Percentage of poor three years in poverty[d]
Canada	28	—	12	12
UK	9	3.8	—	—
USA	37	4.1	14	14
Denmark	21	1.8	30	3
Sweden	18	—	37	—
France	3	2.8	28	2
Germany (West)	9	2.8	26	2
Italy	10	2.8	—	—
Netherlands	6	—	44	1

[a] Monthly average outflows from unemployment in 1993. *Source*: OECD (1996*b*).

[b] Average duration in years (between 1986–91) of being in the lowest earnings quintile among full-time, full-year male workers. *Source*: OECD (1996*b*, Table 3.9).

[c] Data refer to child families only. For France, data refer to Alsace-Lorraine. The exit measure refers to the percentage moving from below 50 per cent of median adjusted household
income to above 60 per cent from year to year t + 1. *Source*: Duncan *et al.* (1993, Table 1).
Danish figure estimated from CLS panel-registry data.

[d] Percentage of child families poor in three consecutive years. *Source*: Duncan *et al.* (1993,
Table 1). Danish figure estimated from CLS panel-registry data.

---

[12] It is, for example, well known that skills and social networks deteriorate with the length of
absence from the labour market. Long periods of poverty are likely to cause a depletion of households' accumulated resources.

[13] Poverty rates among short-term (less than 6 months) unemployed in France, Germany, and
the UK is, respectively, 17, 28, and 29 per cent. Among those unemployed more than one year,
the French poverty rate is 30 per cent; the German, 48 per cent; and the British, 64 per cent
(Nolan, Hauser, and Zoyem, 1998).

labour markets diminish both the levels and the duration of unemployment, but the downside is that people tend to become more easily trapped in low-wage jobs and in poverty.[14] As I noted earlier, the percentage of Americans stuck in prolonged low-paid employment is dramatically higher than among Europeans. Poverty entrapment is similarly much more prevalent in the 'liberal' regime. In fact, among white Americans who were poor in any given year, there is a 30 per cent chance that they will find themselves poor in at least 5 out of the next 10 years; among Blacks, the risk jumps to 50 per cent (Stevens, 1995).

Continental Europe's more 'rigid' labour markets do seem to lock people into long-term unemployment and, to a degree, also into low-wage employment. But the risks of prolonged poverty are modest. On average, the probability of escaping poverty in Europe is five times better than in the United States (Burkhauser *et al.*, 1995; Burkhauser and Poupore, 1993). And, once again, there does seem to be something to the Nordic 'third way' since chances of becoming locked into unemployment, low pay, or poverty are internationally low.

The risks of unemployment and low incomes are clearly concentrating in young households. They bear the brunt of rising inequalities in the Anglo-Saxon world (Gottschalk and Smeeding, 1997; Gottschalk, 1997). And Continental European and, especially, Mediterranean unemployment is overwhelmingly borne by the young, often in search of a first job. The sometimes ambiguous relationship between 'equality and jobs' may therefore be related to the variable ways in which welfare regimes affect youth. In other words, we must examine the nexus of labour market, family, and welfare state support.

Continental Europe's (with the exception of Germany's) youth-biased unemployment is clearly related to high wage costs and strong employment protection for the 'insiders'. It is, however, also an indirect result of how welfare states function. Despite roughly similar levels of aggregate unemployment (and similarly compressed wage structures), youth is considerably better off in the Nordic countries. Why? One main reason lies in active labour market policies, which help absorb unemployed youth in either education or sponsored employment. In the Nordic countries, 2–2.5 per cent of the youth labour force is in active programmes compared to a Continental European average of 1.2 per cent. Similarly, more than 6 per cent of the Scandinavian labour force is in labour market training schemes, compared to 2.3 per cent in Continental Europe.[15] Denmark is a dramatic contrast because, since 1994, it is virtually impossible for any youth to receive passive unemployment aid for more than 3 months—after which

[14] The very low unemployment outflows in Britain cast some doubt on the purported advantages of labour market deregulation.
[15] Calculated from OECD (1997*b*, Table K).

they will receive either subsidized education or jobs.[16] This combination is surely also what accounts for very brief poverty durations among Danish youth.

It is on the income and poverty side that we can locate the reasons for why 'jobs and equality' are not automatic opposites. When we examine the income situation of unemployed youth (aged 20–9), we find a puzzling orthogonality: low poverty in Scandinavia and Southern Europe; high poverty in France and the UK. The low Nordic poverty rates are clearly linked to generous income support from the welfare state; the very high rates in the UK and France reflect very modest social assistance guarantees. But how do we account for the generally low rates in Italy and Spain where, after all, unemployment is concentrated among first-job seekers who have basically no entitlement to social transfers? The answer, of course, lies in familialism.

In Denmark, virtually all (80 per cent) unemployed youth receive welfare state benefits; in Italy only 11 per cent. Yet, in both cases their household income position is basically similar (74 and 77 per cent of average household income, respectively). The level of welfare benefits in Denmark allows them to live independently (92 per cent) while, in Italy, the only realistic shield against poverty is to continue residing with parents (81 per cent of all). The worst-case scenario is found in countries like France and, especially, Britain, where neither the welfare state nor the family provide ample welfare. Hence, in comparison to Denmark, the (logisitic) odds of young unemployed living in poverty is five times higher in France and twelve times higher in Britain.[17]

Familializing social risks like unemployment can be an effective antidote against poverty, but it incurs indirect costs. Familial dependency may actually slow down job search, since the implicit reservation wage, rather than being the difference between social benefits and expected earnings, now includes the value of free room and board. It also implies delayed autonomy, family formation, and fertility and here we can identify one of the principal reasons for Southern Europe's low-fertility equilibrium. In the study cited above, we found that almost 40 per cent of young Danish unemployed are parents; in Italy, virtually no one has children.

---

[16] It is clear that education and training prevent against entrapment. Bjorn (1995) shows for Denmark that some vocational training raises the chance of exiting from unemployment by 30 per cent. In a comparison between Sweden and the UK, Allmendinger and Hinz (1996, Table 7) show that unskilled Swedes have a three times greater chance of moving into skilled jobs than do unskilled British workers, chiefly due to Sweden's accent on active training programmes (see also Esping-Andersen, Rohwer, and Sorensen, 1994).

[17] Calculations based on the 1994 Europanel. For details, see Bison and Esping-Andersen (1998).

FAMILY RISKS AND WELFARE REGIMES

Family instability is the second subversive soldier in the Trojan horse of the welfare state. If traditional causes of lone parenthood, like death of a spouse, have declined in importance, this has amply been made up for by marital instability, divorce, or separation. The new family structure is certainly not exclusively a source of risks. Families have fewer children, many households have none, and this means that there are fewer mouths to feed. The number of households that may find themselves in Rowntree's youthful phase in the poverty cycle is bound to be limited since so few have large numbers of children. Two-earner households have high incomes and are resource-rich compared to the traditional one-earner model. Their phenomenal rise means that more children grow up in riches rather than poverty. Of course, two-career couples are also the ones most likely to divorce.

We have seen how welfare states have responded in radically different ways to the double challenge of women's employment and family instability. Active de-familialization of welfare burdens in the social democratic regime; an essentially passive or, at most, targeted assistance approach in the liberal; and a policy of sustained familialism in Continental Europe—much less in France and Belgium, much more in Italy and Spain. This should influence the profile and intensity of social risks within families.

Duncan *et al.* (1993) compared the impact of job loss and of divorce on the likelihood of falling into poverty. As would be expected, unemployment is generally the strongest catalyst, but divorce also imposes substantial risks. About 15 per cent of divorces in Canada, Sweden, and Germany result in poverty; 6 per cent in Holland and 8 per cent in the USA. The social protection package that families enjoy should, nevertheless, make a huge difference. This comes out in Table 8.4, where I have estimated post-tax and transfer poverty rates for three household types: one-earner, two-earner, and single-parent child families.

There are several important points that emerge from Table 8.4. The first is that the conventional one-earner family is not a very good hedge against child poverty given that its poverty rate is everywhere much higher than the national average. Of course, it hardly exists any more in the Nordic countries, and is also rapidly disappearing in the United States.[18] There are obvious reasons for why the solo bread-winner family is vulnerable. It has only the welfare state (or relatives) to fall back on if child obligations mean reduced hours or make employment altogether impossible.

---

[18] The surprisingly high poverty rates among Swedish and Danish one-earner families is almost certainly due to a selection-bias: this kind of household is now very rare, and most likely found in rural areas.

TABLE 8.4. *Poverty rates in traditional and new child family types*

	Single-parent family	One-earner family	Two-earner family	Total population
USA (1986)	61	33	14	28
Denmark (1987)	6	16	5	6
Sweden (1987)	5	14	4	5
Germany (1984)	28	14	4	10
Italy (1986)	23	23	4	18

Notes: Data include only non-aged ($<$ 65) population. Poverty is measured as less than 50 per cent of adjusted median household income (using an equivalence scale with an elasticity = 0.5 for each additional member).

Source: Luxemburg Income Study data files.

The two-earner household is vastly superior, with child poverty rates that are three or even four times lower (see also Mclanahan, Casper, and Sorensen, 1995). Here we can glimpse a first possible 'win-win' solution. If the contemporary economy generates severe unemployment or income risks, one counter-strategy is to nurture the double-career family. Two incomes makes the household less vulnerable to unemployment or career change. Being less dependent on male bread-winner job security and entitlements, the two-earner family is also more equipped to adapt to labour market flexibilization. And as we have discussed earlier, two-income families are eminent service consumers and, therefore, a source of job creation.

Labour market and family 'failures' may, however, combine to produce zero-earner families, either because of single-person or single-parent households, or when 'unemployment comes in couples'. Due to Southern Europe's familialism and strong job protection of male earners, it is hardly surprising that most unemployed reside in a household with at least one active earner (60 per cent in Italy). This is, however, less the case in Northern Europe (Jacobs, 1998). However, Northern Europe combines countries with strong income guarantees to unemployed households (Denmark, Belgium, the Netherlands, and Sweden), and countries with a weaker safety net (the UK and France). Thus, male unemployment in a two-adult household with no other earner increases the odds of poverty by five times in France and the UK, but not at all in Denmark, Belgium, the Netherlands, or Sweden (Jacobs, op. cit., Table 6a).[19]

Rising divorce rates imply more potentially precarious lone-parent families, almost all of which are headed by women. In Scandinavia, as one

[19] In Italy, the relative odds of poverty are much lower (1.8 times).

would expect, they do quite well with poverty levels that hardly differ from the population average; their mean disposable income falls very close to the national mean. The risk of poverty is steeper in Italy and Germany and, in the United States lone parents are more likely than not to be poor. Given the virtual impossibility for solo mothers to combine child care and work in Italy and Germany, we could have expected even more poverty. In part, they are a rather small stratum; in part, it is very likely that they move in with relatives or parents—the familialistic substitute for welfare state support.[20]

The massive difference between Nordic and American single-parent poverty rates would lead most observers to conclude that, yes, the welfare state is decisive. In the United States, a single parent that relies on AFDC benefits (plus food stamps and Medicaid) will not arrive above poverty level as we measure it. In Sweden, the combined benefit package assures that he or she will. None the less, it is not so much welfare benefits as employment which matters. The employment rate of Swedish lone mothers is twice as high as the American. Since in Sweden they have employment income (in 89 per cent of cases) and receive, in addition, welfare benefits (equal to 30 per cent of their total disposable income), it is in a direct sense the labour market rather than the welfare state which accounts for low poverty. In an indirect sense, of course, this is made possible by welfare state care services. In the United States, only 45 per cent work and they receive very little added public benefits (equal to only 9 per cent of their final income).[21]

Sweden urges lone mothers to work; America 'taxes away' their incentive to do so. The price of 'urging' may be quite high to the Swedish welfare state, but the hidden cost of not doing so may be even higher. If, like in America (and Britain), lone parents leave the labour market and have little incentive or capacity to return, they are more likely to become long-term welfare clients (as we have seen) and the net loss due to forgone lifetime earnings (and inferior life chances of their offspring) may become extremely high.

---

[20] Own analyses of LIS data and Italian family expenditure data suggest that this is true for Italy. As in Scandinavia, their mean disposable income is very close to population average. It turns out that a surprisingly large share of Italian solo mothers work (almost 80 per cent). But here there is a possible 'class effect'. Since divorce is very costly, it is probably a luxury of the wealthier. This, in turn, means that divorced women are more educated and perhaps also more likely to already have a career. Until we know more, the best guess is that lone parents in Italy are a bimodal group with a minority doing poorly, a majority doing very well.

[21] The data derive from Gornick (1994). The importance of the 'work-plus-welfare state' package is even more evident when we examine lone-mother poverty durations. Own analyses of the Danish CLS data show a mean duration of poverty among lone mothers equal to the population mean. Three-quarters escape within two years.

It may be true, as Rosen (1996) insists, that the public cost of maintaining working mothers in Sweden is excessive in the sense that it far exceeds their relative productivity. However, his estimate that maybe 50 per cent of total Swedish expenditure to support working mothers is 'wasted' should be seriously questioned in light of the foregoing discussion. If viewed as a question of women's (and their children's) dynamic life chances and life-long earnings power, the 'waste' may as well be considered productive investment.[22] This, at least, is the reasoning behind Scandinavia's active family policies. They continue to assure that the family and the labour market remain the principal basis of welfare. They can be seen as a pro-active investment against family and market welfare failure.

We can examine more comparatively the relationship between welfare benefits, work, and solo-mother poverty. Although the number of available cases is very small (14), OLS regression is robust because of the excellent fit of the model. As shown in Table 8.5, employment reduces poverty by almost twice as much as do welfare benefits. It is furthermore evident that a sharp decline in social benefits when mothers choose to work provides a substantial negative work incentive. A cross-section regression estimate of its effects on solo mothers' rate of employment (where the independent variable is measured as the differential between welfare benefits to non-working and working mothers) yields a coefficient of $-.99$ (t $= -2.63$) with R-squared $= .464$. In other words, the trade-off is almost perfectly one-to-one: a one percentage ($-.99$) decline in employment for each percentage decline in welfare benefits to working mothers.

WELFARE STATE ADAPTATION TO EXOGENOUS SHOCKS AND NEW RISKS

The post-war welfare state was everywhere income transfer biased and service-lean, i.e. based on the idea that service needs would be met in the family. It was also primarily directed to the aged or large child families, i.e. based on the assumption that most adults would find their welfare through market employment. The Trojan horse at century's end has, as we

---

[22] Welfare dependency among solo mothers in America is, for most, quite shortlived. For 44 per cent it lasts but one year. But this coincides with substantial long-term dependency: 23 per cent remain for two years; almost 12 per cent for seven-plus years. (Gottschalk *et al.*, 1994). Hence, the cumulative cost to the public can be quite high even when, as in the USA, the benefit is meagre and an estimated half of the eligible lone mothers do not even receive benefits. In their classical article Mincer and Polachek (1974) estimated that (American) women lose 1.5 per cent of lifetime income for every year they remain not employed. Exiting for five years implies a 7.5 per cent income loss. More interestingly, a Dutch study estimates that full-withdrawal leads to a 2 per cent loss per annum while remaining in the labour market on part-time leads only to a .5 per cent annual loss (cited in Bruyn-Hundt, 1996: 150).

TABLE 8.5. *The impact of social transfers and employment on single-mother poverty*

	Coefficient	T-statistic	R^2
Constant	146.07	4.87	0.674
Social transfers	−0.79	−2.16	
Employment	−1.29	−4.44	

Note: Poverty is, as in previous tables, measured as below 50 per cent of equivalent median household income.

Source: data taken from Gornick (1994).

have seen, brought with it a host of new social risks. How do different welfare regimes adapt?

Synthetically speaking, the inherent logic of our three welfare regimes seems to reproduce itself. The social democratic nations have responded actively with a redirection of welfare *state* efforts: increasingly emphasizing services and shifting resources towards younger households, both to sustain their incomes and to maximize their employment. The conservative regimes, in contrast, have responded 'passively' in a double sense of the word: firstly, the old transfer bias remains and has in fact strengthened; passive income maintenance has been their major weapon in dealing with new risks. Secondly, the response is passive in the sense that new risks and new responsibilities are largely relegated to the family.

The liberal, deregulatory approach is also passive, but in this case because reliance on markets for welfare solutions has been strengthened. The marketization of risks is evident on several fronts. Besides outright privatization, which is limited, the stress on 'workfare' is one; the move towards some form of negative income tax or 'low-income credit' to *working* families is another (Myles, 1996). In different words, the liberal strategy combines a scaled-back social wage and the 're-commodification' of labour, albeit with subsidies.

These differences are apparent in the emerging shape of contemporary welfare states. The 'proactive' strategy finds expression in a strong move towards servicing and youth welfare in Scandinavia. The 'passive familialistic' welfare states remain transfer biased and are increasingly being reduced to 'pensioner states'. Trends in the liberal group, however, give some support to Castles' (1996) claim that we must distinguish the 'hardcore' liberal welfare states, like the American, from the 'lib-lab' model, like Australia. Although in all cases there is a sustained move towards more welfare state residualism, targeting, and means-testing, Australia and, less so, New Zealand, stand out for their growing attention to young families. See Table 8.6.

TABLE 8.6. *Welfare state adaptation: trends in servicing and age bias, 1980–1992*

	Servicing bias		Age bias	
	Ratio services/cash 1992	Change 1980–92 (% pts)	Ratio youth/aged 1992	Change 1980–92 (% pts)
Liberal cluster	0.12	+0.04	0.80	+0.11
Social democratic cluster	0.34	+0.07	1.02	+0.18
Conservative cluster	0.08	+0.04	0.51	−0.08
Japan	0.08	0	0.18	−0.12

Notes: Health care is excluded from the services–cash transfer calculations. Programmes defined as being youth-oriented include: occupational injury, sickness cash benefits, family cash and service benefits, active labour market programmes, and unemployment benefits. Aged-oriented programmes are old age survivors' benefits and services. Disability pensions and 'other' have been excluded from calculations altogether.

Source: OECD Social Expenditure data base (SOCX).

The regime means presented in Table 8.6 do not disguise large internal deviations except in very few cases: Australia, Ireland, and New Zealand are quite Scandinavian in their bias towards the young. And in the conservative cluster, the Netherlands stands out as less aged-biased than average (see detailed country data in Appendix Table 8A). In brief, the same cases which earlier posed problems for a regime classification, remain ambiguous. Japan, however, reasserts its affinity with the conservative regime.

The startling differences lie not just in the relative weight accorded to youth and services within the three regimes, but also in trends. The liberal group is, as signalled, bifurcated with one youth-oriented group (Australia, Ireland, and perhaps New Zealand) and one that is becoming ever more aged-biased and service-lean (the UK and the USA). The assumption that markets should reign for working-age adults seems especially strong in the latter. The conservative regime (with the possible exception of the Netherlands) is, and remains, service-lean and the age bias is being systematically reinforced. Since this hardly represents a push to prioritize markets—except in the sense that households are assumed to rely on a protected bread-winner—the implicit drift is to reproduce familialism.

CONCLUSION

A 'win-win' adjustment strategy implies managing the new risk structure in a way that no groups become systematic losers. And if I am right in asserting that youth and young families are being disproportionally bombarded from all sides with risks of poverty, low income, unemployment and, perhaps, entrapment in marginalization, what is called for is not more, nor less, welfare state but a major overhaul; a reprioritization of goals, a recast emphasis in favour of young families and, especially, their servicing needs. In order to return to the ideals that Beveridge, Moller, and others implanted in their welfare blueprints, a positive-sum strategy is clearly one in which the state nurtures markets' and families' capacity to maximize welfare.

Perhaps the single greatest obstacle to such a reform strategy comes, paradoxically, from the welfare state's most ardent supporters—the ever-more aged median voter and, where insider-outsider cleavages are especially pronounced, from interest organizations.

It is really only the social democratic welfare states (with Australia) which have responded and adapted themselves in any meaningful way along these lines. Their ability to minimize family 'diswelfare', poverty, and inequalities and to maximize employment during the hard times of the recent decades has not been, as a neo-liberal might believe, because they 'tax and spend' themselves out of everything. Total *public* social expenditure as a percentage of GDP has been stagnant in Denmark and Sweden since 1980; in Norway and Finland, there has been some rise but this is largely a 'catch-up' effect. Neither has the reprioritization of public welfare occurred at the expense of others, say the aged. The latest available data on aged poverty confirm Scandinavia's previous record: internationally extremely low poverty among the elderly.[23]

It is tempting to attribute Scandinavian-cum-Australian welfare state adaptability to their singularly comprehensive and co-ordinated systems of interest representation—especially when we consider that these are, at the same time, comparatively youthful societies. Neither element, taken singularly, seems to offer much of an explanation. Austria and Germany are prototypes of broad, centralized consensus building; they are also unusually 'aged' nations. North America, Britain (and France) are more youthful, but lack any form of comprehensive interest intermediation. In any case, the least adaptable welfare states seem to concentrate in nations, like Italy, that are neither youthful nor co-ordinated.

The contemporary debate is pitched in terms of a perhaps lamentable, but sadly unavoidable, trade-off. Yet, the evidence I have examined suggests that the trade-off differs in terms of intensity and consequences from one regime to another; within regimes, from one country to another. Most

---

[23] Among retired couples, the poverty rates for 1991–2 are the following: Denmark = 3 per cent; Finland = 3 per cent; Norway = 2 per cent; Sweden = 1 per cent. This compares with 5 per cent in the Netherlands, Germany, and UK and 13 per cent in the USA (own calculations from LIS data bases).

nations are currently struggling with how to maximize, or at least maintain existing standards of equality and social citizenship while, simultaneously, generate more jobs and less exclusion. The basic argument I make is that any such objective cannot be attained by simply rolling back or augmenting the welfare state. The contemporary debate is also pitched in terms of a wrong-headed set of political alternatives. If I am right, a positive-sum 'win-win' strategy means rebuilding the welfare state so that it, once again, can assume well-functioning, welfare-producing labour markets and families. This means changing the nexus between state and market as well as between state and families.

In order to identify potential positive-sum strategies, we first need a basic principle for judging the desirability of one option against a rival one. Current thinking is dominated by two rival principles: the more modestly formulated Paretian and the more ambitious Rawlsian. Reduced to the bare bones, a Pareto improvement implies that if someone gains from any change in the status quo there should, at least, be no concomitant loser. The relevant 'someone' may be a group, a social class, a 'chrono-class', or a gender. A Rawlsian improvement (maximum possible justice and liberty), following his 'difference' and 'priority' principle, implies that any change of the status quo should be of greatest advantage to the least well off (Rawls, 1972: 83 ff.).

A Paretian improvement favours 'equity'—closer to the spirit of liberalism; a Rawlsian favours 'equality'—closer to the social democratic spirit. The former suffers from a basic shortcoming as far as welfare state reform is concerned. Since it is perfectly possible to obtain a Pareto improvement when one millionaire doubles his income while the poor continue to starve, this is clearly a rather irrelevant criterion for any welfare state analysis. We must begin with the assumption that we desire welfare state reform in order to improve its capacity to deliver welfare, not in order to make the rich richer. We must also assume that the basic societal objective is to reconsolidate the 'democratic class struggle'; to prevent the emergence of an ever-deepening abyss between the A-teams and B-teams of postindustrial society.

Accordingly, any 'win-win' strategy of welfare state reform must, by definition, lie closer to a Rawlsian principle of justice. It is this which underpins my admittedly more speculative approach in the next, and final chapter. The basic question that guides me is this: What kind of welfare regime will potentially provide positive-sum, or 'win-win' solutions to the dominant dilemmas of postindustrial society?

APPENDIX

TABLE 8A. *Servicing and age bias of welfare states*

	Service bias		Age bias	
	Ratio services/cash 1992	Change 1980–92 (% pts)	Ratio youth/aged 1992	Change 1980–92 (% pts)
Australia	0.20	+0.17	1.16	+0.69
Canada	0.08	+0.01	0.78	−0.52
Ireland	0.16	+0.10	1.12	+0.31
New Zealand	0.07	+0.01	0.91	+0.33
UK	0.13	−0.02	0.50	−0.10
USA	0.06	−0.02	0.30	−0.05
Denmark	0.33	+0.01	1.37	+0.15
Finland	0.21	−0.04	0.94	+0.34
Norway	0.38	+0.23	0.83	+0.17
Sweden	0.45	+0.08	0.92	+0.04
Austria	0.03	+0.02	0.31	−0.09
Belgium	0.08	+0.07	0.61	−0.21
France	0.13	+0.04	0.48	−0.07
Germany (West)	0.12	+0.03	0.43	−0.05
Italy	0.07	+0.03	0.20	−0.09
Netherlands	0.12	0	0.79	−0.28
Portugal	0.10	+0.08	0.55	+0.09
Spain	0.05	+0.02	0.67	+0.04
Japan	0.08	0	0.18	−0.12

Source and explanations, see Table 8.6.

9

Recasting Welfare Regimes for
a Postindustrial Era

If there is one great question that unites all welfare state researchers, it is this: why is it that nations respond so differently to a set of social risks that, all told, is pretty similar whether you are an American, a Spaniard, or a Swede?

Why is it that Scandinavia responds with social democracy and comprehensive welfare states, Continental Europe and East Asia with familialism and corporatist social insurance, and the Anglo-Saxon world with targeted assistance and maximum markets? There is certainly no want of answers. Some point to nation-building traditions and church–state conflicts, some to etatiste initiative, and some to the configuration of class power. These are all compelling explanations but they beg the question of why, in the first place, did state building move in one or another direction? Why was working-class unity and mobilization so thorough in Sweden and not in America? And why, once formed and forged, did the institutions they built last and then reproduce themselves so successfully? The popular answer in latter-day social science is that institutions, once forged, are overpowering and rarely permit the kind of sweeping change that would be observable to the human eye. We may live in a world of path dependencies where social creations, once cemented, are incomparably tougher than the city of Troy. Very well, but who creates and sustains the hegemony of whatever path dependency that obtains?

Economists often draw large benefits from basic simplicity. Their *homo oeconomicus* is certainly not believable, but he can be a convenient tool with which to proceed and eventually make things more complicated. I shall, for the moment, strive for similar minimalism. Sociologists, of course, crave more complexity, and one *Homo* will therefore not do. Let us allow for three ideal typical *homines*: *Homo liberalismus*, *Homo familius*, and *Homo socialdemocraticus*.[1]

---

[1] The ideas for this section of the chapter came from a week-end seminar with Jose Maria Maravall and Adam Przeworski (whom I thank for the idea and to whom I apologize for the result).

Homo liberalismus resembles Mister Economics because he follows no loftier ideal than his own personal welfare calculus. The well-being of others is their affair, not his. A belief in noble self-reliance does not necessarily imply indifference to others. *Homo liberalismus* may be generous, even altruistic. But kindness towards others is a personal affair, not something dictated from above. His ethics tell him that a free lunch is amoral, that collectivism jeopardizes freedom, that individual liberty is a fragile good, easily sabotaged by sinister socialists or paternalistic authoritarians. *Homo liberalismus* prefers a welfare regime where those who can play the market do so, whereas those who cannot must merit charity.

Homo familius inhabits an altogether different planet. He abhors atomism and impersonality and, hence, markets and individualism. His worst enemy is the Hobbesian world of elbows, because self-interest is amoral; a person will find his equilibrium when he puts himself at the service of his family. Freedom, to *Homo familius*, means that he and his kin are immunized from the ceaseless threats that the greater world around him produce. He is not a go-getter with an irresistible urge to challenge the world around him. He is a satisficer, not maximizer, because what really counts is stability and security; a job for life in the postal service is heaven on earth; it will guarantee him and his kin a good life, security and, incidentally, also the means to land a postal job for his daughters and sons. Both *Homo familius* and *femina familia* see patriarchy as a good thing. The family would be unruly without authority and, in any case, respect and status is due to the father, on whose shoulders so much responsibility weighs. To them, the family is the unrivalled source of solidarity and community because it alone knows what its members need. Alas, the family is fragile since so many individuals must depend on the *pater familias*. *Homo familius* is therefore quite happy with the idea that the state—or some higher body—eliminates whatever risk of misfortune may arise. Yet, higher bodies are there to service the family, not to command his loyalties. *Homo familius* wants a welfare regime that tames the market and exalts the virtues of close-knit solidarities.

Homo socialdemocraticus is, like a boy scout or good Christian, inclined to believe that he will do better when everybody does better. Doing good to others is not an act of charity and can, indeed, be coolly calculative. *Homo socialdemocraticus* plans his life around the one basic idea that he, and everybody else, will be better off in a world without want but also without free-riders. Society is something that we all are compelled to share, and so we had better share it well. *Homo socialdemocraticus* is, none the less, also a believer in individual, personal empowerment. Collectivism is not pursued for its own sake, but in order to bring out the utmost in each and every individual soul. That is why collective solutions are always the best. But his individualism is cautionary because no one should be granted favours, advantages, special recognition. *Homo socialdemocraticus* must constantly live with a moral clash between individualism and conformity. He loves the idea that we all be equally endowed; he hates the idea that someone may rise above others, particularly above himself. Solidarity is therefore fragile if someone desires to move beyond the common denominator. *Homo socialdemocraticus* is fully convinced that the more we invest in the public good, the better it will become. And this will trickle down to all, himself especially, in the form of a good life. Collective solutions are therefore the single best assurance of a good, if perhaps dull, individual life.

We all combine the instincts of these ideal typical *homines*; we all have moral conflicts. And all societies combine them in one mix or another. Sweden has its *Homines liberalismi* (although many emigrate to Monte Carlo), and America its *Homines socialdemocratici* (many of which show up regularly in Sweden). But how did a sufficient mass manage to profile itself in collective expression, and thereby sway society towards its preferred welfare regime?

Genetics clearly do not create preferences and beliefs. What might account for this is society itself with all its institutions, incentive systems, and inscribed norms of proper conduct. Society's 'median *Homo*' is created, and this is obviously where labour movements or other collective actors have played a key role. If, originally, a labour movement garnered its strength (or failed to do so) from the available raw material, so it also played a constant historical role in reactivating that very same raw material. Institutional path dependency means that one society is likely to reproduce itself in the image of *Homo socialdemocraticus*, another in the image of *Homo familius*, generation after generation.

Old risks may fade away and new ones emerge, but the response of a welfare regime will, more likely than not, be normatively path dependent. And the norms that our *homines* and *feminae* embody are upheld by power, collective action, and by the median voter's choice. The greater their hegemony, the less power needs to be activated on their behalf. That our three welfare regimes continue to follow an evolutionary logic that for generations has experienced few deviations from the beaten path, suggests that we are here dealing with hegemonic systems.

There have been radical shifts in government and power over the past many decades. The Scandinavian countries have all experienced rightist governments, some even for protracted periods; both the Left and the Right has had its day in France, Germany, Spain, Portugal, Austria, the Netherlands, Australia, and New Zealand; less ideologically clear are the shifts in North America. Political alternation may very well have caused roll-backs in a programme here or some policy redesign there, but there is almost no case of sharp welfare regime transformation.

A few cases do, of course, come to mind. During the Thatcher era Britain appeared to move from social democracy to liberalism; the Antipodes, too. Yet, was this really the case? Appearance may deceive and a longer historical view suggests something else. As I discussed in Chapter 5, the visible similarities between Nordic and British social policy in the aftermath of World War Two are probably better interpreted as Scandinavia's yet incomplete social democratization. As also Heclo (1974) pointed out, Britain failed to take the decisive steps towards a social democratic model already in the 1960s.

If core institutional traits are so unyielding to change, it remains unlikely today—as always—that the contemporary welfare state crisis will produce an avalanche of revolutionary change, no matter how urgent such change is claimed to be. Any blueprint for reform is bound to be naïve if it calls for a radical departure from existing welfare regime practice. The IMF is naïve when it asks that European welfare states adopt, lock, stock, and barrel, the Chilean pension system; American leftists, or emergent democratic governments in ex-communist countries, are equally naïve when they call for the importation of the 'Swedish model'. One thing is to redesign or reform the ways in which the *state* delivers welfare, another to recast the entire welfare regime. Academically speaking, there may exist a blueprint for a 'win-win' strategy, for an ideal postindustrial welfare regime. But unless it is compatible with existing welfare regime practice, it may not be practicable. As I shall argue below, optimizing welfare in a postindustrial setting will, none the less, require radical departures.

WHAT IS TO BE OPTIMIZED?

The Trojan horse has brought us population ageing, unstable families, and a severe trade-off between welfare and jobs, equality, and full employment. These are all long-run and, most likely, unstoppable forces of change. Women's economic independence, novel household forms, and reliance on services are all part and parcel of postindustrial society. We face therefore the challenge of how to redesign our welfare triad so as to convert these changes into something that is societally beneficial. The question, then, is what does each component in our welfare triad need in order to function optimally? The answers are very straightforward:

• The *labour market* craves greater flexibility, and more wage inequality is probably unavoidable if our goal is to restore full employment or, minimally, augment the supply of jobs. It also needs more demand. Since we must count on the tertiary sector to furnish most new jobs, this means demand for services.

• The *welfare state* needs to strengthen its tax base, something that only families and the labour market can produce: a return to higher fertility (to offset ageing), more people gainfully employed, and fewer people reliant on social benefits.[2]

• The *family* needs, above all, adequate incomes and jobs, and it needs access to affordable social services so as to make this possible. Since the emerging labour market implies more inequality and flexibility, optimizing households' welfare requires, as always, social protection to bridge temporary poverty and risks and to prevent these from hardening. To assure against entrapment, however, families need to command skills.

RIVAL REFORM STRATEGIES

The ideal world of *Homo familius* is clearly a suboptimal strategy for reform. Internalizing welfare responsibilities in the family is incompatible with women's demand for economic independence and careers. Today women are becoming more educated than men and heavy unpaid domestic work is therefore threefold irrational: to women and their families, the opportunity cost of domestic labour becomes huge; to society and the welfare state, it means a massive waste of human capital and potential tax revenue; and to the labour market it means suboptimal demand for goods and services.

Moreover, if higher fertility and more flexible labour markets are two important objectives, familialism is arguably counter-productive. Familial reliance on one earner means that the median voter is bound to sustain and even reinforce maximum job security for the individual worker. Moreover, if at least periods of low pay are a realistic prospect for many workers, familialism blocks spouses from increasing their labour supply so as to offset poverty. We have seen that the two-earner household is vastly superior as a guarantee against child poverty. But dual incomes and careers in a familialistic system imply a severe trade-off between careers and children. The likely response is therefore that women reduce fertility.

Therefore, if 'pro-family' policy or, for that matter, 'decentralizing' welfare responsibilities, means that families should assume a greater share of welfare responsibilities and caring burdens, this is a dramatically suboptimal strategy.

---

[2] To avoid any misunderstanding, this does not imply pro-natalist policy. What is at stake is the looming possibility of a permanent low-fertility equilibrium caused by families having fewer children than they actually desire.

THE MARKET STRATEGY

The neo-liberal case for privatization and deregulation is often argued on Pareto-optimal grounds. The reasoning is that too much redistribution, equality, and social protection reduces individuals' incentives and impairs the market's ability to furnish an adequate number of jobs. If income guarantees erode peoples' incentive to save, this raises interest rates and leads to underinvestment; if they erode incentives to work, the economic base of the system is weakened. Too much equality or taxes is harmful if it reduces incentives for education or added effort. And rigidly protected labour markets create jobless growth. Deregulation and welfare privatization hold therefore a promise of benefiting the collectivity: we would all be better-off if more people work, save and educate themselves more, and we would certainly be better-off if all had jobs even if they are not all well-paid. A flexible labour market enhances mobility, and low pay should therefore be only a matter of temporal hardship.[3]

One reason why most neo-liberal writings are so conspicuously void of hard, empirical evidence is because the argument relies on a counter-factual: if only the market were genuinely undisturbed would it all work out. There exists no living case of this in the world, but we can evaluate the merits of the argument through an alternative strategy of comparison. Let us examine two extremes along the public–private continuum: Sweden against the United States. These are arguably the closest living embodiment of *Homo socialdemocraticus*' and, respectively, *Homo liberalismus*' dream.

The difference between the two welfare states could not be more dramatic. In 1990, the American was less than half as large as the Swedish. See Table 9.1. Presumably, social risks in America are as widespread and severe as in Sweden, possibly more. There exist therefore two possible alternatives: either that a huge number of risks are not met, or that the other 'welfare half' is to be found in private social spending. Both turn out to be true.

When we combine the two spheres we find that the two nations pretty much converge. The upper half of Table 9.1 presents macro-economic estimates; the lower half revisits the same phenomenon but from a micro-economic vantage point—the average household. Beginning with the macro comparison, it is clear that the American private economy picks up where the welfare state left off—but not quite: the Swedish total is 35.5 per cent of GDP, the American 29.6 per cent. This is because national accounts statistics do not easily permit us to identify many of those

---

[3] Presentations of the neo-liberal position are abundant. Relatively well-argued works include Lindbeck (1992), Lindbeck (1994), and Murray (1984).

welfare outlays that come out of peoples' own pockets, and neither do they include the total value of tax expenditures which, rightfully, should be added to public outlays.

The micro-accounts must of course take into account what households pay in taxes to the welfare state and what they pay for private welfare. What we miss here are the employer-financed fringe benefits. None the less, we now arrive at close to convergence. The total welfare expenditure package for an average family hovers around 40 per cent in both nations. Tax-burdened Swedes may envy Americans who pay so few taxes, but what they forget is that Americans are forced anyhow to pay for welfare. In Sweden, the state may have crowded out the market; in America, households' spending on private welfare crowds out their ability to buy other things. Likewise, European employers regularly lament the heavy social contributions they have to pay, but they forget that wage-earners in a privatized system are likely to bargain for occupational benefits—if they can. In the primary economy, American employers' combined legislated and negotiated fixed labour costs are quite similar to European.[4]

The contrast offers a perfect example of cost-shifting. What varies is who shoulders the burden, not the total weight of the burden itself. If the burden in a privatized system were distributed so that the losers were few, and their loss not decisive, we would have a case in favour of markets. Empirical data, however, makes this appear unlikely.

We need only turn to 'market failure' theory to see why. The market is perfectly able to absorb the good risks while the bad risks tend to get left behind. This is evident in health insurance where about 40 million Americans have no coverage at all. Medicaid may take care of the really poor (after a means test), and markets do well for the middle class. But there is clearly a huge mass caught in between, and we need not look long to understand why. For an average-income family, private health insurance is expensive but affordable (about 6 per cent of income). For a bottom-quintile family, however, private health would absorb roughly 18 per cent of income.

We also know that private welfare coverage is very unequal (West Pedersen, 1994; Pestieau, 1992).[5] Since the rich can save, the poor not, it is

---

[4] An average American company pays 11 per cent of wages to legislated social contribution, and another 12 per cent towards occupational benefits. This compares to an EU average of 24 per cent to the former and 5 per cent to the latter. Expressed as a percentage of GDP, American employers' combined outlays on legislated and private contributions is 11 per cent. This is quite similar to Finland (11.8) and Germany (10.4), above the Netherlands (7.7), and lower than in France (14.9) and Italy (12.7) (Esping-Andersen, 1996: 28; and OECD, *National Accounts. Detailed Tables, 1994.* Paris: OECD, 1996).

[5] The much-celebrated model of privatized pensions in Chile is increasingly showing signs of severe 'market failure'. Besides such standard problems as very incomplete population coverage, the competitive market logic upon which the private pension funds operate is basically eroding the system itself. To compete for clients, the funds have a huge sales and administration staff.

TABLE 9.1. *Public and private social-protection spending, 1990*

	Sweden	United States
As a percentage of GDP:		
Public social expenditure	33.1	14.6
Tax expenditures[a]	0.0	1.3
Private education	0.1	2.5
Private health[b]	1.1	8.2
Private pensions[b]	1.8	3.0
TOTAL	35.5	29.6
As a percentage of household expenditure:		
Private health, education, and pensions	2.7	18.8
Daycare (child families)	1.7	10.4
TOTAL	4.4	29.2
Taxes	36.8	10.4
Total + taxes	41.2	39.6

[a] Tax expenditures for the USA exclude those for pensions.

[b] Private health data for Sweden are for 1992; American data include 'other social welfare'. Private pensions for Sweden are estimated from employer pension benefits in the OECD national accounts. Swedish tax data are from *Sveriges Statistiska Aarsbok, 1994* (Table T 226). US private pensions and health expenditure data are from *Social Security Bulletin, Annual Statistical Supplement*, 1992 (Table 3A4).

Sources: OECD, *National Accounts. Detailed Tables, 1994*; US Bureau of Labour Statistics, *Consumer Expenditures in 1990*; Mishel and Bernstein (1993, Table 8.37); OECD, *The Caring World*. Paris: OECD (1998, May).

hardly surprising that the private welfare gap is deepening. As we have seen, American occupational pension and health coverage was once quite extensive: about 50 per cent of workers for the former; more than 70 per cent for the latter in the 1970s. A menacing aspect of the American model is that the market seems to shrink in tandem with the public sector. Not only has the percentage of workers covered declined dramatically (occupational pension coverage is now down to about 35 per cent), but there has occurred a simultaneous shift from defined-benefit to individual savings or defined-contribution plans—a case of shifting costs from employers to workers (Myles, 1996).

This means that the average worker pays 30 per cent of his or her contribution payment to cover 'commission costs'. Since the market for clients is limited, the funds compete by pirating each others' clients. One out of four workers shifts funds annually. The consequence is additional transaction costs and, in the long run, oligopolization. From 21 funds in the early 1990s, only about 11 remain today (release from *Oxford Analytica*, 20 December 1996).

And why is private coverage shrinking? Basically for reasons inherent in the model itself. The most cited explanations are, firstly, declining union-ism—arguably a pre-condition for effective deregulation; secondly, occupational plans are rare in smaller and more flexible firms—an obvious correlate of economic adaptation; thirdly, they are equally rare in service industries—the only realistic source of employment growth.

A strategy based purely on deregulation and privatization cannot, like the American example shows, be welfare and efficiency optimizing. On one side, it is clear that privatization does not imply resource savings—quite the contrary. American health care absorbs almost twice as much of GDP as the average European and does not do a better job of delivering health (Navarro, 1996). On the other side, if unregulated labour markets create people who are poor, then it cannot be a welfare-optimizing model if those very same poor people find themselves excluded from social protection.

Homo liberalismus may care about the fate of his co-patriots, but if he inhabits that end of the market where success breeds success, where welfare builds on itself along a cumulative, upward path, he is probably unfamiliar with that other end of the market where failure causes failure to harden, where welfare disaccumulates, where someone who once made ends meet is now homeless.

The neo-liberal strategy has little to say about fertility. Yet, this is a precondition for our postindustrial welfare equilibrium. In any case if, as we have seen, welfare state residualism with de-regulation is associated with alarmingly high child poverty statistics, fertility would have to be reserved for the non-poor to avoid growing social polarization. If growing up poor produces systematic disadvantages that affect the entire life course, and if these continue to be carried over from generation to generation, clearly the greater their fertility the larger the class of losers.

A THIRD WAY?

Is there an alternative strategy? Up to a point, but not further, a 'social democratic' approach might furnish the basis for a new, positive equilibrium. A politics of collectivizing families' needs (de-familialization) frees women from unpaid labour, and thereby nurtures the dual-earner household. And this reduces child poverty, and makes households better equipped to weather the storms of flexibilization, since they will usually have one member's earnings to fall back on if the other is made redundant, needs temporary retraining, or suffers wage decline. Two-earner households have stronger social networks, and are less likely to run them down if one partner becomes unemployed.

avg overall costs expensive

A social democratic de-familialization strategy can reverse fertility decline if it helps employed mothers square the caring–work circle (mainly via daycare), and if it it is willing to cover a good part of the opportunity costs of having children (which means expensive maternity and parental leave as well as generous child allowances). Working mothers may have 'negative productivity' in the sense that their earnings (plus public subsidies) exceed their output. But these costs are potentially recovered via their higher lifelong earnings, the smaller depreciation of their human capital, *and* the resulting fertility dividend.

A fundamental 'postindustrial' dilemma—generally overlooked in contemporary debates—is that families seem no longer inclined to assume the costs of bearing children. As a comparison between fertility in Southern Europe (with Japan) and Scandinavia suggests, the social price of children may be high indeed. Immigration is certainly an alternative, and herein lies a major reason behind North America's (and Australia's) younger age profile. Yet, besides being a rather unrealistic scenario for Europe today, the immigration option poses hard dilemmas of its own. If one of our chief problems is how to absorb masses of low-skilled workers, this would only be compounded by Third World immigration. The advanced economies would clearly prefer highly educated immigrants, yet encouraging such a flow can hardly be considered solidaristic towards Third World nations.

Universalizing the double-earner household (with lots of children) holds yet another promise of welfare improvement. When we add its greater purchasing power to its desperate search for free time, it is a truly promising source of service consumption, from restaurants and leisure parks to child care and home-help services for their aged parents. Thereby families create jobs for waiters, park-keepers, child-minders, and home-helpers. Of course, access to child care is a pre-condition for dual-income families in the first place. This is exactly the point: services beget services; the double-earner household plays the role of employment multiplier. And we saw earlier that the employment multiplier of working mothers can be quite substantial, especially in those kinds of services that are labour intensive.

Encouraging families to consume more external services is therefore part of a potential 'win-win' strategy. Yet, as we know, relative costs can be a major constraint. This is why, despite the virtual universalization of two-earner households, lower-end personal services in Scandinavia grow very little. They would doubtlessly grow if costs were lower, but this implies greater wage inequality.

This is where *Homo socialdemocraticus* must yield to *Homo liberalismus*. Substantial service employment growth outside the public sector depends on flexibility and low wages, something that social democracy cannot easily accept. The social democratic strategy, as I have outlined it so far, will therefore not escape the fundamental 'equality–jobs' trade-off. We need therefore to resolve one last problem: the very same 'equality–jobs' trade-off with which we started.

EQUALITY WITH INEQUALITY?

There is no shortage of proposals for how to resolve this trade-off. There are those who, in adherence to a lump-sum-of-labour assumption, believe that de-industrialization means the end of work. They often advocate a solidarity of work-sharing by sharply reducing hours across the board. This policy was recently applied sectorially in Germany, and is now a national-level objective in France and Italy. It is probably a suboptimal strategy if not accompanied by some proportional reduction in pay, simply because it will raise real-wage costs (which already are widely cited as a major impediment to job growth). But concomitant pay cuts are unrealistic because workers and their families count on their habitual wage cheque to pay their mortgage and maintain their accustomed level of living. Higher wage costs may create inflationary pressures, jeopardize exports, and will above all deepen the cleavage between insiders and outsiders. Work-sharing, as currently proposed is accordingly dangerous and counter-productive. Work creates work; less work creates less work.

A popular alternative to work-sharing is some form of a guaranteed citizen's income. One type emanates from the same 'end-of-work' philosophy, and is meant to secure all those out of work an adequate citizen's wage. Alas, if the goal is adequacy, the proposal is by all accounts impossibly expensive. It would clearly be cheaper if more people work, and less require passive maintenance. This is the premiss of the second type, now becoming a centre-piece social policy in liberal welfare states, namely some form of a negative income tax or, as it is called in the United States, an earned-income credit.

The negative income tax schemes that are now proliferating in North America, the Antipodes, and Britain all seek to resolve a basic dilemma of deregulated economies, namely how to sustain work incentives among low-wage workers when either welfare or crime appear more attractive. The idea is to combat the 'poverty trap' of traditional means-tested assistance by lowering and tapering the tax-bite on each additional dollar earned. The objective is to guarantee a minimal income in recognition of the fact that many work—perhaps even full-time, full-year—at below-poverty earnings. This is the kind of human solidarity that appeals to *Homo liberalismus* because the beneficiary has demonstrated his or her ardent will to be self-reliant; additional effort is rewarded, not punished;

and idleness clearly does not pay. Here is the classical liberal 'help to self-help' philosophy in modern clothing.

Is a negative income tax one way to square the equality–jobs dilemma? This depends on two conditions. One is whether it nurtures a low-skill equilibrium, as Soskice (1994) and Snower (1997) put it. This may very well happen if the real underlying problem is an excess stock of low-skilled, 'untrainable' workers or few incentives for employers to invest in training. Low-wage employment may be the only realistic way to absorb such masses. In many economies, like the American, this skill-less strata is huge and tends to perpetuate itself. A negative income tax, if not coupled to active training policies, does little more than narrow the poverty gap for this population. It certainly will not prevent the problem from being passed on from one generation to the next.[6]

The negative income tax approach is additionally problematic because it implicitly subsidizes low-paying employers. Higher wages might mean that they would have to go out of business (or move to Mexico), or that they would have to augment productivity and quality. If the welfare state reduces employers' incentive to invest in capital or skills, we are clearly dealing with a non-optimal policy. If a negative income tax is coupled to a programme of active skill and educational formation, its role can be positive in the sense of averting temporary poverty in a presumably transitory period of low-wage employment. But the same result could also be obtained through wage subsidies or generous family benefits.

If we face a future with greater wage inequalities, and if these are most likely to afflict younger workers and their families, clearly any prospective welfare policy menu must prioritize strong income guarantees, be it through training or job subsidies, earned income credits, or family benefits. If young families are to be encouraged to have children, it is obviously tantamount that these children not grow up in poverty. The extraordinary aged-bias in many countries' social transfer system is difficult to reverse because the median voter is getting older. Yet, pension benefits may indeed be overly generous in some cases. Take Italy, where average pension income exceeds consumption expenditure by 30 percentage points.[7] Their savings obviously form part of a familialistic–welfare nexus, since they are redistributed to the children and grandchildren—a rather perverse system of redistribution. It is unfortunately not easy to convince *Homo familius* or, for that matter, *Homo liberalismus*, that the welfare state could re-funnel the 30 per cent excess in pension expenditure more effectively to needy youth. In any case, shifting resources from old to young remains a

---

[6] A recent study of basic cognitive capacities, such as minimal literacy, shows a disturbingly high correlation between low parental education and lacking cognitive abilities among their offspring (OECD, 1997*c*).

[7] Own calculations from the 1993 Italian Household Consumer Survey.

basic requirement for any kind of 'win-win' strategy in many welfare states.[8]

Transfers or not, the problem of a more inegalitarian labour market remains. There is in truth only one way out of the impasse, namely to redefine what kind of equality we desire. *Homo socialdemocraticus* must be convinced that we cannot aspire for all kinds of equality at once; that some inequalities can be made compatible with some equalities.

The principle of equality that must go is exactly the same that emerged—most forcefully in Scandinavian social democracy—when welfare states sought to respond to the equality-crisis of the 1960s, namely the promise of equality for all 'here-and-now'. In practice, this may not be so difficult a task. *Homo socialdemocraticus*, like many of his rivals, has surely held any number of lousy jobs in his youth. Like all Scandinavians, he left the parental home very early and lived for years on bread and water (this is what he tells his children). Yet, he is now a respectable citizen with a respectable career. Temporary deprivation is unimportant if it does not affect our life chances.

We can return to Schumpeter's omnibus: always full, but always with different people. Everybody gets off at the next stop, or at least where desired. If, like *Homo socialdemocraticus*, we cling to a notion of equality for all, here and now, we shall never resolve the fundamental dilemma of our times. The kinds of inequalities that are inevitable in the world of *Homo liberalismus* can become acceptable, even welcomed, if they coincide with a welfare regime capable of guaranteeing all citizens against entrapment: no one should find him- or herself in an omnibus with locked doors.

Our search for a postindustrial welfare optimum requires, therefore, some kind of a mobility guarantee. What this will look like depends, in turn, on what are the chief causes of social exclusion and inferior life chances. A room full of academics and experts would, no doubt, draft an endlessly long list of causes. Many standard reasons, such as physical or mental handicaps, do not concern us here because they are not inherently part of the equality–jobs trade-off. From the literature and data that I have surveyed in this book, two sources of substantial life chance problems stand out: one, the risks associated with marital instability and poverty in childhood; two, inadequate skills.

Diminishing family-induced risks calls, as we have seen, for a standard 'social democratic' package of what the feminists call women-friendly policy: child-care services, incentives for mothers to work, and adequate

---

[8] There is growing evidence that welfare states may have overshot their support for the elderly. Recent data indicate that, in many countries at least, the vast majority of pensioners are home-owners and more or less rent-free. They enjoy therefore a substantial amount of capital in addition to generous pensions (OECD, *The Caring World*. Paris: OECD, 1998).

income maintenance to take into account mothers' reduced labour supply and the cost of children. Diminishing labour market induced risks calls for a rethinking of education, training, and marketable skills.

This is not the place to explore the broad issues of education. But there are a number of basic facts that all can agree upon: the returns to skills are rising, as we would expect in a world increasingly dominated by complex technology; the low-skilled are in rapidly declining demand. To exemplify the importance of skills, Bjorn (1995) shows that the probability of exiting from 'marginality' (basically unemployment or low pay) jumps by 30 points with vocational training, and 50 points with some theoretical training. Closing the skill gap is therefore an extremely effective way of catapulting people out of entrapment, of assuring good life chances. And it also pays off to society in the form of a more productive workforce.

There is clearly nothing earth-shatteringly novel about a call for more education. There is virtually no government or international organization today that does not advocate 'active labour market policy' or 'life-long learning'. But there is widespread scepticism about their effectiveness. Active labour market policy with its 'activation' and training programmes does not always appear to pay off if by this we mean that the unemployed eventually find a stable, promising career. Too often, activation looks more like a temporary parking-lot, or one interlude in a never-ending roundabout of unemployment, training, occasional jobs, and then unemployment again.

Effective or not, many believe that training is useless since there are no jobs for the newly trained. In a static sense this is undeniably often true. But they miss the basic point of the omnibus analogy: for any given individual, skills are the single best source of escape from underprivilege. What we are trying to resolve is a dynamic, life-course issue and not where to place everybody today. A new welfare optimum is, in fact, compatible with the possibility that many of us will experience a spell of unpleasantness.

What we really need to understand better is what kinds of skills and what kind of education to promote? We are generally aware of the rising demand for multi-skilling, flexible adaptation, and capacity for life-long learning. A worker with a good theoretical base in his vocational training is much easier to upgrade than someone with a high-school diploma unable to understand instructions on an aspirin bottle. This is why German employers use their skilled workers to run computerized production systems while in England they import engineers. We also face a reality where 'social skills' are more fundamental than muscle because of the direct face-to-face mode of service production. What these are is not easy to define, but they undoubtedly include more than the routine 'have a nice day'. A major problem in the contemporary unemployment structure is that laid-off miners and steel workers are unlikely to possess the kinds of social skills that sell a service.

We know from the OECD literacy studies (OECD, 1997c) that education—even completed secondary education—may guarantee very little if it ends up producing 15 or 20 per cent Americans incapable of even rudimentary reading, writing, and arithmetic. These do not even possess the minimal level of qualifications needed to be trainable. They are a *de facto* human capital waste, a stratum only too obviously condemned to lifelong low-wage employment or, possibly, crime.

It is this kind of result that must be eliminated from any kind of society if we seriously desire an optimal welfare regime. I therefore close this book inviting education experts to design a workable system of skilling entitlements, one that would befit an ideal postindustrial welfare regime. And I invite our political leaders to forge a new coalition of our assorted *homines*, one capable of breaking the deadlock of median-voter support for anachronistic modes of welfare production.

BIBLIOGRAPHY

Adam, P. and Canziani, P. (1998), 'Partial De-regulation: Fixed-term Contracts in Italy and Spain', *Centre for Economic Performance Discussion Paper*, 386.

Adler, M. (1933), 'Wandlung der Arbeiterklasse', *Der Kampf*, 26: 367–82.

Aldrich, H. and Waldinger, R. (1990), 'Ethnicity and Entrepreneurship', *Annual Review of Sociology*, 16: 111–35.

Allmendinger, J. and Hinz, T. (1996), 'Mobilitat und Lebensverlauf', unpub. paper, University of Munich (Jan.).

Alogoskoufis, G., Bean, C., Bertola, G., Cohen, D., Dolado, J., and Saint-Paul, G. (1995), *Unemployment: Choices for Europe*. London: Centre for Economic Policy Research.

Alvarez, R., Garret, G., and Lange, P. (1991), 'Government Partisanship, Labor Organization and Macroeconomic Performance', *American Political Science Review*, 85: 539–56.

Andersen, J. Goul (1992), 'The Decline of Class Voting Revisited', in P. Gundelach and K. Siune (eds.), *From Voters to Participants*. Copenhagen: Politica, 91–107.

—— (1995), 'Velfaerdsstatens folkelige opbakning', *Social Forskning* (Aug.), 34–45.

Anttonen, A. and Sipila, J. (1996), 'European Social Care Services: Is it Possible to Identify Models?', *Journal of European Social Policy*, 6: 87–100.

Atkinson, A. B. (1983), *The Economics of Inequality*. Oxford: Oxford University Press.

—— and Mogensen, G. V. (1993) (eds.), *Welfare and Work Incentives*. Oxford: Clarendon Press.

Auer, P. (1993), 'Sequences in Rigidity and Flexibility, and Their Implications for the Italian Labor Market', in C. F. Buechtemann (ed.), *Employment Security and Labor Market Behavior*. Ithaca, NY: ILR Press, 414–24.

Bairoch, P. (1996), 'Globalization, Myths and Realities: One Century of External Trade and Foreign Investment', in R. Boyer and D. Drache (eds.), *States Against Markets*. London: Routledge, 173–93.

Baldwin, P. (1990), *The Politics of Social Solidarity: Class Bases of the European Welfare States*. Cambridge: Cambridge University Press.

Barbagli, M. (1988), *Sotto Lo Stesso Tetto*. Bologna: Il Mulino.

—— and Saraceno, C. (1997), *Lo Stato delle Famiglie in Italia*. Bologna: Il Mulino.

Barr, N. (1993), *The Economics of the Welfare State*. Palo Alto, Calif.: Stanford University Press.

Baumol, W. (1967), 'The Macroeconomics of Unbalanced Growth', *American Economic Review*, 57: 415–26.

Bean, C. (1994), 'European Unemployment: A Retrospective', *Journal of Economic Literature*, 32: 573–619.

Becker, G. (1981), *A Treatise on the Family*. Cambridge, Mass.: Harvard University Press.

Bell, D. (1960), *The End of Ideology?* New York: Free Press.

—— (1976), *The Coming of Postindustrial Society*. New York: Basic Books.

Bentolila, S. and Bertola, G. (1990), 'Firing Costs and Labor Demand: How Bad is Eurosclerosis?', *Review of Economic Studies*, 57: 381–402.

—— and Dolado, J. (1994), 'Spanish Labor Markets', *Economic Policy* (Apr.), 55–99.

Berger, P., Steinmuller, P., and Sopp, P. (1993), 'Differentiation of Life Courses? Patterns of Labour Market Sequences in West Germany', *European Sociological Review*, 1: 43–64.

Bertola, G. (1990), 'Job Security, Employment and Wages', *European Economic Review*, 34: 851–86.

—— and Ichino, A. (1995), 'Wage Inequality and Unemployment: US versus Europe', *NBER Macroeconomics Annual*, 5. Cambridge, Mass.: MIT Press.

Bettio, F. and Villa, P. (1995), 'A Mediterranean Perspective on the Break-down of the Relationship between Participation and Fertility', unpub. paper, Department of Economics, University of Trento (Dec.).

Beveridge, W. (1942), *Report on Social Insurance and Allied Services*. London: HMSO.

Bison, I. and Esping-Andersen, G. (1998), 'Unemployment and Income Packaging in Europe', mimeo, University of Trento.

Bjorklund, A. and Freeman, R. (1994), 'Generating Equality and Eliminating Poverty, the Swedish Way', NBER Working Paper, no. 4945.

Bjorn, N. H. (1995), 'Causes and Consequences of Persistent Unemployment', Ph.D. diss., Department of Economics, Copenhagen University.

Blackmer, D. and Tarrow, S. (1975), *Communism in Italy and France*. Princeton: Princeton University Press.

Blanchard, O., Dornbusch, R., and Layard, R. (1987), *Restoring Europe's Prosperity*. Cambridge, Mass.: MIT Press.

Blanchet, D. and Pennec, S. (1993), 'A Simple Model for Interpreting Cross-tabulations of Family Size and Women's Labor Force Participation', *European Journal of Population*, 9: 121–42.

Blank, R. (1994), *Social Protection versus Economic Flexibility*. Chicago: University of Chicago Press.

Block, F. (1990), *Postindustrial Possibilities*. Berkeley: University of California Press.

Blossfeld, H. P. (1995) (ed.), *The New Role of Women*. Boulder, Colo.: Westview Press.

Bonke, J. (1995), *Factotum: Husholdningernes Produktion*. Copenhagen: Institut for Socialforskning.

—— (1996), *Arbejde, Tid og Koen I Udvalgte Lande*. Copenhagen: Institut for Socialforskning.

Borchhorst, A. (1993), 'Arbejdsliv og Familieliv i Europa', in S. Carlsen and J. Larsen (eds.), *Den Svaere Balance*. Copenhagen: Ligestillingsraadet.

Bradshaw, J. and Ditch, J. (1995), 'Ireland's Support for Children in

Comparative Context', in J. Blackwell (ed.), *Reason and Reform*. Dublin: Dublin Institute of Public Administration, 346–74.

Braverman, H. (1974), *Labor and Monopoly Capital: The Degradation of Work in the Twentieth Century*. New York: Monthly Review Press.

Briggs, A. (1961), 'The Welfare State in Historical Perspective', *European Journal of Sociology*, 2: 221–58.

Brown, P. and Crompton, R. (1994), *Economic Restructuring and Social Exclusion*. London: UCL Press.

—— and Scase, R. (1991), *Poor Work*. Milton Keynes: Open University Press.

Bruno, M. and Sachs, J. (1985), *The Economics of Worldwide Stagflation*. Cambridge, Mass.: Harvard University Press.

Bruyn-Hundt, M. (1996), *The Economics of Unpaid Work*. Amsterdam: Thesis Publishers.

Buechtemann, C. F. (1993), 'Employment Security and Deregulation: The West German Experience' in C. F. Buechtemann (ed.), *Employment Security and Labor Market Behavior*. Ithaca, NY: ILR Press, 272–96.

Bundesministerium für Familie (1996), *Zeit im Blickfeld*. Stuttgart: Kohlhammer.

Bureau of Labor Statistics (1987), *Handbook of Labor Statistics*. Washington: Government Printing Office.

Burkhauser, R. and Poupore, J. (1993), 'A Cross-national Comparison of Permanent Inequality in the United States and Germany', *Cross-national Studies in Ageing Program Project*, paper 10. State University of New York-Syracuse.

—— Holtz-Eakin, D., and Rhody, S. (1995), 'Labor Earnings Mobility and Inequality in the United States and Germany During the 1980s', *Cross-national Studies in Ageing Program Project*, paper 12. State University of New York-Syracuse.

Burtless, G. (1990) (ed.), *A Future of Lousy Jobs? The Changing Structure of U.S. Wages*. Washington: Brookings Institute.

Bussemaker, J. and van Kersbergen, K. (1994), 'Gender and Welfare States: Some Theoretical Reflections', in D. Sainsbury (ed.), *Gendering Welfare States*. London: Sage, 8–25.

Calmfors, L. (1993), 'Centralization of Wage Bargaining and Macroeconomic Performance', *OECD Economic Studies*, no. 21

—— and Driffill, J. (1988), 'Bargaining Structure, Corporatism, and Macroeconomic Performance', *Economic Policy*, 6: 13–61.

Cameron, D. (1984), 'Social Democracy, Corporatism, Labor Quiescence and the Representation of Economic Interests in Advanced Capitalist Society', in J. Goldthorpe (ed.), *Order and Conflict in Contemporary Capitalism*. Oxford: Clarendon Press, 143–78.

Card, D. and Krueger, A. (1995), *Myth and Measurement: The New Economics of the Minimum Wage*. Princeton: Princeton University Press.

Carroll, G. R. and Mayer, K. U. (1986), 'Job-Shift Patterns in the Federal Republic of Germany: The Effects of Class, Industrial Sector and Organizational Size', *American Sociological Review*, 51: 323–41.

Casey, B. (1991), 'Survey Evidence on Trends in Non-standard Employment', in A. Pollert (ed.), *Farewell to Flexibility?* Oxford: Basic Blackwell, 179–99.

Castellino, D. (1976), *Il Labirinto delle Pensioni*. Bologna: Il Mulino.

Castles, F. (1986), *Working Class and Welfare*. London: Allen and Unwin.

—— (1993) (ed.), *Families of Nations*. Dartmouth: Aldershot.

—— (1996), 'Needs-based Strategies of Social Protection in Australia and New Zealand', in G. Esping-Andersen (ed.), *Welfare States in Transition*. London: Sage, 88–115.

—— and Mitchell, D. (1993), 'Worlds of Welfare and Families of Nations', in Castles (ed.), *Families of Nations*.

CENSIS (1995), *Rapporto sulla Situazione Sociale del Paese, 1994*. Roma: Francoangeli.

Chiesi, A. (1993), 'L'uso del Tempo', in M. Paci (ed.), *Le Dimensioni della Disuguaglianza*. Bologna: Il Mulino, 215–44.

Clark, C. (1940), *The Conditions of Economic Progress*. London: Macmillan.

Clark, T. and Lipset, S. M. (1991), 'Are Social Classes Dying?', *International Sociology*, 4: 397–410.

—— Lipset, S. M., and Rempel, M. (1993), 'The Declining Political Significance of Class', *International Sociology*, 3: 293–316.

Cobalti, A. (1993), 'La Classe Operaia nella Societa Postindustriale', *Polis*, 3: 477–502.

—— and Schizzerotto, A. (1994), *La Mobilita Sociale in Italia*. Bologna: Il Mulino.

Coleman, J., Campbell, E., and Hobson, E. (1966), *Equality of Educational Opportunity*. Washington: Government Printing Office.

Commission of the European Community (1993), *Social Protection in Europe*. Luxemburg: EC.

Crompton, R. and Jones, G. (1984), *White-Collar Proletariat: Deskilling and Gender in Clerical Work*. London: Macmillan.

Crouch, C. (1985), 'Conditions for Trade Union Wage Restraint', in L. Lindberg and C. Maier (eds.), *The Politics of Inflation and Economic Stagnation*. Washington: Brookings Institute.

—— and Pizzorno, A. (1978), *The Resurgence of Class Conflict in Western Europe since 1968*, i and ii. New York: Holmes and Meier.

Dahl. R. (1966), 'Some Explanations', in R. Dahl (ed.), *Political Oppositions in Western Democracies*. New Haven: Yale University Press, 348–87.

Dallago, B. (1990), *The Irregular Economy*. Aldershot: Dartmouth.

del Boca, D. (1988), 'Women in a Changing Workplace: The Case of Italy', in J. Jenson, E. Hagen, and G. Reddy (eds.), *Feminization of the Labour Force*. Oxford: Polity Press, 120–36.

Dolado, J., Kramarz, F., Machin, S., Manning, A., Margolis, D., and Teulings, C. (1996), 'The Economic Impact of Minimum Wages in Europe', *Economic Policy*, 23: 319–72.

Drèze, J. H. and Snessens, H. (1994), 'Technical Development, Competition from Low-wage Economies and Low-skilled Unemployment', *Swedish Economic Policy Review*, 1: 185–214.

Duncan, G., Gustavsson, B., and Hauser, R. (1993), 'Poverty Dynamics in Eight Countries', *Journal of Population Economics*, 6: 215–34.

Eisner, R. (1988), 'Extended Accounts for National Income and Product', *Journal of Economic Literature* (Dec), 1611–84.

Elfring, T. (1988), 'Service Employment in Advanced Economies', Ph.D. diss., University of Groningen, Department of Economics.

Elster, J. (1989), *The Cement of Society: A Study of Social Order*. Cambridge: Cambridge University Press.

Elmeskov, J. (1998), 'The Unemployment Problem in Europe', paper presented at the Department of Economic, European University Institute, Firenze, 6 Mar.

Erikson, R. and Aberg, R. (1985), *Welfare in Transition*. Oxford: Clarendon Press.

—— and Goldthorpe, John H. (1992), *The Constant Flux: Class Mobility in Industrial Societies*. Oxford: Clarendon Press.

—— Hansen, E. J., and Uusitalo, H. (1991), *Welfare Trends in Scandinavian Countries*. Armonck, NY: M. E. Sharpe.

Espina, A., Fina, L., and Lorante, J. (1985), *Estudios de Economia del Trabajo en Espana*, pt. I. Madrid: Ministero de Trabajo e Securidad Social.

Esping-Andersen, G. (1990), *The Three Worlds of Welfare Capitalism*. Cambridge: Polity Press.

—— (1992), 'The Making of a Social Democratic Welfare State', in K. Misgeld, K. Molin, and K. Aamark (eds.), *Creating Social Democracy*. University Park, Pa.: Pennsylvania State University Press.

—— (1993) (ed.), *Changing Classes: Stratification and Mobility in Postindustrial Societies*. London: Sage.

—— (1994), 'Welfare States and the Economy', in N. Smelser and R. Swedberg (eds.), *Handbook of Economic Sociology*. New York: Russell Sage.

—— (1997*a*), 'Hybrid or Unique? The Distinctiveness of the Japanese Welfare State', *Journal of European Social Policy*, 7/3: 179–89.

—— (1997*b*), 'Welfare States at the End of the Century', in OECD, *Family, Market and Community*. Paris: OECD, 63–80.

—— (1998), 'The Effects of Regulation on Unemployment Levels and Structure', *Report to the European Commission DG XII*, Brussels: EU.

—— Rohwer, G., and Sorensen, S. L. (1994), 'Institutions and Class Mobility: Scaling the Skill Barrier', *European Sociological Review*, 10/2: 119–33.

European Commission (1993), *Employment in Europe*. Brussels: EC.

Evers, A. and Svetlik, I. (1991), *New Welfare Mixes in Care for the Elderly*. Budapest: European Centre for Social Welfare Policy and Research.

Feist, U. and Liepelt, K. (1990), 'Dynamik des Arbeitsmarkts und Wahlerverlhalten' in M. Kaase and H. D. Klingemann (eds.), *Wahlen und Wahler*. Opladen: Westdeutcher Verlag.

Ferrera, M. (1994), *Modelli di Solidarieta.* Bologna: Il Mulino.

—— (1996), 'Il modello Sud-Europeo di welfare state', *Rivista Italiana di Scienza Politica*, 1: 67–101.

Feur, R. (1991), 'Emerging Alternatives to Full-time and Permanent Employment', in P. Brown and R. Scase (eds.), *Poor Work*. Milton Keynes: Open University Press, 56–70.

Freeman, R. B. (1993), *Working Under Different Rules*. New York: Russell Sage Foundation.

—— (1994), 'Labor Market Institutions and Economic Performance', *Economic Policy*, 3: 63–80.

Freeman, R. B. (1996), 'Why Do So Many Young Americans Commit Crimes and What May Be Done About It?', NBER Working Paper, no. 5451.
—— and Katz, L. F. (1995), *Differences and Changes in Wage Structure*. Chicago: University of Chicago Press.
Fritzell, J. and Lundberg, O. (1994), *Vardagens Villkor. Levnadsforhallanden I Sverige under tre Decennier*. Stockholm: Brombergs.
Fuchs, V. (1983), *How We Lived*. Cambridge, Mass.: Harvard University Press.
Gallie, D. (1991), 'Patterns of Skill Change. Upskilling, Deskilling, or the Polarization of Skills?', *Work, Employment and Society*, 3: 319–51.
Garret, G. and Lange, P. (1986), 'Performance in a Hostile World: Economic Growth in Capitalist Democracies 1974–1982', *World Politics*, 38: 517–45.
Garrido, L. (1992), *Los Dos Biografias de la Mujer en Espana*. Madrid: Ministerio de Asuntos Sociales.
Gauthier, A. (1996), *The State and the Family*. Oxford: Clarendon Press.
Gershuny, J. (1978), *After Industrial Society: The Emerging Self-service Economy*. London: Macmillan.
—— (1991), *Changing Times: The Social Economics of Postindustrial Societies*. Report to the Rowntree Memorial, University of Bath, June.
—— (1993), 'Postindustrial Career Structures in Britain', in G. Esping-Andersen (ed.), *Changing Classes: Stratification and Mobility in Postindustrial Societies*. London: Sage, 136–70.
Giersch, H. (1985), 'Eurosclerosis', Kiel Discussion Paper, no. 112. Institut für Weltwirtschaftsforschung. University of Kiel.
Ginsburg, N. (1992), *Divisions of Welfare*. London: Sage.
Glyn, A. (1995), 'Unemployment and Inequality', Science Center Berlin Discussion Paper, FSI 95–303.
Goldey, D. (1993), 'The French General Election of 1993', *Electoral Studies*, 12/4: 291–314.
Goldin, C. (1990), *Understanding the Gender Gap: An Economic History of American Women*. New York: Oxford University Press.
—— and Margo, R. (1991), 'The Great Compression', NBER Working Paper, no. 3817.
Goldthorpe, J. (1982), 'The Service Class, its Formation and Future', in A. Giddens and G. Mackenzie (eds.), *Social Class and the Division of Labour*. Cambridge: Cambridge University Press, 162–87.
—— (1984), 'The End of Convergence: Corporatist and Dualist Tendencies in Modern Western Societies', in J. Goldthorpe (ed.), *Order and Conflict in Contemporary Capitalism*. Oxford: Clarendon Press, 315–43.
—— Lockwood, D., Bechhofer, F., and Platt, J. (1968), *The Affluent Worker*. Cambridge: Cambridge University Press.
Goode, W. J. (1963), *World Revolution and Family Patterns*. New York. Free Press.
Gordon, D., Edwards, R., and Reich, M. (1982), *Segmented Work, Divided Workers*. Cambridge: Cambridge University Press.
Gornick, J. (1994), 'Economic Gender Gaps in the Industrialized Countries', Luxemburg Income Study, unpub. paper (Nov.).
—— Meyers, M., and Ross, K. E. (1997), 'Supporting the Employment of Mothers', *Journal of European Social Policy*, 7: 45–70.

Gottschalk, P. (1993), 'Changes in Inequality of Family Income in Seven Industrialized Countries', *American Economic Review*, 2: 136–42.

—— (1997), 'Inequality, Income Growth and Mobility: The Basic Facts', *Journal of Economic Perspectives*, 11: 21–40.

—— and Smeeding, T. (1997), 'Cross-national Comparisons of Earnings and Income Inequality', *Journal of Economic Literature*, 35: 633–81.

—— Mclanahan, S., and Sandefur, G. (1994), 'The Dynamics of Intergenerational Transmission of Poverty and Welfare Participation', in S. Danziger, G. Sandefur, and D. Weinberg (eds.), *Confronting Poverty*. Cambridge, Mass.: Harvard University Press.

Gough, I. (1979), *The Political Economy of the Welfare State*. London: Macmillan.

—— Bradshaw, J., Ditch, J., Eardley, T., and Whiteford, P. (1997), 'Social Assistance in OECD Countries', *Journal of European Social Policy*, 7/1: 17–43.

Gouldner, A. (1979), *The Future of Intellectuals and the Rise of the New Class*. London: Macmillan.

Graebner, W. (1980), *A History of Retirement*. New Haven: Yale University Press.

Guerrero, T. and Naldini, M. (1996), 'Is the South so Different? Italian and Spanish Families in Comparative Perspective', Mannheimer Zentrum für Europaische Sozialforschung Working Paper, no. 12.

Gustafsson, S. (1994), 'Childcare and Types of Welfare States', in D. Sainsbury (ed.), *Gendering Welfare States*. London: Sage, 45–61.

—— (1995), 'Single Mothers in Sweden: Why is Poverty Less Severe?', in K. McFate, R. Lawson, and W. J. Wilson (eds.), *Poverty, Inequality and the Future of Social Policy*. New York: Russell Sage, 291–326.

Hakim, C. (1997), *Key Issues in Women's Work*. London: Athlone.

Hansen, E. J. (1995), *Velfaerdsgenerationen*. Copenhagen: Institut for Socialforskning.

Harrison, B. and Bluestone, B. (1988), *The Great U-Turn*, 2nd edn. New York: Basic Books.

Heclo, H. (1974), *Modern Social Policies in Britain and Sweden*. New Haven: Yale University Press.

—— (1981), 'Towards a New Welfare State?', in P. Flora and A. Heidenheimer (eds.), *The Development of Welfare States in Europe and America*. New Brunswick, NJ: Transaction Books, 383–406.

Hernes, H. (1987), *Welfare State and Woman Power*. Oslo: Norwegian University Press.

Hicks, A. (1988), 'Social Democratic Corporatism and Economic Growth', *Journal of Politics*, 50: 677–704.

—— Swank, D., and Ambuhl, M. (1989), 'Welfare Expansion Revisited: Policy Routines and Their Mediation by Party, Class, and Crisis, 1957–1982', *European Journal of Political Research*, 17: 401–30.

Hirsh, F. (1976), *Social Limits to Growth*. Cambridge, Mass.: Harvard University Press.

Hoem, B. (1995), 'Gender-segregated Swedish Labour Market', in V. Oppenheimer and A. Jensen (eds.), *Gender and Family Change in Industrialized Countries*. Oxford: Clarendon Press, 279–96.

Hout, M., Brooks, C., and Manza, J. (1993), 'The Persistence of Classes in Postindustrial Societies', *International Sociology*, 3: 259–78.

Huinink, J. (1995), *Warum Noch Familie?* Frankfurt: Campus Verlag.

ILO (1943), *Yearbook of Labour Force Statistics*. Geneva: International Labour Office.

Ingelhart, R. (1990) 'Values, Ideology, and Cognitive Mobilization in New Social Movements', in R. J. Dalton and M. Kuechler (eds.), *Challenging the Political Order*. Oxford: Polity Press, 43–66.

Ingerslev, O. and Pedersen, L. (1996), *Marginalisering 1990–1994*. Copenhagen: Institut for Socialforskning.

INSEE (1990), *Données Sociales*. Paris: INSEE.

ISTAT (1997), *Rapporto sull'Italia*. Bologna: Il Mulino.

Jacobs, S. (1998), 'Characteristics of Unemployed, Risks of Unemployment and Poverty in the European Union'. Paper prepared for *The Employment Precarity, Unemployment and Social Excusion Project*, Nuffield College, Oxford University.

Jencks, C. and Peterson, P. E. (1991) (eds.), *The Urban Underclass*. Washington: Brookings Institute.

—— Smith, C., Ackland, H., and Bane, M. J. (1982), *Inequality: A Reassessment of the Effects of Family and Schooling in America*. New York: Basic Books.

Jensen, P. (1997), 'Ledighedens dynamik', in L. Pedersen (ed.), *Er der Veje til Fuld Beskaeftigelse?* Copenhagen: Socialforsknings Instituttet, 39–62.

Jimeno, J. and Toharia, L. (1994), *Unemployment and Labor Flexibility: The Case of Spain*. Geneva: International Labour Office.

Jones, C. (1993), *New Perspectives on the Welfare State in Europe*. London: Routledge.

Kangas, O. (1991), *The Politics of Social Rights*. Stockholm: Swedish Institute for Social Research.

—— (1994), 'The Politics of Social Security: On Regressions, Qualitative Comparisons, and Cluster Analysis', in T. Janoski and A. Hicks (eds.), *The Comparative Political Economy of the Welfare State*. Cambridge: Cambridge University Press, 346–64.

Kern, H. and Schumann, M. (1984), *Das Ende der Arbeitsteilung?* Munich: C. H. Beck.

Kirscheimer, O. (1957), 'The Waning of Opposition in Parliamentary Regimes', *Social Research*, 24: 127–56.

Kitschelt, H. (1994), *The Transformation of European Social Democracy*. Cambridge: Cambridge University Press.

Kohli, M., Rein, M., and Guillemard, A. (1993), *Time for Retirement*. Cambridge: Cambridge University Press.

Kolberg, J. E. (1992) (ed.), *Between Work and Social Citizenship*. Armonck, NY: M. E. Sharpe.

—— and Uusitalo, H. (1992), 'The Interface Between the Economy and the Welfare State', in Z. Ferge and J. E. Kolberg (eds.), *Social Policy in a Changing Europe*. Boulder, Colo.: Westview Press, 77–94.

Korpi, W. (1980*a*), 'Approaches to the Study of Poverty in the United States:

Critical Notes From a European Perspective', Swedish Institute for Social Research Working Paper, no. 64.

—— (1980*b*), 'Social Policy and Distributional Conflict in the Capitalist Democracies', *West European Politics*, 3: 296–315.

—— (1983), *The Democratic Class Struggle*. London: Routledge.

Kuhnle, S. (1981), 'The Growth of Social Insurance Programs in Scandinavia', in P. Flora and A. Heidenheimer (eds.), *The Development of Welfare States in Europe and America*. New Brunswick, NJ: Transaction Books, 125–50.

Kurz, K. and Müller, W. (1987), 'Class Mobility in the Industrial World', *Annual Review of Sociology*, 13: 417–42.

Lange, P., Ross, G., and Vanicelli, M. (1982), *Unions, Change and Crisis: French and Italian Union Strategy and the Political Economy, 1945–1980*. London. Allen and Unwin.

Lash, C. (1977), *Haven in a Heartless World*. New York: Basic Books.

Laslett, P. and Wall, R. (1972) (eds.), *Household and Family in Past Time*. Cambridge: Cambridge University Press.

Layard, R., Nickell, S., and Jackson, R. (1991), *Unemployment: Macroeconomic Performance and the Labour Market*. Oxford: Oxford University Press.

Lazear, E. (1990), 'Job Security Provisions and Unemployment', *Quarterly Journal of Economics*, 105: 699–726.

Lebergott, S. (1984), *The Americans: An Economic Record*. New York: W. W. Norton.

Le Grand, J. (1991), *Equity and Choice*. New York: HarperCollins.

Leibfried, S. (1992), 'Towards a European Welfare State: On Integrating Poverty Regimes in the European Community', in Z. Ferge and J. E. Kolberg (eds.), *Social Policy in a Changing Europe*. Frankfurt: Campus Verlag, 245–80.

Leo XIII (1891), *Rerum Novarum*, Papal Encyclical, Vatican City.

Lesemann, F. and Martin, C. (1993), *Home-Based Care, the Elderly, the Family and the Welfare State*. Ottawa: University of Ottowa Press.

Lessenich, S. (1995), 'Espana y Los tres Mundos del Estado del Bienestar', Universitat Pompeu Fabra Working Paper, no. 95/9.

Levy, Frank (1988), *Dollars and Dreams: The Changing American Income Distribution*. New York: W. W. Norton.

—— and Murnane, Richard (1992), 'U.S. Earnings Levels and Earnings Inequality: A Review of Recent Trends and Proposed Explanations', *Journal of Economic Literature*, 30: 1333–81.

Lewis, J. (1993), *Women and Social Policies in Europe*. Aldershot: Edward Elgar.

Light, I. and Karageorgis, S. (1994), 'The Ethnic Economy', in N. Smelser and R. Swedberg (eds.), *Handbook of Economic Sociology*. Princeton: Princeton University Press, 647–71.

Lindbeck, A. (1992), *The Welfare State*. London: Elgar.

—— (1994), 'The Welfare State and the Employment Problem', *American Economic Review* (May), 71–5.

—— and Snower, D (1988), *The Insider-Outsider Theory of Unemployment*. Cambridge, Mass.: MIT Press.

Linder, S. (1970), *The Harried Leisure Class*. New York: Columbia University Press.

Lipset, S. M. (1960), *Political Man*. New York: Doubleday Anchor.
—— (1964), 'The Changing Class Structure and Contemporary European Politics', in S. Graubard (ed.), *A New Europe?* Boston: Beacon Press, 337–69.
—— (1991), 'No Third Way: A Comparative Perspective on the Left', in D. Chirot (ed.), *The Crisis of Leninism and the Decline of the Left*. Seattle: University of Washington Press, 183–232.
—— and Bendix, R. (1959), *Social Mobility in Industrial Societies*. Berkeley: University of California Press.
McFate, K., Lawson, R., and Wilson, W. J. (1995), *Poverty, Inequality and the Future of Social Policy*. New York: Russell Sage Foundation.
McKinley, L., Blackburn, D., Bloom, E., and Freeman, R. (1990), 'The Declining Position of Less Skilled American Men', in G. Burtless (ed.), *A Future of Lousy Jobs?* Washington: Brookings Institute, 31–76.
Mclanahan, S. and Sandefur, G. (1994), *Growing Up With a Single Parent*. Cambridge, Mass.: Harvard University Press.
—— Casper, L., and Sorensen, A. (1995), 'Women's Roles and Women's Poverty', in V. Oppenheimer and A. Jensen (eds.), *Gender and Family Change in Industrialized Countries*. Oxford: Clarendon Press, 258–78.
Maddison, A. (1964), *Economic Growth in the West*. London: Allen and Unwin.
Marchand, O. and Thelot, C. (1997), *Le Travail en France*. Paris: Nathan.
Marimon, R. and Zilibotti, F. (1996), 'Actual Versus Virtual Employment in Europe: Is Spain Different?', European University Institute Working paper, ECO no. 96/21.
Marshall, T. H. (1950), *Citizenship and Social Class*. Oxford: Oxford University Press.
Martin, A. (1973), *The Politics of Economic Policy in the United States*. Beverly Hills: Sage.
Masnick, G. and Bane, M. (1980), *The Nation's Families*. Boston: Auburn Press.
Maurau, G. (1993), 'Regulation, Deregulation and Labor Market Dynamics', in C. F. Buechtemann (ed.), *Employment Security and Labor Market Dynamics*. Ithaca, NY: ILR Press, 358–73.
Mayer, K. U. (1993), 'Changes in European Life Courses and their Social, Political and Economic Determinants', Paper presented at the *European Science Foundation Conference*. Schloss Ringberg, 22–6 Nov.
—— (1997), 'Political Economies and the Life Course', mimeo, Max-Planck Institute, Berlin.
—— and Müller, W. (1986), 'The State and the Structure of the Life Course', in A. B. Sorensen, F. E. Weinert, and L. Sherrod (eds.), *Human Development and the Life Course: Multidisciplinary Perspectives*. Hillside, NJ: Lawrence Erlbaum Associates, 217–45.
—— and Carroll, G. R. (1987), 'Jobs and Classes: Structural Constraints on Career Mobility', *European Sociological Review*, 3/1: 14–38.
Miliband, D. (1994) (ed.), *What is Left?* Oxford: Polity Press.
Mincer, J. and Polachek, S. (1974), 'Family Investments in Human Capital', in T. W. Schultz (ed.), *Economics of the Family*. Chicago: University of Chicago Press.

Mishel, L. and Bernstein, J. (1993), *The State of Working America*. Armonck, NY: M. E. Sharpe.

Mitchell, D. (1991), *Income Transfer Systems*. Avebury: Aldershot.

Moffit, R. (1992), 'Incentive Effects of the US Welfare System', *Journal of Economic Literature*, 30: 1–61.

Murray, C. (1984), *Losing Ground*. New York: Basic Books.

Myles, J. (1984), *Old Age in the Welfare State*. Boston: Little, Brown.

—— (1996. 'When Markets Fail: Social Welfare in Canada and the United States', in G. Esping-Andersen (ed.), *Welfare States in Transition*. London: Sage, 116–40.

—— and Turegun, A. (1994), 'Comparative Studies of Class Structures', *Annual Review of Sociology*, 20: 103–24.

Myrdal, G. (1954), *The Political Element in the Development of Economic Theory*. Cambridge, Mass.: Harvard University Press.

Navarro, V. (1996), *The Politics of Health Care Reform*. Oxford: Basil Blackwell.

Netherlands Ministry of Social Affairs (1996), *The Dutch Welfare State from an International and Economic Perspective*. The Hague: SZW.

Nickell, S. (1997), 'Unemployment and Labor Market Rigidities: Europe versus North America', *Journal of Economic Perspectives*, 3: 55–74.

—— and Bell, S. (1995), 'The Collapse in Demand for the Unskilled Across the OECD', *Oxford Review of Economic Policy*, 11: 40–62.

Nolan, B., Hauser, R., and Zoyem, J. P. (1998), 'The Changing Effects of Social Protection on Poverty', Paper prepared for *the Employment Precarity, Unemployment and Social Exclusion Project*, Nuffield College, Oxford University.

O'Connor, J. (1973), *The Fiscal Crisis of the State*. New York: St. Martin's Press.

O'Connor, J. (1996), 'From Women in the Welfare State to Gendering Welfare State Regimes', Special Issue of *Current Sociology*, 44/2.

OECD (1981), *The Welfare State in Crisis*. Paris: OECD.

—— (1992), *Employment Outlook*. Paris: OECD.

—— (1993), *Employment Outlook*. Paris: OECD.

—— (1994a), *The OECD Jobs Study: Part I and II*. Paris: OECD.

—— (1994b), *Economic Outlook*. OECD: Paris (Dec.).

—— (1994c), *Women and Structural Change*. Paris: OECD.

—— (1995a), *Education at a Glance: OECD Indicators*. Paris: OECD.

—— (1995b), *Income Distribution in OECD Countries*, Social Policy Studies no.18. Paris: OECD.

—— (1995c), *Employment Outlook*. Paris: OECD.

—— (1995d), *Taxation, Employment and Unemployment*. Paris: OECD.

—— (1995e), *Historical Statistics*. Paris: OECD.

—— (1996a), *Literacy, the Economy and Society*. Paris: OECD.

—— (1996b), *Employment Outlook*. Paris: OECD.

—— (1997a), *Family, Markets and Community*. Paris: OECD.

—— (1997b), *Employment Outlook*. Paris: OECD.

—— (1997c), *Literacy, Skills and the Knowledge Society*. Paris: OECD.

—— (1998), *The Caring World*. Paris: OECD.

Offe, C. (1972), 'Advanced Capitalism and the Welfare State', *Politics and Society*, 4: 479–88.

Offe, C. (1984), *Contradictions of the Welfare State*. London: Hutchinson.
—— (1985), *Disorganized Capitalism*. Cambridge, Mass.: MIT Press.
Olson, M. (1982), *The Rise and Decline of Nations*. New Haven: Yale University Press.
Oppenheimer, V. and Jensen, A. (1995), *Gender and Family Change in Industrialized Countries*. Oxford: Clarendon Press.
Orloff, A. (1993), 'Gender and the Social Rights of Citizenship', *American Sociological Review*, 58: 303–28.
Ostner, I. and Lewis, J. (1995), 'Gender and the Evolution of European Social Policies', in P. Pierson and S. Leibfried (eds.), *Fragmented Social Policy*. Washington: Brookings Institute, 1–40.
Paci, M. (1973), *Mercato del Lavoro e Classi Sociali in Italia*. Bologna: Il Mulino.
Palme, J. (1990), *Pension Rights in Welfare Capitalism*. Stockholm: Swedish Institute for Social Research.
Palmer, J. (1988) (ed.), *The Vulnerable*. Washington: The Urban Institute.
Parsons, T. and Bales, R. (1955), *Family, Socialization and Interaction Processes*. Glencoe, Ill.: Free Press.
Pedersen, P. and Smith, N. (1995), 'The Welfare State and the Labor Market'. CLS Working Paper, no. 17, Aarhus University.
—— —— (1997), 'Arbejdsudbud og incitamenter', in L. Pedersen (ed.), *Er der Veje til Fuld Beskaeftigelse?* Copenhagen: Socialforsknings Instituttet, 91–114.
Pempel, T. J. (1989), 'Japan's Creative Conservatism: Continuity Under Challenge', in F. Castles (ed.), *The Comparative History of Public Policy*. London: Polity Press, 149–91.
Pestieau, P. (1992), 'The Distribution of Private Pension Benefits: How Fair Is It?', in E. Duskin (ed.), *Private Pensions and Public Policy*. Social Policy Studies, no. 9. Paris: OECD.
Phelps, E. (1997), *Rewarding Work*. Cambridge, Mass.: Harvard University Press.
Pierson, P. (1994), *Dismantling the Welfare State?* Cambridge: Cambridge University Press.
Ploug, N. and Kvist, J. (1994), *Recent Trends in Cash Benefits in Europe*. Copenhagen: Socialforsknings Instituttet.
Polanyi, K. (1944), *The Great Transformation*. New York: Rhinehart.
Pontusson, J. (1992), 'The Role of Economic-Structural Change in the Decline of European Social Democracy', Paper presented at the *American Political Science Association Meetings*, 3–6 Sept.
Presidenza del Consiglio dei Ministri (1993), *Terzo Rapporto sulla Poverta in Italia*. Roma: Istituto Poligrafico dello Stato.
Pugliese, Enrico (1993), *La Sociologia della Disoccupazione*. Bologna: Il Mulino.
Ragin, C. (1994), 'A Qualitative Comparative Analysis of Pension Systems', in T. Janoski and A. Hicks (eds.), *The Comparative Political Economy of the Welfare State*. Cambridge: Cambridge University Press, 320–45.
Rawls, J. (1972), *A Theory of Social Justice*. Cambridge, Mass.: Harvard University Press.
Regini, M. (1992), *Confini Mobile*. Bologna: Il Mulino.
—— (1988) (ed.), *The Effects of Labor Market Regulation on Unemployment*. Report to the European Commission, DGXII, Bruxelles.

Rein, M. and Rainwater, L. (1986), *The Public-Private Mix in Social Protection*. Armonck, NY: M. E. Sharpe.

Renner, K. (1953), *Nachgelassene Werke*, iii. *Wandlungen der Modernen Gesellschaft*. Wien: Wiener Volksbuchhandlung.

Reskin, B. and Padavic, I. (1994), *Women and Men at Work*. London: Pine Forge Press.

Rhodes, M. (1996), 'Globalization and West European Welfare States: A Critical Review of Recent Debates', *Journal of European Social Policy*, 6/4: 305–26.

Rimlinger, G. (1971), *Welfare and Industrialization in Europe, America, and Russia*. New York: Wiley.

Rodgers, G. and Rodgers, J. (1989), *Precarious Work in Western Europe*. Geneva: ILO.

Rose, R. and Shiratori, H. (1986), *The Welfare State East and West*. Oxford: Oxford University Press.

Rosen, S. (1996), 'Public Employment and the Welfare State in Sweden', *Journal of Economic Literature*, 34: 729–40.

Roussel, L. (1992), 'La famille en Europe Occidentale: Divergences et convergences', *Population*, 1: 133–52.

Rowntree, S. (1901), *Poverty: A Study of Town Life*. London: Longman.

Rowthorne, R. (1992), 'Centralization, Employment and Wage Dispersion', *Economic Journal*, 102: 506–23.

Roy, C. (1984), 'Le temps et les activités quotidiennes', in INSEE, *Donées Sociales*.

Sainsbury, D. (1994), 'Women's and Men's Social Rights: Gendering Dimensions of Welfare States', in D. Sainsbury (ed.), *Gendering Welfare States*. London: Sage, 150–69.

Saint-Paul, G. (1996), 'Exploring the Political Economy of Labor Market Institutions', *Economic Policy*, 23: 263–316.

Sala-i-Martin, X. (1992), 'Transfers', NBER Working Paper, no. 4186.

Salamon, L. M. and Anheier, H. K. (1996), *The Emerging Non-profit Sector*. Manchester: Manchester University Press.

Salido, O. (1996), 'La Movilidad Ocupacional Femenina en Espana: Una Comparacion por Sexo', Ph.D. diss., Universidad Complutense de Madrid, Facultad de Ciencias Politicas y Sociologia (June).

Saraceno, C. (1996), 'Family Change, Family Policies and the Restructuration of Welfare', Paper presented at the OECD Conference *Beyond 2000: The New Social Policy Agenda*. Paris: OECD, 12–13 Nov.

Saunders, P. (1994), *Welfare and Inequality*. Cambridge: Cambridge University Press.

Scarpetta, S. (1996), 'Assessing the Role of Labor Market Policies and Institutional Settings on Unemployment'. *OECD Economic Studies*, 26: 43–98.

Scharpf, F. (1987), *Sozialdemokratsche Krisenpolitik im Europa*. Frankfurt: Campus Verlag.

—— (1990), 'Structures of Postindustrial Society or Does Mass Unemployment Disappear in the Service Economy? in E. Applebaum and R. Schettkat (eds.), *Labor Market Adjustment to Structural Change and Technological Progress*. New York: Praeger, 17–35.

Schettkat, R. (1997), 'Employment Protection and Labor Mobility in Europe', *International Review of Applied Economics*, 11/1: 24–41.

Schizzerotto, A. (1993), 'La Porta Stretta: Classe Superiori e Processi di Mobilita', *Polis*, 1: 15–44.

Schumpeter, J. (1964), *Imperialism and Social Classes*. New York: Meridian Books.

Sen, A. (1992), *Inequality Reexamined*. New York: Russell Sage Foundation.

Shalev, M. (1996), *The Privatization of Social Policy? Occupational Welfare and the Welfare State in America, Scandinavia, and Japan*. London: Macmillan.

Shaver, S. and Bradshaw, J. (1993), 'The Recognition of Wifely Labour by Welfare States', Social Policy Research Centre Discussion Paper, no. 41. Sydney: University of New South Wales.

Shavit, Y. and Blossfeld, H. P. (1993), *Persistent Inequality*. Boulder, Colo.: Westview Press.

Siebert, H. (1997), 'Labor Market Rigidities and Unemployment in Europe', Institut für Weltwirtschaft Working Paper, no. 787. University of Kiel.

Singelmann, J. (1978), 'The Sectoral Transformation of the Labor Force in Seven Countries, 1920–1970', *American Journal of Sociology*, 83/5: 224–34.

Skocpol, T. (1995), *Social Policy in the United States*. Princeton: Princeton University Press.

Smeeding, T., O'Higgins, M., and Rainwater, L. (1990), *Poverty, Inequality and Income Distribution in Comparative Perspective*. New York: Harvester/ Wheatsheaf.

Snower, D. (1997), 'The Low-Skill, Bad-Job Trap', in A. Booth and D. Snower (eds.), *Acquiring Skills*. Cambridge: Cambridge University Press, 109–26.

Socialstyrelsen (1991), *Vaard och Omsorg i Sex Europaiska Lander*. Stockholm: Ministry for Social Affairs.

Soskice, D. (1990), 'Wage Determination: The Changing Role of Institutions in Advanced Industrial Countries', *Oxford Review of Economic Policy*, 6: 36–61.

—— (1994), 'Reconciling Markets and Institutions: The German Apprenticeship System', in L. Lynch (ed.), *Training and the Private Sector*. Chicago: University of Chicago Press.

Standing, G. (1993), 'Labor Regulation in an Era of Fragmented Flexibility', in Buechtemann (ed.), *Employment Security*.

Stephens, J. (1979), *The Transition from Capitalism to Socialism*. London: Macmillan.

—— (1996), 'The Scandinavian Welfare States: Achievements, Crisis and Prospects', in G. Esping-Andersen (ed.), *Welfare States in Transition*. London; Sage.

—— Huber, E., and Ray, L. (1994), 'The Welfare State in Hard Times', Paper presented at the Conference on the *Political Economy of Contemporary Capitalism*. University of North Carolina, 9–11 Sept.

Stevens, A. H. (1995), 'Climbing Out of Poverty, Falling Back In'. NBER Working Paper, no. 5390.

Stigler, G. (1956), *Trends in Employment in the Service Industries*. Princeton: Princeton University Press.

Streeck, W. (1992), *Social Institutions and Economic Performance*. London: Sage.

Svallfors, S. (1998), 'Worlds of Welfare and Attitudes to Redistribution: A Comparison of Eight Western Nations', *European Sociological Review*, 13/2: 283–304.

Sveriges Statistiska Aarsbok, 1994. Stockholm: Statistiska Centralbyron.

Swenson, P. (1989), *Fair Shares: Unions, Pay and Politics in Sweden and West Germany*. Ithaca, NY: Cornell University Press.

Taylor-Gooby, P. (1996), 'The United Kingdom: Radical Departures and Political Consensus', in V. George and P. Taylor-Gooby (eds.), *Squaring the Welfare Circle*. London: Macmillan, 95–116.

Tilly, L. and Scott, J. (1987), *Women, Work and Family*. New York: Methuen.

Titmuss, R. (1958), *Essays on the Welfare State*. London: Allen and Unwin.

Toharia, L. (1997), 'The Labor Market in Spain', unpub. MS, Universidad Alcala.

Ultee, W., Dessens, J., and Jansen, W. (1988), 'Why Does Unemployment Come in Couples?' *European Sociological Review*, 4: 111–22.

United Nations (1991), *The World's Women, 1970–1990: Trends and Statistics*. New York: United Nations.

—— (1995), *Human Development Report*. New York: United Nations.

United States Department of Commerce (1976), *Historical Statistics of the United States, 1776–1976*. Washington: Government Printing Office.

van de Kaa, D. (1987), 'The Second Demographic Transition', *Population Bulletin*. 42: 3–57.

van Kersbergen, K. (1995), *Social Capitalism*. London: Routledge.

van Parijs, P. (1987), 'A Revolution in Class Theory', *Politics and Society*, 15/4: 453–82.

Velfaerdskommissionen (1995), *Velstand og Velfaerd-En Analyse Sammenfatning*. Copenhagen: Ministry of Commerce.

Visser, J. (1992), 'The Strength of Union Movements in Advanced Capitalist Democracies', in M. Regini (ed.), *The Future of Labor Movements*. London: Sage.

—— (1996), 'Unionization Trends Revisited', mimeo, University of Amsterdam.

—— and Hemerijck (1997), *A Dutch Miracle*. Amsterdam: University of Amsterdam Press.

Vogel, E. (1980), *Japan as Number One*. Cambridge, Mass.: Harvard University Press.

Wagner, M. (1996), *Ehestabilitat und Sozialstruktur im Wandel der Ost- und Westdeutschen Gesellschaft*. Free University of Berlin, Habilitatsschrift in Sociology.

Waldinger, R., Aldrich, H., and Ward, R. (1990), *Ethnic Entrepreneurs*. Beverly Hills: Sage.

Wall, R., Robin, J., and Laslett, P. (1983), *Family Forms in Historic Europe*. Cambridge: Cambridge University Press.

Wennemo, I. (1994), *Sharing the Costs of Children*. Stockholm: Swedish Institute for Social Research.

West Pedersen, A. (1994), 'What Makes the Difference?', in P. Kosonen and P. K. Madsen (eds.), *Convergence or Divergence? Welfare States Facing European Integration*. Brussels: European Commission, 125–56.

Wilensky, H. (1975), *The Welfare State and Equality*. Berkeley: University of California Press.

—— (1981), 'Leftism, Catholicism, and Democratic Corporatism', in P. Flora and A. Heidenheimer (eds.), *The Development of Welfare States in Europe and America*. New Brunswick, NJ: Transaction Press, 345–82.

—— and Lebeaux, C. (1958), *Industrial Society and Social Welfare*. New York: Russell Sage.

Wood, A. (1994), *North–South Trade, Employment and Inequality*. Oxford: Clarendon Press.

Wright, E. O. (1989), *The Debate on Classes*. London: Verso.

Zweig, F. (1971), *The Worker in Affluent Society*. New York. Free Press.

INDEX

market strategy of 175–8
occupational benefits 17–18
occupations distribution 109, 110, 111
personal services 105, 116
productivity gap 112
professional-technical jobs 107, 108, 109
single parents 163, 164 n.
social exclusion 158
subsidies 66
unemployment entrapment 159
union decline 121
unique model 141
unregulated markets 23
welfare capitalism 76
welfare regime typology 88
welfare state bias 169
Workfare 80
universalism 13–14, 17, 18, 41, 78–81
upward class mobility 30, 108–9, 149

Visser, J., trade union coverage 19
vocational training 160 n.
voluntary sector 35 n.

wage arbitration system 89
wage regulation 125–8
welfare capitalism, types of 13–14, 76
welfare production 54–5
welfare regimes 60–7, 74–86

definitions 34–5, 36–40
families 35–6, 60–7, 92–4
fourth world 89–91
typology 86–92
see also individual welfare regimes
welfare state:
crisis in 2–3, 145–6
de-familialization 45–6, 61–2
equality 32–3
familialism 70
industrial relations 20–1
needs of 174
post war 15, 34, 148–50
public opinion 147–8
Wood, A., low skilled 101
workers' rights 21–3
working class 15, 41
working hours 53, 180
work-sharing policy 180

youth unemployment 126–7, 133
bias 157, 158
disproportionate risks 167
family obligation 69–70
generation clash 147–8
labour market regulation 137
parents 62–3
temporary contracts 151